HOM

how to start a home-based

Web Design Business   **fourth edition**

Jim Smith

Guilford, Connecticut

This book's purpose is to provide accurate and authoritative information on the topics covered. It is sold with the understanding that neither the author nor the publisher is engaged in rendering legal, financial, accounting, or other professional services. Neither The Globe Pequot Press nor the author assumes any liability resulting from action taken based on the information included herein. Mention of a company name does not constitute endorsement.

Text designed by Sheryl P. Kober

Library of Congress/Cataloging-in-Publication Data is available on file.

ISBN: 978-0-7627-5955-2

Printed in the United States of America
10 9 8 7 6 5 4 3 2 1

I dedicate this book to the memory of my father and mother, who raised a family of entrepreneurs. They taught my three brothers and me the value of being in charge of our own destinies. They also taught us the value of taking responsibility for our mistakes and learning from our frequent blunders.

Moreover, they gave each of us the gift of humor—the ability to laugh and to find our own happiness in a world filled with opportunities.

We learned through our parents' example that integrity is everything in business and that although superiority in products and services may appear to be expendable luxuries when starting a business, that same superiority assures long-term success.

My dad was in the construction business. His ventures were varied, and his failures became lessons for later successes. He and my mother worked hard and as a team—each one helping the other. My mother appeared to be the perfect entrepreneur's wife—supportive, encouraging, and portraying a positive image of her husband's business for all to see. Yet, she also had the entrepreneurial spirit. She ran the business end of my dad's company. In her "spare time"—after keeping the records for my dad's business, taking care of four growing boys, and selling encyclopedias—she decided to open a kindergarten to bring in more money. After several years of successful business growth, my mother and dad were both able to sell their respective businesses and retire, travel, and enjoy themselves.

I draw strength from the memory of my mother and dad and all the good that they represented. If you are blessed with similar role models, take counsel from them, whether in person or in spirit—you won't go wrong.

Help Us Keep This Guide Up to Date

Every effort has been made by the author and editors to make this guide as accurate and useful as possible. However, many things can change after a guide is published—new products and information become available, regulations change, techniques evolve, etc.

We would love to hear from you concerning your experiences with this guide and how you feel it could be made better and be kept up to date. While we may not be able to respond to all comments and suggestions, we'll take them to heart and we'll make certain to share them with the author. Please send your comments and suggestions to the following address:

The Globe Pequot Press
Reader Response/Editorial Department
246 Goose Lane
P.O. Box 480
Guilford, CT 06437

Or you may e-mail us at:
editorial@GlobePequot.com

Thanks for your input!

Contents

Foreword

If a successful business was just about knowing the technical details, of being able to fit tab "a" into slot "b," then you'd be able to put this book down right now and get on with building cool Web sites for clients and earning lots of money.

Hold on, though!

It's not clear sailing at all, and there's a reason why so many small businesses are unsuccessful—particularly in the service sector. A successful Web design business has to first and foremost be a successful business, which means, like it or not, you're going to have to become at least a part-time businessperson in addition to being a Web designer.

You won't need to subscribe to the *Harvard Business Review* or enroll in a prestigious executive MBA program, but you really do need to learn how to draw up a contract, negotiate, manage deadbeat clients, back out of bad relationships, balance a checkbook, and much more.

That's why you're lucky to have picked up Jim Smith's splendid book *How to Start a Home-Based Web Design Business*!

With his breezy writing style and engaging sense of humor, Jim not only tells you everything you need to know and do to have a successful business and be a successful Web designer, he also shares his horror stories and explains what happened, how he dealt with it, and how he now avoids the problem.

I spent years running a home-based Web design firm from the perspective of "if I know more about HTML than you do, I'm ready to run a business." It was mostly good, with interesting clients, a steady paycheck, and engaging work. Except when it wasn't, when the client bailed halfway and decided not to pay me, or found that his niece or nephew could do the work for half the price, or when changes and updates were a ceaseless flow, eating up all my time and costing me lost opportunities, or when clients simply didn't live up to their side of the relationship.

I didn't have the benefit of Jim's book, so I had to learn through experience, which is valuable but slow, and often expensive. You have a smarter path ahead of you, because you can read *How to Start a Home-Based Web Design Business* and learn all the details involved with having a successful and sustainable business. Less pain, more profit. Sheesh, I wish I'd had this when I was in the thick of things!

As a fellow home-based business entrepreneur, I also appreciate Jim's explanation of why he hasn't hired lots of employees, taken on more work than he can comfortably fit into his lifestyle, or sold his business to a larger firm. One of the greatest benefits of being a home-based Web designer is that you have the flexibility to make the job fit your life, not vice versa.

Being able to work at home with minimal overhead while simultaneously coming across as a professional and being competitive with fancier, higher priced firms is critical, and that's another lesson you'll learn as you read this.

The only mistake you can make at this juncture is not to read this book cover to cover. Grab a highlighter, too. You'll need it.

Dave Taylor
Intuitive Systems, Inc.
www.intuitive.com

Acknowledgments

My gratitude goes to my many clients—without whom there would be no Web design business. However, this book, as well as much of my success, is only possible through the strength I receive from my wonderful wife, Cindy Smith. As someone who has more than thirty-five years of service with the same employer, she frequently, and understandably, is mystified by my entrepreneurial drive. She has always been, however, right beside me as my cheerleader, advisor, and confidant.

While running a business may appear simple on the surface, it is often because of a team effort that the business runs smoothly. My key team player is my wife. When I meet an obstacle, I can count on her perspective to help me overcome it. When business is in a slump, she gives me the enthusiasm to keep going. Her support and encouragement have given me the necessary motivation to write this book, while simultaneously designing Web sites.

A tired cliché states, "Behind every successful man, there is a woman." I do not like this expression. Cindy has neither been behind me, nor quietly working behind the scenes. She stands beside me as an independent and accomplished individual. I like standing side-by-side with her as well. Because of her, this book was possible.

Introduction

So, you're considering going into business as a Web site designer. Maybe you've greatly enjoyed the process of designing your own site or you've had some experience building sites for others? You think this might be the right time to turn your creative energy into an income-producing business. Great idea—as long as you put together a plan that ensures a good chance of success.

Opportunities for intriguing design work abound in today's Internet marketplace. The World Wide Web has opened doors (or perhaps windows is the better metaphor!) for well-trained, creative minds to launch enterprises unheard of in earlier decades. Your dreams may include starting a company whose design work is generated by a team of colleagues, or you may simply desire a modest income developed by your own steady attention to a small number of hand-picked clients. In either case, this book will start you on the path to success.

In the pages that follow, I describe the structure of a small, independent Web site design shop and offer my choices and experiences as guidelines for you designers who are planning to open or improve a shop of your own. You may find that you are well rounded in the five personality traits that I've iden-tified as the best qualities of the entrepreneurial Web site designer. Or you may discover that those are traits you'll need to develop, and you'll start out small. If you follow the many tips I offer from my own firsthand trial and error, you may avoid the most common pitfalls of small-business ownership and be on your way to achieving your dream.

In *How to Start a Home-Based Web Design Business*, I will show you several different approaches for running your own Web design shop. Some designers want to be on the cutting edge of technology, while others, myself included, forgo the flashier options available and focus on building Web sites that give a great experience to a wide range of computer users. Since there is no right or wrong beyond delivering Web sites that satisfy your clients, you will need to determine your own Web design style, based on your strengths and the markets you want to tap into. You may also find that your style changes over time. The point is to discover your own style and what works for you and your clients.

With confidence gained through the worksheets, quizzes, tip lists, and appendices provided within these pages, you can look forward to many years of personally and professionally rewarding work. As you peruse the topics listed in this guide, you'll notice the book is crammed with valuable advice on the nitty-gritty of shop setup, equipment, business structures, accounting, marketing, advertising, contracts, and much more. More importantly, this book also provides encouraging ideas for the maximum enjoyment of having your own business. My goal is to help you define your goals, develop a sound plan, and achieve your highest potential—personally and professionally. So, let's get started!

01 Overview of a Web Design Shop

Let's begin by defining the basics for those who like to start at square one. A Web design shop is a business that offers services related to setting up, modifying, and maintaining Web sites on the Internet. In this book, the focus is on Web design shop activity for commercial Web sites rather than personal ones. If you find that you have a market for personal Web site development, you will be able to easily adapt your practices for that market.

What Size Shop Is Best for You?

A Web design shop can be any size from a one-person business to a large company with many employees working on varied aspects of multiple projects. This book addresses the needs of those who want to open a Web design shop with either a single worker or a limited staff.

In addition to designing Web sites, many Web design shops offer a variety of related services. These can include Internet consulting and training, Web site hosting (putting the Internet files on a server that is connected to the Internet), Web-based programming, graphic design, e-commerce development, search engine optimization, marketing, and other services. You may need to provide some or all of these additional services, depending on your area of focus and the needs of your market.

Your Web design shop can be located in your home, in a commercial office building, or virtually—on your laptop! I have found that a Web design shop need not be located in a luxurious office with high overhead. Chapter 3 discusses some of the pros and cons of having a Web design shop in an office complex, as well as some of the issues with other locations.

As my client list for my Web design business increased, I began to wonder whether to expand my business beyond a one-person shop. Many large Web design shops started out small, grew, then merged their way into multimillion-dollar businesses. The temptation can be great to do likewise. In my own case, after much research and discussion, I decided that the advantages of a small shop worked best for my personality and lifestyle.

Following on page 3 is a list I created to help me make that decision. All the statements are worded positively so they can be weighed fairly. Some of these points may be more important to you than others, and you may have additional issues to consider.

I might be able to make more money by merging or by expanding my business, but one-on-one contact with my clients is important to me. The decision to keep my business small was the right one for me.

If you want a couple of good resources for understanding larger Web design shops, read *Web Project Management: Delivering Successful Commercial Web Sites* by Ashley Friedlein and *Secrets of Successful Web Sites: Project Management on the World Wide Web* by David Siegel. Friedlein's book delves into the how-tos of leading a team of developers through the various design functions, from the planning to the testing and ultimately to the launch of a Web project and ongoing support and maintenance. Friedlein has created a textbook of valuable information for anyone thinking about opening a large Web design shop. Although it is a great reference book, Friedlein's book lacks useful examples of projects she has handled. This is where Siegel's book excels.

Although Siegel's book was written in 1997, the information and examples are still helpful today. He describes specific projects that he has worked on, as well as the various sizes of design businesses and some of the pros and cons of each. He also provides an idea of how larger Web design shops handle their projects.

Both of these books stay in a prominent spot on my bookshelf. They have been a handy reference as I looked at jobs that were larger than those I typically accept. Sometimes their suggestions gave me the confidence to accept larger jobs. Other times, their advice made me realize that some projects should be referred to a larger team of designers.

SMALL SHOP ADVANTAGE	LARGE SHOP ADVANTAGE
I can make my own decisions without requiring a team discussion.	Responsibility for decision making is shared.
I control the jobs coming in and can take some time off whenever I decide to.	With others to depend on, I can get the coverage I need to take time off when I wish to.
When I'm feeling fired up and eager to work, I can take on extra work and enjoy the extra income.	When I feel good, others around understand those good times and enjoy sharing in them.
When I'm not feeling inspired, I can take a day off to recharge my battery.	When I'm in a slump, there are others around to help me snap out of it.
If I get a job that requires a skill I don't have, I can hire an outside contractor to assist in the project.	I can tap into a large pool of diverse resources.
If a client is happy, I enjoy knowing I'm directly responsible. Conversely, if there is a problem, I know that I have the authority to take care of that problem.	Satisfied customers are the result of teamwork. Colleagues work together to correct problems.
I can settle in and focus on my work for hours without interruption.	There are others around to help keep the feeling of isolation from overwhelming me.
I am directly responsible for the flow of money. The harder I work and the more satisfied clients I have, the more I make.	A steady stream of clients and revenue means a steady paycheck. I don't need to worry as much about where the next job will come from.
I get to see projects go from start to finish. It is rewarding to begin a project and know that I'll be able to see it through to the end.	I can focus on my area of expertise knowing that others will focus on theirs. Even though I do only specific tasks, the entire job will be expertly done.

Is This a Good Time to Start a Web Design Business?

In 1859 British novelist Charles Dickens penned, "It was the best of times, it was the worst of times."[1] Some people will say that this is a good time to start a Web design business; others will say it is the worst of times to start your own business.

Although some of your decision depends on where you are located and the market you are going after, much is based on your ability to meet potential clients' needs. I'm in Connecticut and have noticed that the larger Web design companies have slowed down, whereas my business and other small design companies are doing well.

In the early 1990s when I started my Web design business in my local area of Hartford, many businesses were very successful. I was told that it was a bad time to start an Internet company since most businesses were doing well and didn't need a Web site or my services. When the downturn came in the mid-1990s, I was told that it was a bad time to be in the Internet business due to the downturn.

In the early 2000s we were once again hearing that it was a bad time to be in business due to the uncertainty in the economy. And after the tragedy of September 11, 2001, many larger firms decided to make cutbacks, including having their existing staff take over much of their Web design and update work. Since this was the bread and butter of larger Web design companies, the larger Web companies found themselves hurting. These larger companies tried to scale down their services to meet the needs of smaller businesses needing Web designs, but even today most smaller businesses have smaller budgets (made even smaller by the market slowdown) and can't pay enough to make their business worthwhile for the larger Web design companies.

So, what happens to my smaller business is that, after a potential client has had a couple of bids from the "big guys" for $8,000 to $20,000 or more, my Web site start-up price of $1,000 to $2,000 starts looking very attractive.

Starting any business is not easy, and there is no "perfect" time to do so. But based on my experience and what I'm hearing from others, if you make that "leap," your chances increase if you go after smaller businesses and keep your costs down so you can give your customers a good deal for their money.

A smaller Web design business has some flexibility that larger ones are missing. When times are tight, you are helping other businesses that want to stay in business

---

1 A Tale of Two Cities, *bk. 1, ch. 1 (1859)*.

during a tough economy. Your job is to advise them on their Internet strategy. You will help them succeed since this is the time when they will be eager to set up or upgrade their Web sites. As economic conditions improve, your clients will be eager to add new features to their Web sites. So whether it is the worst of times or the best of times, you should focus on helping your clients improve their business. This will make it the best of times for you.

Who Should Start a Web Design Shop?

A leading Web design magazine on the Internet[2] offers a tongue-in-cheek recommendation that the first step to take in setting up a Web design business is to make an emergency appointment to see a mental health professional so he or she can talk you out of it. Certainly some would agree with this advice. However, certain personality traits have helped me in owning and successfully operating my Web design shop. This book will help you identify your strengths as well as those areas in need of fortification, which may spare you a visit to those mental health professionals.

To successfully operate a Web design business, you must either hire many people or wear many hats. Since you probably won't start out with a full staff of people, you will need to use your gift of gab to sell your services while keeping that pencil sharpened to make sure the business expenses are met and simultaneously pondering the scripts needed to design the Web sites. While carrying out your various roles you may decide that my euphemism of "changing costumes" sounds much better than "having multiple personalities," although on some days the difference may seem slight.

Imaginary "costumes" can help you understand the five major behavior traits you will need in your Web design business. In the computer arena, the popular name for the first personality trait is the propeller-head. This trait is symbolized by a beanie hat with a propeller on top. I wear my propeller hat when I am working with the code and scripts of a Web site. The second outfit I wear is my ponytail. This is the costume of the creative artist working with the graphics and the layout of a Web site. I put on my rainmaker costume when I need to stir up a storm of customers; then I quickly change to my green visor cap, sharpen my pencils, and calculate how to turn my flood of customers into dollars. Finally, there is one more essential outfit—my suit. This allows me to become the wise businessperson who makes the

---

2 *Charlie Morris,* Web Developer's Journal, *November 24, 1999; (http://web developersjournal.com/articles/set_up_a_web_design_shop.html)*

tough decisions to guide my business to meet my goals. Let's take a closer look at these various costumes.

The Propeller-Head: Programming, Scripting, and Computerizing

Many of you wishing to set up your own Web design shops will start out as propeller-heads. You may have been working as a programmer in a dark corner of a corporate computer department. You may have been tweaking a database for the company Web site or working with the massive servers that provide storage and security for a corporate site. Over time you have branched out to learn about the layout and design of a Web site. This training, coupled with strength in programming or computer networking, is a powerful combination.

Although most propeller-heads are very happy staying behind the scenes, keeping Web sites safe and operating smoothly, some may wish to break away. If you are a propeller-head, study the other "costumes" you will need to wear and decide if you can either handle those areas of the business or find a partner or employee who can do so. If you are a propeller-head, you are probably very analytical and detail-oriented. This is the antithesis of our next personality, the ponytail.

The Ponytail: Artistic Design and Layout

If you are a creative and artistic person, you are probably known in computer circles as a ponytail. You may be a graphic designer or a layout artist for a company newsletter. You may be an administrative assistant who has been asked to create or update your department's section of the corporate Web site. If you are a ponytail currently working on Web sites, you probably arrange the sections and you may create logos and graphics for the site. You also probably have a team of propeller-heads that takes care of programming and networking the site.

As you do more work and learn more about the Internet, you will begin to pick up some of the skills to write scripts that make Web sites not only attractive but also interactive. With your strength in the creative and artistic areas, you may find it tedious to work on code one line at a time to try to fix a problem area. However, you probably will enjoy putting on the rainmaker outfit and using your creative talents to talk to potential clients about how great a new Web site can look.

The Rainmaker: Selling Your Services

The rainmaker is probably the most easily overlooked of our five Web shop personalities. But it's as important as any other role you carry out. Whether you're a propeller-head learning how to be creative or a ponytail learning about programming, you will eventually discover that if you don't take the time to create rain, or clients, you will go through many dry spells and your business will wither.

It takes a special person to turn a lukewarm potential client into a motivated, enthusiastic customer. If you are a propeller-head, you are accustomed to using logic repeatedly, but this may not be what a potential client needs to make a decision. You may need to translate the complexity and teach your customer using very basic terms and easily understood analogies. Alternatively, as a ponytail, you may be most comfortable selling the Web site as an artistic masterpiece. Again, this may not be what your client needs. Your client may need to know how her site will translate into dollars and cents.

You will need to take off your beanie cap or ponytail outfit to put on your rain-making gear and start helping your potential client make a decision. In my own business, once I became comfortable swapping these different costumes—or aspects of my business—I was much more effective in my interaction with clients. Chances are you'll notice the same effect. Whether a client (either one person or several representatives from one company) asks about your creative abilities or programming skills, or just needs some facts to show that you're the right person for the job, you can successfully respond to his or her needs. Good rainmaking skills will help you not only to acquire new customers, but also to keep a steady volume of work and thus avoid nerve-wracking feast-and-famine cycles.

The Green Visor Cap: Bookkeeping

Your Web design shop may have creative talents, skillful programs and scripts, and the ability to bring in a steady flow of business. However, unless you regularly put on the green visor cap, grab the sharpened pencils, and look at profitability, everything else may be a waste of time. No one expects you to be an accountant in order to run a Web design business. (In fact, in chapter 3 you can discover why you may want to pay someone else to do this job.) However, as the owner of a Web design business, you do need to spend some time making sure your business is profitable. Whether you do your own bookkeeping or farm out that task to someone else, ultimately you are responsible for your business and you should have an idea of its financial status.

It is reasonable to expect that you are computer savvy and that you may wish to computerize most aspects of the bookkeeping and accounting. However, you will find that many of your accounting tasks require a certain amount of manual intervention. Every time you do some work for a client on an hourly basis, you must track that time carefully. You must make sure that you transfer your time to an invoice and submit the invoice to that client. For your clients on a monthly or quarterly contract, you must make sure they get their invoices on time. You must also make sure clients pay those invoices. You also need to deposit those payments into your business bank account and record the deposits.

Before you can bill one cent to a client, you need to be able to estimate how much time you will spend on a project, what your expenses will be, what profit you need from the project, and finally, how much to charge the client. Once you have established a budget for that project, you need to put in milestones to make sure the project remains profitable. If you are adding features that were not in the original specs, you need to be able to go to the client and sell him on the extra cost, showing him how the additional features will enhance his site.

Did you see a switching of costumes in the example just discussed? While wearing your green visor cap, you calculated that additional features would require additional funding, so you put on your propeller-head cap and listed all the neat benefits of this great script. You then put on your rainmaker outfit and set out to flush out the necessary additional funding. With all of these personalities working together, the only piece missing is the one that holds it all together by making the tough decisions—the "suit."

The Business Suit: The Decision Maker

There are times when you must make tough decisions to further the business, becoming the hard-core businessperson who looks only at improving the bottom line. Do you need to take on some undesirable clients to give a boost to your cash flow? Do you need to sit down with a client who is fun to work with and tell him that in order to continue making improvements to his site, you must charge him more? Do you need to settle a debate between your programming propeller-head and your creative ponytail? This is all part of being the suit. Some people love the stress and tension of making hard business decisions; most of us would rather avoid them. But no matter how you feel, there are many times when a detached, unemotional opinion is needed to keep the business running successfully.

Balance: Putting It All Together

My experience has proved that the five different personality traits or costumes need to work together in a Web design business. There may be times when you want your creative talents to take center stage and other times when you need to sharpen your pencils, put on your green visor, and try to figure out how to make a profit on a project that's on the table.

Many of my clients have made me realize the benefit of having all my strengths readily available. With my propeller cap on, I can work with their technology department to assure them that their needs for security can be met. With a switch to ponytail mode, I can show the great-looking graphics they can have on their new Web site. The green visor cap personality can figure out what it will cost them, while the rainmaker can show them why that price is a great bargain. If negotiations are necessary, the "suit" can tell a client that although the neat graphics will really enhance his site, those can be pared down to lower the cost a bit. (Meanwhile the imaginary ponytail is in the background mumbling!)

By now it should be clear how each of the five personality traits benefits your Web design business, and why you need to be able to balance those traits. However, what happens if you hate to make decisions? Or you enjoy decision making but do not like to spend your time on the "artsy" part of designing Web sites? Or, what if you enjoy creating Web sites but do not feel comfortable trying to sell your services? Does this mean that you should not open your own Web design business? Not necessarily.

It's unlikely that many Web designers have a perfect balance of every trait. Most of these costumes are behaviorally opposite others. Since we are all human, we need to determine where our strengths are and explore ways to build up the areas that need improvement.

How Will You Fare in a Web Design Business?

The following quiz will help you identify your business strengths and weaknesses. Once you know them, you can learn how to maximize the strengths and compensate for the weaknesses. This exercise is for your benefit, and the more candid you are, the easier it will be to spot the areas you want to develop.

For each behavior, rate yourself on a scale of one to five. One means the statement is nothing like you, and five means it fits you perfectly. Add up your points for each section to see what areas need work.

Your Rating	Propeller-Head
	"I could spend hours tweaking a program just to see it run successfully."
	"I am familiar with and can use many programming languages such as Java, C++, Perl, PHP, ASP, and more."
	"I've worked with many networks and computer systems. I'm familiar with terms like TCP/IP, router, ATM, and DSL."
	"I like to study many of the methods used to prevent crackers from breaking into computer systems on the Internet. I feel confident in working to maximize security on a Web site."
	"I have taken computers apart and feel I know a lot about how the memory works, how a hard drive functions, and how it all works together."
	Total out of 25 possible points

Your Rating	Ponytail
	"I feel I have a good sense of color, balance, and eye appeal, and I enjoy laying out a Web site."
	"I am very comfortable with one or more popular graphic design programs used to create and modify graphics for the Internet."
	"I am familiar with terms like pixels, Web-safe colors, screen resolution, jpeg, gif, and dither."
	"I could spend hours blending a group of photos into a collage for a Web site."
	"I like to do creative and artistic things, such as painting, drawing, sculpting, designing newsletters, photography, and landscaping. I just enjoy being creative."
	Total out of 25 possible points

Your Rating	Rainmaker
	"I love to talk to potential clients about the Internet and its benefits and the great opportunities."
	"I am amazed when I meet someone who is not on the Internet. I look forward to figuring out how their business can change if they get on the Internet."
	"When I go to social gatherings, I find myself talking excitedly about the Internet and what the future will bring."
	"I enjoy selling a service I believe in. I find a big thrill in getting a prospect to make a commitment and sign a contract."
	"If someone else were cranking out Web sites, I'd enjoy running out and beating on doors to sell as many as they could generate."
	Total out of 25 possible points

Your Rating	Green Visor Cap
	"I enjoy figuring how much money I can make, whether by designing Web sites or selling widgets."
	"If a client wants a Web site, I can always find a way to work it into his or her budget while still making money for myself."
	"I'm familiar with the difference between accounts receivable and accounts payable in business. I know what cash flow is and what tax forms I need to file."
	"I've tended to the books for a business and have been responsible for keeping track of some of the accounting needs of a business."
	"It would drive me crazy to not have a clear picture of how much money I make and how much I spend."
	Total out of 25 possible points

Your Rating	Business Suit
	"When I have something of value that someone else needs, I enjoy negotiating a deal to make us both happy."
	"I would much rather make a decision, right or wrong, than leave a matter undecided. I hate indecisiveness."
	"I have broad shoulders. I am willing to take full responsibility for everything that happens in my business and personal life."
	"When a decision must be made, I'm not against making someone uncomfortable. That heightened stress level is what makes things happen."
	"I've owned or managed successful businesses before. I enjoy directing a business unit."
	Total out of 25 possible points

How to Score the Quiz

Propeller-Head: How did you score for programming, scripting, and computerizing?

Points	Comments
21–25	Congratulations; you are a propeller-head! Use these strengths to your advantage by getting contracts that need a lot of scripting or database work that others may not be able to handle. You may find that you are not as strong in some other areas of this quiz. If so, you may want to find another Web designer with those strengths who needs a partner with your skills.
16–20	You have a strong background in programming or scripts that will give you a firm foundation in your Web design business. Do not be afraid to market your skills when promoting your business.
11–15	Your skills as a propeller-head are probably very adequate for designing Web sites. You might find that, as you get projects that are beyond your capabilities, you need to either brush up on some of the needed techniques or find some assistance. Keep in your contact list the name of at least one propeller-head who is willing to help on occasional projects either as an employee or on a contract basis.

5–10	You will need some help from a propeller-head! You should consider either taking some courses to strengthen your skills or finding a propeller-head to work with on a regular basis.

Ponytail: **How did you score for artistic design and layout?**

Points	Comments
21–25	You are an Internet ponytail! You have strong artistic and creative skills that you will be able to bring to Web site designs. If you need some help with other aspects of your business, use your layout and design skills and find an associate with other strengths for projects that are more complex.
16–20	You have a very strong creative and artistic background. This will serve you well in layout, design, and improvement of Web sites. In selling your services, be sure to highlight your skills as a creative designer. But keep in mind that the goal of most Web sites is to inform or sell a product or service. Avoid creating great-looking Web sites, known as "eye candy," that do not accomplish their goals.
11–15	You have good skills that will help you in designing Web sites. As long as you work on Web sites that do not require advanced skills in design or graphic artwork, you should be fine. If you find you are getting projects that require advanced skills, you may wish to contract with a graphic artist.
5–10	Keep the names of some good ponytails in your contact list! You may also want to spend some time experimenting with a good graphic design program. Most have tutorials available either on the Internet or on a CD-ROM. If you are not interested in the creative side of Web design, or feel you don't have the necessary talent, make sure you have a strong partner, contractor, or employee to give you help with the creative tasks.

Rainmaker: **How did you score for selling your services?**

Points	Comments
21–25	You have the ability to create rainstorms of customers! Your strength in selling is a great asset. Be careful that you don't

oversell your services and then find you can't keep up with the work. You may wish to combine forces with either a propeller-head or a ponytail so that you can concentrate on keeping work flowing.

16–20	You have a talent for selling. If you combine that with some design skills and try to enhance any other traits that need boosting, you should have a great future in owning a Web design shop.
11–15	Your sales ability is probably adequate to maintain your business. You might want to spend some time learning new sales and marketing skills. Try to find a niche market (for example, focus on being a hardware store Web designer or health care provider Web designer) and become the expert in that area. This will allow you to concentrate on a smaller market while building your skills in sales.
5–10	Like me, you need to really sharpen your skills in sales and market-ing or find someone to assist you with that. There are many books and seminars on marketing your business and on creating sales strategies. (Be aware, however, that you may have a tendency to *read* how to market and promote your business rather than actu-ally doing so!) If you know someone who can create a rainstorm of customers, you may wish to hire him or her on a contract basis to help you get started, or have him or her work part-time selling for you.

Green Visor Cap: How did you score for number crunching?

Points	Comments
21–25	Congratulations; you can track your Web design shop's profit-ability. Typically, you may also have strength in programming or, if not, have the focus to do so. Also, you can probably handle the business decisions, but be careful that you don't lose customers by making business determinations based solely on numbers and logic with customers who operate on instinct.
16–20	You have a good foundation for making sure the numbers make sense in your business. Keep your eye on those numbers while making sure that you don't neglect the other facets of your

business. You may wish to make a schedule to determine when to sit and "crunch the numbers." Then make sure that you maintain a balance between knowing your financial status and keeping the sales coming in and design work going out.

11–15   You know enough about your business numbers to keep track of what is there. You may want to get someone to help maintain your books so you can focus on other areas of the business. Don't be afraid to ask questions of others who understand the accounting process better than you do.

5–10   Your green visor cap is down over your eyes and you will need some help! You may want to hire an accountant (not the most expensive one with the fanciest office when you are starting out!). Read the section in chapter 3 about hiring professionals, and be ready to get the assistance you need. Much like using the gauges on your car, if you don't know what the gauges in your Web design shop mean, you might run out of fuel even though, with some planning and forethought, you could have simply filled up the tank.

Business Suit: **How did you score as a decision maker?**

Points	Comments
21–25	Congratulations; you are able to make high-level decisions to keep your Web design shop running smoothly and profitably. You may find that, although you are strong in decision-making skills, you can't sell to indecisive individuals. Alternatively, you may have difficulty in the artistic design of a Web site or the tedium of troubleshooting a script. Most Web designers are not strong decision makers, so you may want to team up with someone who can use your expertise.
16–20	You have no problem making decisions and negotiating deals. Use your skills in creating a professional shop to your advantage. Evaluate the areas in which you need help, and decide whether it is better for you to focus on strengthening yourself in these areas or to bring on some assistance.
11–15	You have enough business experience to run your business. If you feel you are entering into difficult negotiations, prepare yourself

as much as possible and decide ahead of time what your bottom line is. If you find yourself losing important points in contracts, mentally put on your suit and tough it out. Periodically you may find that you have trouble making some decisions. This is normal but it shouldn't get in the way of running your business. If you find, however, that it is affecting your business, find a trusted ally to use as a sounding board. In your Web design business, you don't need people to agree with you—you need people who will give you their honest opinions and tell you when you are deluding yourself.

5–10   You may wish to have someone around to make some of those tough decisions with you. Drawing straws and flipping coins can work in some cases, but when your business depends on evaluating information and making an educated decision, you don't want to leave it to chance. Consider taking some courses on how to evaluate data and make effective determinations. You also should look into assertiveness training classes. Some clients will be happy to take advantage of a skilled but indecisive Web designer. Be ready to negotiate a fair decision with those clients. You may wish to find a mentor through your local Small Business Administration's SCORE chapter to give you periodic advice and act as a sounding board for your business.

Putting Your Score Together

If you scored a total of more than 75 points on this quiz, you are probably in great shape to start your own Web design business. If your score was between 50 and 75 points, look at some of the areas where you need support.

If you are strong in designing and programming but need help in the business aspect or in selling yourself, consider taking some business-related courses. If you are great at selling and at running a business but less skilled at creating Web sites or writing scripts, you may wish to hook up with designers who are interested in either contracting work or partnering.

If you are fortunate enough to have a relatively level score for each of the five areas, you will be able to take care of a wide variety of client needs. You will find that it is to your advantage to have a broad knowledge not only of Web design skills but also of business-related skills. In addition to the obvious benefits of having business skills to run a business, you will also find it helpful in marketing Web sites to other business owners. You will be able to convey the benefits of a Web site to an apprehensive businessperson.

If your total score is much below 50 points, you should either supplement this book with courses on business and Web design or consider working with other Web designers to build up some of the necessary skills. Although you may not find it possible to be totally frank at all times, you will be able to pick up more from others if they know in advance that your goal is to learn from them so that you can go out on your own. Once you increase your confidence with some further education and experience, you'll be better equipped to define your own business.

02

Deciding What Services to Offer

First among the decisions to make when creating a Web design shop is the number and kind of services to offer. Luckily, many clients will approach you with a clearly defined list of needs. Your level of expertise, however, will determine what services you can actually offer. When I started my business, I offered only limited services based upon my experience. If someone needed a Web site designed or repaired, I was the right person for that job. If someone needed any database work or programming done, I declined. Over time, I discovered which services were most appealing to clients and either added those to my repertoire or found someone to do the work either as a subcontractor or by referral. Some clients want to deal with only one individual; others would rather break a job into segments and try to get the lowest bid on each piece. For clients who want you to take care of all of their Internet needs, your best strategy is to develop the additional skills or locate subcontractors to supplement your abilities.

Web Site Hosting

When I started my Web design shop, many of my customers knew nothing about the Internet. They had no idea what to do after their Web sites were designed. I could help them upload their files onto the Internet company or host that they had lined up, but many of them didn't know which Web hosts were good or bad. Naturally they looked to me for an expert opinion on who should host their Web sites. I knew that hosting the Web site referred to the computer in which the Web files are stored, and I knew that the server needed to be connected to the Internet. Beyond that, my understanding was not very clear of the Internet.

Even though my own knowledge of Web hosting was not extensive at the time, hosting seemed to be an important service to offer. I knew it was important to find a good hosting company that I could recommend to my clients, and after researching the possibilities, I decided to become a reseller.

The prices my clients were being quoted for Web site hosting ranged from nothing to a generous sum. I knew with some Web hosts charging no fee, I couldn't compete on price. I also knew that due to low margins, many Web designers were offering hosting only to their own clients. As Web designer Sean Oskouie, said, "We have ceased offering hosting to non-design clients altogether . . . it is not worth it, unless you own your own servers and have the required staff to maintain them, and then it still is not worth it." Sean elaborated on the kind of service that he includes in his hosting and asserted that "no one can steal my customers even if they offer the same hosting package at half price."

Like Sean and many others, I also decided to offer hosting only to my design clients and compete on service and features of hosting rather than price. I looked for a company that could offer great service, reliability, and reasonable prices (the cheapest is probably not the most dependable), and one that had a track record for speedy connectivity. Because I knew little about Web servers, I also wanted a company that made the process easy for me to understand and work with. (If you have experience with servers, that may not be as important to you.)

I realized that I had two possibilities: I could get my own equipment and do everything myself, or I could resell hosting through another company. Since I'm lacking as a propeller-head with the skills needed to do everything myself, I decided not to host using my own servers but instead to resell using someone else's servers.

Hosting with Your Own Servers

If you are lucky enough to be a hands-on propeller-head with experience in networks and servers, you will probably be ready to host your clients on your own servers. There are several benefits to doing so. If you have your own servers, you can probably beat the prices offered by resellers like myself. You have a tremendous amount of control over what happens to your servers, what to load, when to upgrade, and how to troubleshoot any problems.

One of the major considerations is the initial cost that you will be making to buy, upgrade, and maintain the equipment and connections. You also must decide if you are offering around-the-clock monitoring and repairs to the servers; if a server goes down at 3:00 a.m. (and after bedtime seems to be a popular time for problems), you will need to make sure you or someone else is available to get the server back up and running quickly. If you are on vacation, someone must be available to monitor and fix any problems.

If you are taking care of your own servers, you must be very familiar with languages and tools available for the operating system(s) you have available, whether UNIX, Windows NT, Linux, or others. You also need to be on top of security issues and maintain your system with security patches. You also must stay informed of the latest security breaches so you can prevent them from reaching your system.

Marketing Your Servers

With your own servers in the basement of your office, you have a lot of work to do, but your profits will likely be greater than those of someone who is reselling hosting services. However, to get the sales, you will have to convince your clients that your hands-on care and your ability to take care of your clients' needs has enough value to make your services more appealing than the arsenal of support people and equipment that I have backing up the hosting packages that I'm reselling. Once you are aware of my marketing strategies to entice your hosting clients away from you, you can adjust your sales presentation accordingly.

When I talk with potential clients, I tell them that I will cost a bit more than smaller multipurpose servers offered by local Internet service providers. I explain that their files should be put on a major Web server that is connected directly to multiple main feeds of the Internet. Often I will run some tests to show clients in real time what my commercial server's Web page delivery time is compared to some of the more popular local servers. (Make sure you pick a very fast hosting company if you are going to try this as a selling technique!) I explain to my clients that the Web server that holds their files is secured inside a concrete reinforced fortress-like building that only authorized employees can access. Palm-scanners and other security devices safeguard the server room, which is staffed and monitored twenty-four hours a day. It's important to reassure clients that if something goes wrong with any server, there are multiple backup plans. All servers have instant power backup units attached in case of a power outage. For an extended outage, a huge power generator on standby outside in a semitrailer can supply the entire hosting company with electrical power. Multiple lines connect everything directly to the Internet, so if one feed goes down, others instantly take up the load (this is known as redundancy). All files are backed up each night to protect against loss or corrupted data.

I remind potential clients that, like other forms of information exchange, their Internet site should be of top quality. If they saw a TV commercial that was having technical difficulties or was otherwise of poor quality, they would not think too much of the company being promoted. Or if they went into a store to make some purchases and had to abandon their shopping cart because of a power outage, they wouldn't be very happy shoppers. The Internet experience is the same; if visitors have trouble accessing the Web site, they may not come back.

By the time I finish a sales pitch to potential clients, they usually see the value of paying a little more to get peace of mind that their Web site is being well cared for. If you are a propeller-head with your own servers, you will have to convince your clients that your hands-on care has enough value to make your services more appealing.

Becoming a Value Added Reseller

Since I don't have the skills of a propeller-head, I decided to become what's known as a *value added reseller* (VAR) of Web hosting services. By serving as a VAR, I increased my value to my clients and made some extra income as well. The key to the term "value added reseller" is the *value* you add, not simply being a reseller. If you aren't able to add any value for your clients, you will have trouble convincing them to pay you extra simply to be a middleman.

Part of the value that you can add for your clients is the knowledge and research about the best server for their needs. The servers that I use are heavy-duty, commercial grade servers. They almost never go down or slow down. For most of my clients, the monthly cost is not an issue because they get "something extra." They may not want to take the time to understand what is special about these servers, but they know that the value I offer is peace of mind and a good, reliable service.

I tell my clients that, although they can go with a lower-priced local server or one of the free services, I think their business is important enough to put it on a dependable, secure server. I ask them what would happen to their site if someone found a security hole, hacked into the local server, and changed all or part of their site. If they go with a "Blarneystone" server, they don't have to worry. Their Web site is monitored by experts and housed in the same secure fortress as huge megamillion-dollar corporations, so they get the same protection the big guys do.

If clients want to go with another hosting company, I graciously go along with their wishes but remind them that each hosting company does things a bit differently. If I am making changes to their Web site in the future, since I charge by the hour, they will be paying for me to work on a server that I'm not familiar with. And if there are any problems with the other server company, I won't be able to use my influence to get things fixed faster.

Basically, I always reassure potential clients that if they purchase their hosting through me, I'm responsible for those servers . . . period! If they have a problem, I won't be shunting them off to someone else or blaming it on those servers; I'll be fixing the problem!

Hosting Companies That Offer Reseller Packages

If you decide to become a reseller, there are numerous hosting companies available for you to choose from. You should first decide how quickly you will be trying to grow. Some companies allow you to start with one or two clients and grow from there. RapidSite is one hosting company that I've used that allows you to start small and add new clients as you grow. Another option is companies that charge you for space on a server; it is up to you how quickly you add customers. If you get a larger server, the price per unit of storage space goes down, but you need more customers to make it cost effective.

The difference between these two types of services is that the start-up cost with a company like RapidSite is less if you expect to have only one or two sites within the next several months. With RapidSite, you pay a start-up fee and then a monthly charge for each site they host for you. If you don't grow any larger than a couple of hosted sites in the next year, you only pay for those sites plus that start-up cost. For the other option, you rent a block of space on a server. You pay the same amount for that space whether you have two sites, twenty sites, or two hundred sites, limited only by the capacity of that server. Depending on what you charge, everything beyond your server rental cost is profit.

There are many companies offering these services. Two of the largest ones that I'm most familiar with are viaVerio and Alabanza. Alabanza has a very attractive reseller package with a full-featured "control panel" for each client that you sign up. A control panel is basically a Web page full of icons for options available to your client. You control the icons that each client has available so you can offer many add-ons that are convenient for your client to select. Some add-ons are free and others have a charge associated that adds more profit for you when someone chooses those features. A few years back I was discussing hosting with Alabanza's sales executive, Tommy Murphy, who stated that "no one comes close to us in automation." Many of their competitors have come a long way since then but Alabanza is still offering plenty of great packages.

With most automated control panels your clients can automatically add a variety of online editors or remove them. They can order a new domain name and pay online or make changes to an existing domain name. With numerous options for your clients to work with, you can upsell features and offer free features that appeal to your clients. Your server package should offer all the tools and support you need to get started. Tommy Murphy offers some details on their control panel, known as a Domain System Manager:

> Our Domain System Manager (DSM) allows you as a partner/client to have your entire business automated. The software handles domain registration, package creation, billing, reporting, databasing, collections, and much more. With this solid infrastructure in place, you can sleep at night and have the functions of your business running. The DSM handles all of the time consuming tasks so you can grow your business instead of running it. Our service reduces the cost of running a business to increase your profit margins.

One potential downside to a large server that you should be aware of is that you will be paying a large monthly fee for the server, so you need to make sure you have enough customers to keep you from going in the red. The people selling you server space should be able to help you figure out how many customers you need to start making a profit based on how much you intend to charge each customer. Based on a normal pricing structure, I need to bring in around twenty customers before I start making any profit on my servers. You may feel that you don't want to take this large of a step when first starting out.

If you like the idea of having some control of your server but don't want to start out quite as large, you could look at the servers offered by viaVerio. These are Virtual Private Servers (VPS), which means they are shared servers, with each reseller having its own protected turf. Depending on the price that you sell your hosting services for, you should be able to start making a profit after your third or fourth hosting customer.

The other option that I recommend to you if you are starting out in reselling hosting services is to pay a little extra to have a "server guru" or server manager on your team. I use http://ServerPros.com to help oversee all my servers. Their prices are nominal, and I like having someone else as my server guru who knows about things like MX records, CNAMES, SSL, SSI, Mutt, TOP, etc. When a client calls me to ask whether I can set up cURL or SSI or something like that, it is nice to be able to e-mail or call my "server experts" to get a quick answer.

Income from Reselling Hosting Services

I find that as I build the hosting business, the steady income helps level out the empty spots in my business's cash flow between Web design jobs. You should decide whether you want to offer hosting based on low prices or hosting based on top grade servers. Rather than competing on prices, I decided to deal in top quality servers. By doing that, I don't need to worry about competing with the low prices (or freebies) but rather can charge for professional commercial server space (averaging $30 to $50 in my area versus $10 to $20 for the low-cost servers). If you go for the higher-priced servers, just make sure your clients understand what they are paying for. In my experience, once they know what they are paying for, they will almost always pay a bit more for the peace of mind of a dependable server company.

For my servers, I use viaVerio and add in the services of a server management company to help me manage my servers. With this combination, I start making money when I get my fourth customer signed up for hosting. Although there is no minimum number of customers I need to sign up, I am renting a block of server space, so the faster I can sign up clients, the faster I can get them to pay me rent rather than myself paying it out of my pocket!

It costs me $150 a month to "rent" server space for a block of Web sites. I charge clients $40 per month, which means that I need at least four customers before I start making money on hosting. I also charge $50 for each customer as a one-time setup fee and pay the server company half of that. Once I load my server to a comfortable capacity of around twenty clients, I am bringing in $800 each month and paying the server company $150. After I fill one server, I start setting up another server. I then go back in the hole for a few weeks while I scramble to get those first four paying clients lined up for the next server. Then I can breathe easier and continue to build up the next server.

If you charge $40 per month, you will be competing with some cheap server companies charging $20 or less and some more expensive ones that charge $50 or so. You can charge less and go for the low-end profit margin, but I've found that if I gain my clients' confidence, I can show them that once they've had their site on my server, they'll never go back to a cheaper one.

Some Web hosts encourage their clients to pay annually by offering a discounted rate. I decided that because my focus is on Web design rather than hosting, billing annually distances me from my clients for a long stretch of time. When hosting a Web site, I send invoices out quarterly and usually touch base with those clients to make sure everything is satisfactory with their hosting. By doing this, instead of designing a Web site and then letting the client forget about me and the Web site for an entire year, I frequently get updates and some new referrals through this follow-up contact. When I invoice my clients, some are reminded of updates that they want and send me an e-mail requesting extra work for me to do. I've noticed that my requests for updates generally increase shortly after sending the quarterly hosting invoices. After a while, you will get more and more repeat business from a select group of clients that have placed a value on keeping their sites fresh and updated.

How to Get Started with Hosting

You should already have a few customers to start hosting Web sites and feel that you will be able to add more as time goes on. Mark Sharkey, the server manager with http://ServerPros.com, describes some of the information that server management companies typically need to set up Web sites on a server:

> Although a server can be set up without any Web sites, I would recommend that someone starting to host Web sites should have two to four Web sites ready to put on a server. That way they aren't starting with an empty server but are already close to, or above their breakeven point where they will start making money. After talking with a new reseller to determine the size server they need, all I need is an ID and password they want me to use to set up their server.

> For each Web site they are adding, they need to give me the domain name(s), and whether they are ordering those or if they want me to do so. I also will want to know if any of the sites will need special modules or add-ons.

> If they want me to set up the e-mail boxes I will need some information on that or I can teach them how to do that for themselves. E-mail can either be forwarded to another e-mail system or we can set up e-mail accounts (POP3 accounts) on their server. If they want e-mail forwarded, I need the incoming e-mail addresses (i.e., john@newaccount.com) and where to forward them (i.e., john@aol.com). If they want POP3 accounts, I will need the e-mail address (i.e., john@2ndnewaccount.com), the ID (john) and a password for accessing that POP3 account. For each domain name I also need to know if they want

a catchall address for any e-mail that isn't addressed to anyone specified. In other words, if someone sends e-mail to BobByrd@newaccount.com instead of RobertByrd@newaccount.com, should those incorrectly addressed e-mails be dumped, sent to someone within the organization, or returned as unknown.

If they will be using other software on the server, I will need to know which ones to install for them. For example, if they need to use Perl or PHP, or if they will be using a secure certificate, or need a database like MySQL or PostgreSQL, I can install whatever it is that they want. If they aren't sure, we can do a basic installation and, as time goes on, we can install programs as they are needed.

As server managers we can either take care of their entire server environment or we can provide them with a login and a password that gives them complete access to their entire server. With a server management company behind them, they can stay as "hands on" as they want.

Transferring a Web Site

If I am hosting a client's preexisting Web site over to my server, after I get a signed contract in hand (very important for protection!), I create a duplicate of the client's Web site on my server. I then check all links and pages to make sure it functions correctly on my server. Sometimes this is a simple process; at other times I spend awhile tweaking pages to make it work correctly. If I am going to be updating the Web site as well, I create a draft sub-directory to build the new Web site. I set up the client's e-mail records on my mail server. I then contact the registrar holding the domain name or I have my client do so, to change the DNS (Domain Name System) records over to my server. The DNS records tie together domain names such as www.blarney stone.com with hard-to-remember IP addresses such as 161.58.14.144. Once that has been approved it takes a few days for the change to appear. If I've done a good job of copying the original Web site onto my server, it is a seamless transfer and no one notices the changeover. I usually change a period or space or something small on the home page so I can easily detect the swap when I'm looking at the Web site on the new server.

You usually don't have to contact the previous hosting company during the changeover. However, when the domain name registrar gets the request to change the DNS records, they will notify the admin and technical contact via e-mail of the pending change to give them time to protest it. So eventually the former hosting company will know about the transfer anyway. If that company does protest the transfer (I've never had that happen), your client will have to contact the registrar directly to confirm that the change is authorized. It can be a big pain if that happens, and your new client will likely depend on some help and advice from you.

There are two things to point out to your newly transferred clients:

1. If the client has a long time left on a contract with the other company, you'll want to remind the client to cancel that once you are up and running to avoid paying double. It isn't your fault if that happens, but this just makes things less messy!

2. I didn't make it clear how the transfer process worked when I was dealing with one new client. I contacted the domain name registrar to change the records. The registrar contacted the previous host. The previous host took that as a hostile act by its ex-client, trying to sneak away "after all we've done for you." This created hard feelings between my client and the ex-host. Naturally I ended up in the middle because my new client wanted to break the news to the outgoing hosting company in its own way; instead there were bad feelings between them because I wasn't clear about when the transfer would become public knowledge. Not a lingering problem, but something that I'm now sensitive to, and you should be as well.

Other Considerations in Hosting Web Sites

■ As a Web host, you usually have access to update your clients' Web sites unless you don't want it. You are considered the "admin" (or "server god"), with complete control over the entire server. You ultimately are responsible for your server and what goes on there, securely setting up passwords for clients, determining what e-mail addresses to add (and remove) and what mailbox sizes to allocate for your clients, etc. This is a monumental amount of information to grasp all at once, which is why I prefer having someone helping to manage and advise me when I get in over my head. Whatever you decide, make sure you take the responsibility seriously. You have a business's main communication pipeline in your control. That company is depending on you to make all the right decisions. You have access to the company's passwords and possibly some confidential information. Be sure to treat the server information with the respect and privacy it deserves.

- In this quickly changing business, there may come a day when you become dissatisfied with your hosting company, so don't get so locked into the one that you are using that you can't switch to another one if needed. I would never switch without good reason, and if that became necessary, I'd test out the new hosting company first; if all went well, I'd contact my clients, tell them that I will be switching everyone over to the new servers, and explain why this will benefit them. Fortunately, I've only had to do this once, but I have heard horror stories from Web designers who have locked their clients into one hosting service and couldn't swap them without major interruption of service.

- Although I use the servers by viaVerio for my hosting solution, I recommend you research the market to find some hosting resellers that meet your specific needs and then try one or two. If you find a good match, build your business around that hosting company. However, if you don't like the first one(s), try others until you get one that meets your needs. Once you have found the one that you want to use, settle in and build a client base using that hosting company. You will find over a period of time that you become very familiar with the servers, what you can and can't do with them, and what their strengths and weaknesses are, and will be able to plan your work schedule knowing, for example, that it takes a certain amount of time to get a new account set up and to get changes made in the accounts as your clients' needs expand.

- Some people think that they are required to learn various programming languages as well as UNIX and/or NT to host Web sites. I didn't know any UNIX commands at the time I started hosting, yet most of my clients were on UNIX servers. If you are a ponytail such as I tend to be and lack an intimate knowledge of servers, you need to find a server guru to take care of some of that. After hosting for as long as I have, I've learned some UNIX commands, but I can still put in a phone call to my server manager and say, "I'm knee-deep in directories and can't remember what command tells me what the path is." It would be better if I knew all the UNIX commands, but second best is knowing how to get the help needed.

- In addition to the access you have to the server as a reseller of hosting services, you will also need to consider how much access you want to give your clients to their Web server. Many resellers give their clients total access to the server. Some, like Alabanza, include a control panel that gives a variety of configuration options on the server. I typically don't offer complete access unless a client specifically requests it. My reasoning is this: Most of my clients are very busy and don't have the time or the interest to make their own changes. They would rather pay someone to take care of everything for them; they don't want to feel compelled to learn how to change an e-mail address or password themselves.

Shared Updates

I let my clients know that when I'm the only one with access and there is something messed up on the back end, I know it is either the hosting service or me. Otherwise, if the client has access, I generally first suspect that the client did something to botch it up (which is frequently correct).

I then tactfully tell clients that if there is a problem that they've created and they want me to fix it, I bill hourly. If they don't want access and something breaks, it is my responsibility to fix it. Consequently I have very few clients with access to their own control panels. If yours are more hands-on or Internet savvy, you may wish to have them take more responsibility for their Web servers.

Domain Name Services

To some degree, you should be involved in purchasing domain names for your clients. Some of your clients won't have a domain name and will not know anything about them. They expect you to handle the details for setting up a Web site; searching for and purchasing a domain name is part of that service. At one time, buying a domain name was not a complex deal. There was one company that controlled all of the "dot-com" domains. That has changed. Now several companies sell domain names. Most are dependable, but be sure to check the reputation of any company from whom you are considering buying a domain name.

Occasionally horror stories circulate about the same domain name being accidentally sold to two companies. If I find the name my client wants is available and I purchase it, I don't want any complications. My client may be signing agreements to put that name on business cards, brochures, vehicles, TV ads, and more. Don't shop for the cheapest price for domain names—it isn't worth the potential for problems. An angry client who has already started the process of promoting a domain name, only to find out that there was a mix-up, will probably blame you, since you sold it to him. That could potentially create enough headaches and expensive lawsuits to keep an attorney in nice clothes for years to come. Look for a company with a clean record, not for the best price.

There are some other things to be aware of when registering domain names for clients. First, when you register a name for a client, make sure you have a reliable method to remind yourself a month or two before that name is going to expire. Don't depend on your registrar to remind you. If you change your e-mail address or have a typo on the form or the e-mail gets misdirected, you may not get the notification. Nothing will upset a client as much as assuming that you have everything under control, only to find out that her domain name has expired! There is a grace period with most registrars before the domain name goes back into circulation, but you should treat your clients' domain names as valued assets. If a client loses a domain name to someone else, that client probably won't be very understanding about your excuse.

Domain Name Ownership

I always list the clients as the owners of their own domain names. A client has paid for the name, so I feel it belongs to her. Besides, if there is a trademark fight, I don't want to be in the middle! I usually put my name as the billing and tech support and the client as the admin support. That way, if a client owes money and tries to quietly move a site (this has only happened a couple of times), as the tech contact I am notified. I would never (for legal reasons) hold a client's domain name hostage for nonpayment, but it is nice to be put on notice that someone is pulling up stakes and sneaking out.

Some designers try to put their own names as the only contact, but that can easily backfire and build up some distrust when another Web designer (such as myself) points out that even though the client "owns" her domain name, all control of making changes and such has been taken away from her. My clients appreciate knowing they can gain control over their domain names even though they and I know that they probably will never really need to.

If you are involved in managing domain names for your clients, be prepared to answer some questions from them due to the confusion created by outside companies trying to trick your clients into switching their domain names away from your service. Your clients will get written, faxed, or e-mailed notices that their domain names are about to expire (in six months or so) and, rather than lose them, they should send a check to this other company along with authorization to secure their domain names for the next five years or so. Usually I get a phone call from a confused client asking what this letter, e-mail, or fax means. Periodically I get a notice from the other company that my client's domain name is being moved somewhere else. As advocate for my client, I call the client immediately and explain what she was tricked into doing. I then suggest that she have her credit card company reverse the charge and that whoever is listed as the admin on the record block the switchover. So far this has worked well in those cases. However, there are always new scams being created, so make sure you stay alert to potential problems.

Search Engine Placement and Marketing Advice

If someone goes to a search engine and types *Webmaster,* he or she probably won't find your company in the top three results, or even the top ten. No matter how good you are at search engine placement, it probably won't happen. It would be like going to the library and asking to see any ten library books, hoping to find a particular one. There are too many books, and without being more specific, you probably wouldn't get the one you want. Whether books in a library or Web sites listed on a search engine, you need to be specific or really hunt through the listings to find the right one.

You may wish to offer a search engine placement service for your clients. I offer a one-time start-up listing with the major search engines as part of my design package, and do complimentary minor tweaking from time to time for sites that I've hosted. I also offer a quarterly add-on package with my Web hosting for people who recognize the value of search engine monitoring and placement.

Search Engine Report

As an additional service, I offer clients a tool I call the Quarterly Search Engine Rating and Analysis Report. This includes a report showing where the major search engines place my client using a predetermined key word or phrase. This shows whether any of the search engines have added, improved, reduced, or dropped their listing since the last report. If minor revisions are needed to improve a Web site's position, I often do them at no additional charge. (You may decide either to charge separately for changes or include all changes in your package deal.) In my quarterly report I also include some marketing tips specific to the client's type of business, along with suggestions that may help her utilize her Web site to build her business.

A few big search engines handle the vast majority of Internet searches. Listing your clients' Web sites with them brings the most value for the clients. Although most of the currently popular search engines (Google, Yahoo!, and Bing, for example) are likely to remain popular for some time to come, you should do research to make sure that you list clients on the top ones. The only time to vary from this plan is when there are significant local directories or even directories specific to a particular client's needs that make sense to target.

My search engine rating and analysis report comes in two parts. The first is an e-mail sent to my client with a summary of the report. It includes a link to the second part, a full documentation of the report through a series of Web pages located in a password-protected section of the client's Web site. This search engine report is usually bundled for a special price with another report I generate, my quarterly Web Site Statistics Report and Analysis. Should you create a similar system, always try to make the summary e-mail as informative and focused as possible because, for many busy business owners, that summary may be the only part of the report they have time to review. As informative as the full report is, it is admittedly an extensive amount of information. If you can't give a concise list of highlights, the client might overlook important parts of the report. By providing a summary, you give the client your opinion of the highlights and your analysis. She can then refer to the full documentation to back up those highlights if needed for marketing or budget meetings.

With these two reports each quarter, my clients are able to accurately assess the activity they can expect from their Web sites on the Internet. They can also forecast and budget for changes to improve the position and impact of their Web sites.

Competitors' Search Engine Reports

There are a multitude of companies that send unsolicited e-mail offering to perform amazing feats to improve a client's placement in search engines. These companies charge a wide range of prices, some as much as thousands of dollars. Some offer guarantees that they will place your client high on the listings of search engines. These offers work in several different ways. You should be aware of them so that you can respond to clients when they inevitably ask what you think of these amazing offers.

Many search engine placement companies offer to place a Web site with several hundred search engines. This is overkill. It will generate a lot of unsolicited junk e-mail for very little return. If you can get a good, solid placement with the top three search engines, your client will be well served. Many of the smaller search engines will pick up your client's site through the major engines anyway.

Some search engine placement companies offer to improve the listing of your business. It sounds plausible to think that if someone typed *Webmaster* on Yahoo! that my company could come up at the top of the list—after all, someone has to be at the top of the list! But there's a catch. When these companies promise to improve my rating, they don't guarantee I will stay there for any length of time. Furthermore, their strategies frequently include rearranging my Web site, often to the detriment of its appearance and navigability.

Daniel Wedeking, owner of Electronic Surfer Website Maintenance, Inc., offers his no-nonsense ideas for attracting the search engines when he says to:

> Build a site with a lot of textual content. No fancy tricks. No hidden code. No text the same color as the background. Use the meta tags properly (don't abuse). Use alt tags to emphasize what the graphics are about and how they relate to your product (e.g., if you sell boats, then put "boat sales" as the alt tag of a picture of a boat). Build pages targeting certain keywords relating to your site. For example, build a page that talks about fishing boats and tag that site appropriately. Make these pages have the same look as your site and make them a part of your site.
>
> If you use tricks that don't sell your product, who cares how much traffic you get. For example: Your description meta tag is displayed by the search engine under the title of your site when a search is done. With this description tag you must (1) make your site capable of being found; and (2) make the person viewing your description want to click on that link and go to your site. If you follow these commonsense rules you will see meaningful traffic. Also, you won't have to change your site every week when a new "trick" is invented, or change it back the following week when the search engines figure out the trick and demote you for it.

Pay-Per-Click Service

A Pay-Per-Click (PPC) service is an effective way to place your client's Web site at the top of the major search engines. There are two separate services that, when used together, cover most of the major search engines. One is by Google and the other by Yahoo!. Here's how they work. When people go to Yahoo!, AltaVista, MSN, etc., they see "sponsor sites" at the top. If anyone clicks on one of those, it costs the sponsor money per click.

For example, you have a client selling mercury switches. In www.Yahoo.com there are around twenty million listings for "mercury switch." Your client may not want to wait for the search engines to elevate her listing to the top of the list.

With the PPC program, her link will be at the top in the "sponsored results" box, and for each person who clicks on her link, she pays a dime or more, depending what others have bid. If she has a budget of $20 per month, Yahoo! will send two hundred people to her site each month. These are not random people looking for bicycles or Roman gods; these are people who have typed in "mercury switch" in a search engine, seen the blurb, and clicked on that link to go to your client's Web site. That is very well-targeted advertising.

If other people selling mercury switches bid higher than a dime per click, your client would need to bid higher to keep in first place. Also, some terms are more popular than others, so if your client wanted everyone who typed in "switch" to see her listing, she might need to pay $3 or more per visitor for that word.

Of course, if you sign up your client for several related search terms and just keep an eye on the results, you will usually get a better response than just doing a single word. With some well thought out key words and some carefully worded content, this becomes a very focused and powerful means of directing traffic to the area of the Web site that you want.

You can get more details on these programs at http://advertising.yahoo.com/smallbusiness/ or http://adwords.google.com.

Web Site Statistics Report and Analysis

As I do with the Quarterly Search Engine Rating and Analysis Report, I also offer a Web Site Statistics Report and Analysis, and I send an e-mail summary of this report. The full documentation is available on a password-protected section of the client's Web site.

There are many good statistics programs available with varying degrees of information. I use Urchin, Google Analytics, or Webalizer to develop my Web Site Statistics Report and Analysis. They allow me to turn my log files into useful and impressive graphics that I can use to quickly analyze many aspects of a Web site's performance. It's possible, for instance, to figure out which of the site's pages were most popular and which least popular. These programs can compute how much time each visitor spent at the popular pages, which tells me whether people are reading the content or bouncing in and right back out again. I can see whether visitors are looking for pages that are not at the Web site, or whether they are using a link that is pointing to a nonexistent Web page. These programs can also identify which search engines bring the most people to the site and whether a link from another site is pulling in viewers. I can even tell which key words people use to find the site. If the words *suit* and *tie* are being used together in a search that leads to the Web site of an attorney who specializes in lawsuits, I can determine why people left the site quickly—they were probably looking for clothes. I can tell which browser and operating system people used, so I can advise my client on how high-tech or low-tech we should make the Web site when updates are needed.

Some of the Web statistics packages are pricey, but the information these packages can provide makes it a service add-on you should consider. Most clients probably know that a little "hit counter" script on a Web site can count the number of times a Web page has been clicked on. I show potential clients what a meaningless number the "hits" is and how easily it can be distorted by some unscrupulous Web designer using her "reload" button to inflate the total. Then I show them all the valuable information they can get from my statistics package. After that, clients usually are not satisfied with a simple counter.

Graphic Design

When skills were being handed out, I was fortunate to get a good share of "ponytail" talent for artistic design work. When designing sites, I don't have to rely heavily on templates, so my sites are distinctive. There are some very good templates available, but when I do utilize those, I modify them to make the appearance unique. Graphic design software like Photoshop and Paint Shop Pro helps me create and enhance pictures and logos. If you enjoy that part of the Web design business too, you can charge extra to design logos and do layout work for brochures and flyers. I usually concentrate my efforts on Web work, but you may want to offer your clients design and layout services for printed material as well. If you meet a talented graphic designer, you may be able to get some Web development work from her in exchange for sending some logo design and Web site layout work to her.

Scripting, Databases, and Programming

Since I consider myself "programming challenged" and can't get much deeper than one layer of "if" and "then" and "else," I prefer to hand off most of my programming work to others. Out of necessity, I have learned some of the basics of programming, databases, and scripts. If your strengths are not in these areas either, you may want to become proficient at being a "copy and paste" programmer and scriptwriter. There are plenty of snippets of free or very cheap scripts that will take care of many of your needs.

Existing scripts serve me well, but when I get a contract that delves deeper than I can deal with, I turn to my Rolodex of names of people to hire as programming sub-contractors. When I started my business, I turned down any design jobs that required anything resembling propeller-head work. However, I came to feel that since I could do better designing sites than most propeller-heads, it was better for a potential client if I worked with others to offer a combined skill set at a reasonable price. An additional benefit of this team approach is that some of my programmer colleagues refer clients to me who need my skill set.

Maintenance Contracts

Some Web design shops offer maintenance contracts to their clients based on a sliding scale, with the lowest hourly rates for clients who guarantee the most work. For example, Linda Titus of www.netsitesworldwide.com shares her version of a maintenance agreement:

> I call my maintenance agreement a "Webmaster Account," and I offer it to every client who requests continuing maintenance, and to every client whose Web site obviously needs ongoing maintenance. Each month I bill for what is essentially two hours' worth of work, except at a 10 percent discount. This covers *up* to two hours' worth of work, and if they need additional work, I bill them for the extra time at the 10 percent discounted rate.

The benefit that Linda has found from her agreement is guaranteed income every month, even if her clients don't give her enough work to fill two hours' worth of time. Linda, however, always does some work for her customers every month, such as removing stale information or doing search engine marketing. She doesn't carry over hours that are not used. Linda has found that this encourages clients to give her assignments in order to keep their Web sites fresh. The latter is especially good for returning visitors to the sites, and it helps keep the search engine listings active.

On the other hand, for most of my clients a maintenance agreement has limited appeal; my clients would rather pay for any change at the time it is needed. If you work with businesses that need routine updates such as announcements, schedule changes, and special offers, you may wish to offer these clients a maintenance contract with a discount in your hourly rate.

E-Commerce

It is difficult to have a Web design shop without offering e-commerce site-building services. Many people are caught up in the dream of owning their own online store. I frequently need to dispel potential clients' unrealistic expectations of getting rich quick. Some Web design shops feel that if a client wants an e-commerce site, it should be built regardless of what the site builder thinks the outcome will be. I like to go beyond just building the e-commerce site. I try to make my advice and experience available, especially if a client seems to be proceeding without all the facts. E-commerce sites can be extremely successful and profitable for a storekeeper who is armed with the right tools and information.

Once he has heard my thoughts, he can make his own decision. If he decides to proceed, I will help him build his e-commerce store and make his dream a reality. I plan to be in business for a long time, and one of my goals is to offer my clients the best chance at their own success.

If you decide to offer e-commerce site-building and maintenance, you will need several skills. You must be familiar with photographing, scanning, and modifying pictures of products. You must have a certain amount of scripting, programming, and database knowledge to get the site up and to keep it maintained. You must be knowledgeable about security issues, online shipping and taxation, credit card acceptance, Payment Card Industry (PCI) compliance for credit card security, and online marketing.

E-Commerce Packages

There are some very good e-commerce software packages available. These may cut into your profit margin more than building an e-commerce solution from scratch, but their proven track record will assure your clients of their reliability. Since my propeller-head skills of programming an e-commerce site are not as strong as my other skills, I prefer to use prebuilt packages. There are some good reseller packages with "turnkey" (turn the key and go) solutions at a reasonable price. For example,

Yahoo! will set you up with a small e-commerce store for $50 plus $39.95 per month. You can go to http://smallbusiness.yahoo.com/merchant/ to learn more about it. If you want to, you can become an "affiliate" with Yahoo! Small Business and get a finder's fee for each customer you sign up. To learn more about that program, go to the very bottom of that Small Business page and you'll see a link for their Affiliate Program. With a program like this, you can learn more about their options and charge your clients a fee to advise them along the way.

Customized E-Commerce Sites

If my client has some specific needs not provided in a turnkey package, or if I have a client with a larger budget who wants a more powerful solution, I recommend creating a custom-designed e-commerce site for him, even if it means bringing in a subcontractor to help with the scripting and programming. This way we can build the e-commerce solution to meet the client's needs without apologizing for features that aren't available. If the client wants something and has the budget for it, a custom site can usually accommodate those needs.

Rather than building the custom site from the ground up, there are some programs that can give you a starting point to build from. A good foundation for a custom Web site that I use is called Zen Cart (www.zencart.com). It was developed as "Open Source" software. There is no charge for the software. Everyone using it is expected to tweak it and improve it for their own needs while sharing those improvements with others. That way, everyone benefits in the continuous evolution of the program. It was developed using PHP, so if you are familiar with PHP and are interested in developing an e-commerce solution for a client, this might be a good option for you. It is not for the beginner without any programming experience unless you have a propeller-head that you can call on as a resource.

Internet and Networking Security

Finally, some of your clients may inquire about their Web site security. If you have had experience safeguarding site security, you may wish to offer that as part of your Web design business. As both e-commerce sites and security breaches proliferate, business as a consultant on security matters should grow, too.

If you are experienced in networking matters, you may decide to use your own Web servers. This will give you a better profit margin than a network and security novice like me who resells space on a commercial server. However, this will be a big responsibility, and you should be prepared to combat any situation or threat to your clients' sites that arises. You will also need to be able to compete against resellers like myself who give their clients round-the-clock monitoring and protection.

Regardless of which add-on services you decide to offer, you will probably discover that some of your competitors will charge more, while others will charge less for the same types of services. As long as you can offer good services for a good value, you will find that most of your clients will prefer working with you for their various Internet needs rather than hiring many individuals to achieve their goals.

03

Planning Your Web Design Shop

For most businesses, location is critical. However, I have found that a Web design shop can be almost anywhere. As long as a few concessions can be made to accommodate customers, your business could even be in the desert. Of course, if you are in a remote area, you may initially need to commute into a large metropolitan area to gather new clients. Later, as your customer base grows, it won't be as essential to run around finding clients. As your reputation spreads, so will your ability to use short meetings—many times by phone or e-mail—to gather the information you need.

Facilities for a Web Design Shop

Location

What do you do for a temporary office when you travel into a metro area from your home office? I was once told that you can drink coffee anywhere but a coffee shop is there for conducting business! If you have been to a metro-area coffee or donut shop mid-morning, you've probably noticed business people conducting business there. I find that if I meet with a potential client in his or her office, the phone is ringing, people are coming in with requests, and it is very difficult to get a few words in. If the client's office is not near my home office, I usually offer to meet him at a coffee or donut shop. That way we can evaluate his needs, plan for future growth, and do all the other things that are so difficult to do uninterrupted. We can also have private conversations about the client's business and his plans for its future that might be too confidential for curious employees.

As an alternative, sometimes I rent a small office in a building that offers daily or hourly shared space. These shared offices often offer mailboxes, voice mail, photocopiers and fax machines, and other amenities. This way, in addition to my fully equipped home office, with the use of a laptop I can create a virtual office anywhere.

Equipment
Virtual office equipment
My most important tool is my laptop. I invested in a dependable laptop with a large hard drive (at least, the 100 GB seemed large last year!). I boosted the RAM memory to 1 GB so I can load several windows at once and flip between them quickly. My laptop has a large screen that rivals many desktop monitors for clarity and brilliance.

With my laptop, a wireless connection, and my car, I have a mobile virtual office whose convenience can't be beat. Before a client meeting, I preload that client's Web site on my laptop's hard drive, along with my Web page editor and any competitors' sites I want to use for comparison. During the meeting, we review the client's site, and I get the information on any necessary changes. If I have another appointment scheduled for that day, I drive to a parking lot and make the updates to the first client's Web site. Then next time I go to my home office, I upload the modified Web files to the client's Web server and test them. That's the advantage of a virtual office!

A few other investments have also enhanced my virtual office. An AC adapter that plugs into the cigarette lighter in my car recharges the laptop battery when I've been away from a power supply for too long. I can work and recharge simultaneously.

A digital camera and a tripod have been helpful. When I visit a client, periodically there is an opportunity to take a photograph to add to the Web site. Inevitably, if I don't have my camera with me, that's when someone requests a photo, so I've made it a practice always to take it along.

In the early days of my Web business, each day I packed in my computer case the file folders that I would need for that day's appointments. But I found that I frequently received phone calls while on the road, asking me to stop by a client's office or to make some changes to a Web site. Since I hadn't anticipated the requests, I didn't have the needed files with me. And, as my client base grew, my computer case got more and more stuffed and it became harder to swap folders. I started to kid about how I needed a file cabinet with me . . . and then I stopped kidding about it. I bought a heavy plastic file holder that can hold quite a few folders. I bought a sturdy hand cart to replace the lightweight one I had been using. I then strapped the file holder on the cart with a heavy, rubber strap and placed my laptop on top of that. I then secured my laptop with a bungee cord. Now I can wheel my office anywhere! I can usually leave the file holder in my car and take just the laptop with the specific file I need when I visit a client. However, when I do need an assortment of files, being able to wheel around my file holder has saved me from back strain and many return trips to my office and allowed me to make the best use of my time.

Home office equipment

My home office is where I keep all the business records I don't need on a daily basis. All my accounting records are stored at the home office, as well as my original software, documentation, and licensing authorizations.

In my home office, there's always a stack of newspaper articles, trade publications, and other information that I'm trying to make time to read. Anyone with a Web design business should subscribe to industry publications. Try to regularly sift through your collection of periodicals, tear out the most significant articles, and throw the rest away. Otherwise, you will find yourself rereading the same articles, trying to recall if you've read them before.

No home office should be without a scanner. For Web design work, you don't need to shop for the highest resolution possible. A large, 17-inch computer screen shows graphics at a low resolution, around 82 DPI (dots per inch). A scanner typically scans an image at 300 to 600 DPI. So buy your scanner for convenience of use and other features rather than the highest resolution. (If you want more great tips about scanners, look at Wayne Fulton's reference site www.scantips.com.)

Consider getting a good-quality, name-brand ink jet color printer for your home office. They are reasonably priced, and most of the name brands produce very good images. My Epson Workforce 600 is an all-in-one printer, scanner, and copier that connects wirelessly to my laptop anywhere in my house and office. It was less than $200 and has all of the features I need. You can use standard printer paper most of the time, but keep some high-performance ink jet paper on hand for special presentations. Brilliant white ink jet paper, combined with the high-resolution setting on your printer, will give you a printed page that looks both clean and sharp.

If space permits, it can be very useful to have an older 486 PC in your office. It's a good practice to check out how Web pages you're designing will perform on an older PC. If you set up a 486 PC with a dial-up modem and an older version of Microsoft's Internet Explorer, you can see what happens when potential site visitors with older equipment try to view your Web site. (Once in a while it is very scary to see what an older browser without any scripting capability can do to your fancy, shining, high-tech Web site.) You say you don't think your clients care about people viewing the site with older PCs? Ask if they mind losing a few potential customers here and there because their Web site is inaccessible to those visitors. Very few clients are willing to lose customers to their site if they can prevent it. You needn't gear all your design work to accommodate owners of older computers, but don't ignore them totally.

Your home office may also include firewall computers, test servers (large or small), and related hardware. I myself don't have large servers—my focus is on design work and I don't require them. Some Web design shops, however, would be lost without their own servers for testing everything. You will need to decide for yourself based on your business's focus what equipment you need, but I consider large test servers an option rather than a necessity.

Software

Software to be used by a Web designer is a very individual thing. In some circles it is discussed with almost religious fervor. Rather than tell you what is "right," I'll give you my opinions based on my experience. In Internet terms there is an expression that applies here, "YMMV": your mileage may vary.

In my opinion, Microsoft Expression Web, and its precursor, FrontPage, are good beginner's tool but not taken seriously for most commercial Web design work. I started designing back in the dark ages using Notepad and creating the HTML code by hand. When I got my first edition of FrontPage, I thought it was amazing. I then realized that as long as I was in control of what the client got, FrontPage worked well. When a client requested something unusual I would spend hours trying to create a workaround using FrontPage. I finally switched to Dreamweaver several years ago and have found it meets my needs for most design work. It is a much better tool for clean coding, and although not quite as easy to use without training as Expression Web, it is much more powerful and not difficult with a bit of training. If you just plan on dabbling in some Web sites as a hobby, Expression Web is fine and easy to use. Otherwise, look at a more powerful solution such as Dreamweaver.

Included with Dreamweaver is a cascading style sheet (CSS) editor. The more you use CSS in your Web design, the easier it will be when your client wants all the two hundred captions under the photos to be a shade darker. Make the change once in the style sheet and it takes care of the captions on the entire site.

For graphic design software, PhotoShop by Adobe is the top name. It retails for over $600, which is out of reach for most beginning Web designers. If you are starting out and want a powerful but much less expensive alternative, try Paint Shop Pro by Corel or Adobe Elements, either for around $100. Or you can get Fireworks as an add-on to Dreamweaver. Whether you get PhotoShop, Paint Shop Pro, Fireworks, or one of the other graphics programs available, plan on spending some time learning how to use it. Like most other aspects of your Web design business, being able to create good graphics that work well within the Web site can make the difference between a good Web site and a great one.

Depending on the type of Web designs that you use, you will probably run into a need to make Flash files. These are the large, impressive animation files you see in Web sites. For a while it was very popular to create a giant Flash file to start a Web site. These are known as "splash pages." Many of those have been eliminated to make way for less dazzle and more content-rich sites. Although Flash looks great and is fun to work with, I always try to talk clients out of using Flash unless there is a sound business need to do so. Although Flash is now viewable on most browsers, there are still some people who will miss the show. The full version of Flash by Adobe costs around $700, but if you want to start out with a less expensive product while you save up for Flash, try SWiSHmax by SWiSHzone.com, based in Sydney, Australia, for around $100. Either product has a learning curve, so plan on spending some time studying it.

Another software program you will need is an FTP or File Transfer Protocol program. A couple of popular ones are WS_FTP Pro and CuteFTP for around $45 to $60, however I use an open source software called FileZilla which meets all my needs. An FTP program works much like Windows Explorer does with files: You select the files from one site and upload them (drag and drop or select "copy") to your hard drive. When they are on your hard drive, you move them to the other server you want. If you use Dreamweaver, it has an FTP feature in it. When you set up an account it will ask you where it is and the ID/password. Put that in, designate a directory on your computer to work on the files, and then download the site onto your hard drive with Dreamweaver. The only time that won't work is if the site was created with Expression Web or FrontPage, in which case you would need to use that program to transfer the files. Even if you use Dreamweaver, Expression Web, FrontPage, or another program, there will probably be times when you will want to have an FTP program available.

There are numerous other software programs, many of them shareware or freeware that you can add to your arsenal as you need them. Most software programs have a trial period of thirty to sixty days before making a purchase. This is usually helpful to prevent turning software into "shelfware" that sits on your shelf unused.

Keeping in Touch

As the owner of a Web design shop, you are in the communications business. It is important not only that you stay in touch with your clients, but also that you make it convenient for them to contact you. If it is easy for clients to reach you, they probably won't notice that; however, if they have difficulty contacting you, they will definitely notice!

Always answer your telephone like a business phone, even if it's also your home line. Clients who call you will not be impressed by young children answering your phone, or by a TV blaring in the background. That folksy feeling is fine for some home businesses, but it is inappropriate when you are trying to portray an image of being on the cutting edge of technology. It is essential that your main phone number have voice mail. You must also have either a second phone line or call waiting so you don't miss calls that might lead to new clients.

Voice mail works well for me. In the past I used answering services, with varying degrees of success. I switched to voice mail because I found that many people would rather leave a detailed voice mail message for me than give a message to an operator. Most of my operator-assisted messages ended up being, "Please call Mr. Jones. He has something to talk about with you." These days most people are comfortable talking to voicemail, but if you feel your clients would rather speak with a real person, get references from some answering services and try out the services until you find one that meets your needs.

You may also prefer voice mail service to answering machines. I used an answering machine for a while, but found that many times I was on the phone with an important call that I didn't wish to interrupt using my call waiting. The answering machine couldn't pick up the call, so the caller would hear endless ringing. After weighing possible solutions, I decided to get a voice mail service from RingCentral for around $25 per month. Now, when a call comes in, my computer pops up a window that allows me to select a custom message if I can't answer the call. A Web-based control panel directs calls made to my toll-free number to my home phone, cell phone, office phone, and several others. This can be done in sequence, known as call hunting, or it can ring all the numbers at the same time. This saves me from having to give out several different phone numbers and allows me to be seamlessly connected even when I'm at a family function or sitting in a hotel room in another state. There are a full range of features and add-ons to these services so it is best to shop around based upon your particular needs.

If your home office is removed from many of your clients and you travel to see them or to try to get new clients, make sure you have quick access to your messages. Although occasionally I will get a "junk" voice mail message, most of the time when people leave me a voice mail I like to know about it right away.

The final piece to my complete phone connectivity is my cellular phone. When I'm on the road and my phone alerts me to a voice mail, I can quickly check the message and either return the call immediately or make a note to return the call when I get back to the office. For my cell phone, I use one of the smartphones that allows me to check email and to look at Web sites while on the road.

Exchanging Information

E-mail is usually the best way for clients to send you information, whether text or graphics. Clients can send you information as an attachment. (If you are using a free e-mail service that doesn't allow attachments, change it quickly!) This should spare you from rekeying text or rescanning images.

There are various advantages to having your own domain name. One advantage is that it makes it easier for clients to remember your e-mail address. (Make sure your Web host allows you to use your domain name in your e-mail address.) Another advantage is that if you change Internet service providers, you don't need to change your e-mail address.

Although I prefer not to get faxes, some businesses are still most comfortable sending information that way. You should either buy a fax machine, use a shared fax service, or sign up for one of the fax-toe-mail programs that are available (www.jfax .com or www.efax.com). If you find that you're getting a lot of your work via fax, you may want to invest in OCR (optical character recognition) software to work together with your faxes. By scanning a faxed document into your computer and then running the OCR program to try to convert into text, you may save yourself much typing time. I seldom use this option—most of my documents arrive electronically—but if your business warrants it, a good OCR program is a real time-saver.

Now that CD-ROM and DVD burners (machines to record information on a compact disk) and rewriteable CD-ROMs are more affordable, that is a good way for sending you data. You may wish to consider purchasing a CD-ROM or DVD burner for your Web design shop as well. In addition to creating backups, you can use the burner to create an advertising disk for potential clients. It will hold a lot of data and be readable by anyone whose computer has a CD-ROM player. USB flash drives are another great way to exchange data. I keep a few small inexpensive ones on hand so I can send and receive information from clients.

Warehousing digital images is another practical application for a CD-ROM/DVD burner. If you use a digital camera or scanner as much as I do, you will find that huge files accumulate on your hard drive. When I go to a client's place of business for a photo session with my digital camera, I take more pictures than I think I will need. This reduces the return trips for retakes. I take these pictures on the high-resolution setting so I can manipulate them when I get back to my office. Although this strategy is a time-saver for me, it creates blocks of large graphics files on my hard drive. When a client's working directory on my hard drive reaches approximately 500 megabytes, I burn it onto a CD-ROM and delete most of the huge source graphics files from my hard drive. I don't have to waste time retaking photos that I deleted to free up hard drive space.

How to Create a Good Business Plan

Plans are nothing. Planning is everything!

— *Dwight D. Eisenhower*

A business plan is as necessary for a business as an itinerary, maps, and credit cards and/or cash are for a cross-country trip. It is entertaining to listen to the tales of those who set out on a journey without any money, plans, or goals in mind. I did that kind of traveling when I was younger, and at the time I recognized that it was irresponsible, somewhat reckless, and yet a lot of fun. I started to apply that same approach to my business ventures, but I learned that the level of risk with a business is much greater than with a road trip and winging it isn't the best approach—or as much fun. It had been an adventure when I ran out of money while traveling across the country and had to stop and work at a local carnival. It was a difficult day when I had to tell my full-time employees—people who trusted in my ability to run a business—that my company had run out of money and that they (and I) would have to go work elsewhere. Forgive my enthusiasm for business plans; I've learned the hard way.

If you are like many people wanting to start a business, you may have been told to put together a business plan. You may feel that this is an academic exercise with little value, as I did at one time. Now I've put together enough businesses, some good and some bad, to know that the same reason I resisted a business plan is the reason I needed one. Stepping out of a secure job into the world of running a business can be stressful and worrisome. Without a positive and enthusiastic attitude, your new business probably won't succeed. (I do understand the reluctance to sit down and play devil's advocate with yourself over the business—it's enough to put a damper on your enthusiasm. But I guarantee that seeing your business fail from lack of a clear plan will make you feel far worse.)

Tips for Creating and Implementing Your Business Plan

Think of your business plan in two stages: the fact-finding stage and the analysis stage. Fact-finding takes a lot of time (congratulations; reading this book is part of that process). Analysis may not take as long, but it is easy to overlook it and problematic if you do gloss over it. Your opinions and your ability to assess the information you received in the fact-finding stage form your analysis. If you do your analysis well, your business has a great chance of doing well, too. If you shortchange your analysis by using it only as a selling tool for a banker, partner, or spouse, you may find yourself wondering how your business could have gone so wrong.

Analyze your business plan when you can sit quietly and look carefully for solutions to problems. If you feel you don't have enough information to make your decisions, gather more information. If you aren't sure what something costs, or whether products are available, investigate these things. Remember that everything that is unknown at the time you craft your business plan might be even more difficult to determine when you are busy running your Web design shop. Plan everything you can in advance to avoid surprises later.

Some people are great at creating gloomy scenarios, and these people have their place when you are planning your business. However, I don't recommend that you put the analysis portion of your business plan together with the "help" of anyone like that, or you might not get far. During the initial stages of developing your business plan, beware of what may happen if someone begins to poke holes in your ideas.

(This balloon bursting can come from a spouse, business partner, parent, or friend.) More than likely you will be defensive about, rather than receptive to, any "what if" questioning, and will try to defend your plans with your current knowledge instead of doing some research to provide concrete solutions. For example, someone may question whether there will be enough of a demand for Web design work in your area for your first year of operation. Instead of flatly denying the possibility of this, you should incorporate that contingency into the business plan and decide how you would compensate (Web hosting, training classes, desktop publishing, or other services). Overall, you should resist the temptation to react to pointed questions and, instead, honestly assess your plans. You are not like a big bank, waiting for your next huge government bailout. You need to plan well for your own survival and success.

After you have your business plan drafted, there will be plenty of time to present it to the doomsayers. You will be much better prepared to listen and much more responsive to suggestions if you have a complete and cohesive plan. Do your homework first and then invite the critics to analyze the plan for areas you missed or shortchanged. You won't have all the answers, but you will be better prepared to decide whether their concerns will cause problems for the success of the business. As you gain a new perspective from the pessimists, see how this affects your business plan and make any necessary adjustments.

Remember that a business plan is a living, dynamic tool for your business. You aren't expected to have all the answers when starting your business. It took me more than two years to create my business plan. (Of course, I was simultaneously getting Web design jobs and testing out various revenue producers.)

Don't be afraid to update your plan periodically as you discover new information and as situations change. There are still times in my business that I feel I'm losing direction or I see that the business has changed from the way I perceived it. At those times, I look at what has changed and whether the business is benefiting. Since it is usually a positive change, I analyze the impact the change has on the business. This is not too intense, just a sanity check to make sure the change is desirable and won't negatively affect another aspect of the business.

Using Your Business Plan

If you are required to put together a business plan for a bank loan officer or for some other purpose, it will most likely be a positive, polished selling tool rather than an honest, unpolished statement of facts. Indeed, if you included all possible

Online Resources for Business Plans

There are many great references that you can use to help you create a business plan for a loan officer or for use as a selling tool. Here are some online resources to get you started.*

www.sbaonline.sba.gov/starting_business/
The Small Business Administration (SBA) has some good references and suggestions.

www.nolo.com
From Nolo's main page, use the search engine to search for "business plans" to view many good articles. Nolo is a book publisher with a focus on legal matters, so its Web site also provides articles on many legal and small business topics.

www.paloalto.com/ps/bp/
Palo Alto Software, Inc., is a respected software company offering programs to help you create your own business plan. If you are overwhelmed by the thought of creating a business plan, this company offers hundreds of sample plans with easily followed wizards to make the task more manageable. If you get a software package such as Palo Alto's Business Plan Pro, do not plan on rushing through a "fill-in-the-blank" format. You should allocate enough time to it to develop your plan fully and create strategies to lead you toward a successful business. A business plan is your road map to that success; make sure you take enough time to create a good map!

www.inc.com
From *Inc.* magazine's Web site, use the search field to find the phrase, "business plan" (with the quotes). "Build a Strong Business Plan" is a very thorough how-to blueprint for creating your own business plan.

www.sbdcnet.org/SBIC/businessplans.php
Business plan–related links from the Small Business Development Center, including some examples of specific business plans.

www.bplans.com/
A one-stop shop for business plans, with great tips and ideas; a good resource to use when putting together your plan.

*The Web is always changing, and if these sites shut down, a search using one of the major search engines will yield others.

contingencies and your plans for handling them, you would probably worry a loan officer unnecessarily.

If you do need a business plan to use as a selling tool, I encourage you to have two separate business plans. One should be an upbeat plan for promoting your business, and the other should be an honest appraisal and road map for your own use. My usual litmus test is that if you feel compelled to put a nice report cover on the business plan (usually to impress someone like a banker), you should sell that person using a polished version of the plan with all the bells and whistles. If you are strong in marketing or know a marketing guru, this is the time to use those skills. If your business plan is for yourself or others for whom you don't need to put on a fancy cover, you can use a "real" business plan. This will be the one that helps you plan for not only the great business that you expect to build but also the obstacles that may come up!

Since there are many resources available to help you create a business plan for your loan officer, let's look instead at how to design a business plan for yourself. Your plan can consist of several files on a computer or an array of papers in a file folder. Just be sure to label it as your "plan" so you can find it easily to review and update. What if your business already exists—can you still create a business plan? Absolutely.

When I started my business, I was working full-time for a Fortune 500 company. In the evenings and on weekends, I did Web design work for my budding business. For a while, I didn't feel compelled to create a full business plan. Designing Web sites was a fun, challenging, and interesting sideline, but it wasn't a vital part of my income. When I decided (with some help from a major corporate downsizing) to expand my Web design activities to a full-time business, it became essential to know where the business was going. Fortunately, I already had an idea of what the Web design market was like, from having worked in it part-time. What I needed to do was put together the information I had and research any missing pieces. This would help me confirm that I was making a wise decision by starting my own Web design shop. That is what a business plan is for.

You can't create a business plan in a single evening while sitting at the kitchen table. When I drafted my initial plan, I spent months talking to corporate human resources people about corporate contracts. I also met with corporate recruiters, spoke with trainers, attended meetings, and read trade publications.

You may be wondering where you could possibly get the time to do all of this research without an income. Don't go without an income—get paid to create your business plan! Part of my research led to contracts. When you speak with corporate recruiters, you will probably find some small contracts through them. When you talk with corporate Web people, you may find opportunities to grab small contracts to fill in short-term gaps.

Although you will make some money during this planning stage, you should expect to do some belt-tightening as well. No matter how much you try to maintain a financial status quo, there may be gaps in income when you hit a dry spell. However, you should think of this period of fact finding and preparing your business plan as a time for training or learning how to run your business. I know that I could have taken formal classes on setting up a business, but I opted for hands-on experience. If you have a spouse, children, or others who will be affected, discuss your plans with them and keep the communications open.

How My Business Plan Evolved

To begin, I evaluated my skills and how that would impact my new business. I knew that I was not a strong propeller-head; I had little programming experience and only a limited knowledge of networks. I enjoyed and was good at the design work, layout, art, and other ponytail-related tasks. Since I had owned and operated several businesses in the past, I also knew I was strong in the suit tasks of business operations and negotiations. I had enough experience with number crunching to know that I did not like it, so I decided to hire an accountant to handle everything except the day-by-day bookkeeping. I also realized that I have never been a great salesman/rainmaker, so I red-flagged that aspect of the business so I could plan around it.

Next, I looked at the market to determine where I could find a good fit. Working for large corporations can be more secure and stable than working for small companies. There is usually more funding in large companies, and some projects last a long time. Smaller companies usually offer more flexibility and are more receptive to innovative suggestions. Although my personal preference was to work with smaller companies, I knew that I might benefit from the larger projects; I wouldn't need to sell my services as frequently.

Then, I looked into what contracts were available in corporations. I looked at the listings of several online job search firms. Although many of the Internet-related jobs called for a full-time staff person rather than an independent contractor, some jobs were available for contractors. Most of the contracts were for propeller-heads—either for programming, which was at the bottom of my skill list, or for a variety of networking tasks, for which I had limited experience. I contemplated investing in a series of classes to learn a skill I wasn't excited about, in order to work in large corporations, which wasn't my preference. I decided that in order for my business to be successful, I needed to explore other options.

I chose to refocus on small to midsize businesses. I knew that some small businesses needed Web sites and that many more would in the future. I knew that although I wasn't good at sales, I did enjoy teaching and presenting information to businesses about Web sites. I considered working as a trainer or lecturer, but after much exploration, I decided I could make more money as a Web designer.

Positioning

I considered positioning myself as a Web artist, but many of the small businesses I had dealt with didn't recognize the value of my artwork as much as they did my ability to evaluate their Internet business needs. My best selling point was my ability to design a Web site that would have the maximum marketing impact for a client. Sometimes that impact was the result of great graphics; other times it was through maximizing a client's position on search engines. Many times, it was simply that a professional image on the Internet helped validate a client's business.

I decided that my key market would not need me as a network expert, a phenomenal scriptwriter, a security guru, or even a wonderful Internet artist. The market that could benefit most from my skills needed an Internet business consultant who could design Web sites. Although I've reevaluated and modified this focus from time to time, it has been a good foundation.

I now teach Internet-related topics in classes, lectures, and small business presentation series. Although I offer a certain amount of free advice to small businesses, I don't hide the fact that I'm hoping they will hire me as their Web designer and Internet consultant. Aside from training disadvantaged children to use computers, all my computer-related work is either for pay or in anticipation of future business. I enjoy the work that I do, and my clients are happy to refer me to others. It took some planning (remember that business plan?), but now my business enables me to do what I enjoy and allows me to offer my talents to a market that appreciates them. That's why I encourage you to plan your business rather than let the business point you in whatever direction it wants.

Crafting Your Business Plan

In appendix A you will find a sample business plan for a Web design shop. It illustrates what you should think about and include when you create your own plan. Among the most important parts of any business plan are a mission statement, advertising and marketing strategies, profit and loss projections, and such financial plans as the structure of the business and methods for accounting, banking, insurance, and payroll. In a Web design business, you may also want to write a vision statement, a personal evaluation of your skills and talents, a business image plan, and a description of your products and services. All of these are described in appendix A.

In crafting your plan, you should start out by assessing your skills—not only what you are good at, but also what you enjoy. List everything, no matter how trivial it may seem. Are you good at gardening? Are you an expert coin collector or a race car enthusiast? Do you enjoy yoga or fly fishing? You are starting a business that might allow you to combine some of your favorite things! Maybe you can design Web sites for yoga instructors, or set up sites to catalog people's coin collections. I enjoy getting in front of a group of people and teaching them something new. At first, I didn't realize I could incorporate that into my business. I was pleased to discover that I could. So, try to expand your plan to include pleasurable skills and talents that you may have.

Combining your skills and interests is a part of the second step in your business plan: evaluating the market. What segment of the market is the best fit for your talents and interests? Put some ideas together and test them. If you enjoy cooking, try to get a contract designing a Web site for a kitchen supply company or a restaurant. Use that as a learning experience by asking for feedback. Look at other similar sites to see what they've done. Ask many questions. Although in the client's eyes you are designing a Web site at a reasonable price, you also are trying to decide if there is a market for you to do others. Maybe this client's Web site will be so successful that you know that others will be interested. This is the time to find out!

Once you have decided on a market for your skills, you must decide how you will make it work. You've discovered a huge market for designing Web sites for yoga instructors. How are you going to make that work? Do you attend the conventions and get to know the influential figures? Is there someone who has assured you of business? What are the risks? What will happen if the person you're depending on to feed you business bows out? How can you expand the business beyond its current limits? Do you have other skills or interests you can tap into to grow the business? How certain are you that this will work—have you tested it thoroughly?

A Pilot Program

Many people assume that their theories will work but never test them. As the builder of a Web design business, you can and should test your theories. Some businesses call this test phase a pilot program. Others call it a market test, and still others, research and development. I call it "going out and getting contracts to see if it is possible." That can move you out of the realm of theory very quickly! If you get several signed contracts in a market that you wondered about, you no longer need to assume your idea works; you have your indicator. However, if you try to get contracts and run into obstacles, you can evaluate the reasons. Are you using ineffective selling techniques? Are clients reluctant to deal with an unknown person? Are clients not interested in your services? Once you have improved the selling techniques or modified your services to match the need, retest your theory. Eventually, you will fine-tune this aspect of your business plan to be a certainty.

Much of the remainder of your business plan will come from your decisions about issues common to all business plans. By now, you probably have a good idea of what the focus will be for your business. You know not only that you want to open a Web design shop, but also what market you will target and how you will use your skills to succeed in that market. Following are some other issues to address. Many of these are covered elsewhere in this book.

- The type of business you want (sole proprietorship, LLC, corporation, or other).
- Where you will be located (home office, shared space, rented office).
- What your competitors are doing right, and what you would do differently.
- The amount of revenue you will bring in during the first week, month, and year. (This is difficult to predict, but if you don't have a realistic estimate, you won't be able to plan for the hills and valleys that are normal in the growth cycle.)
- What your expenses will be. (Much like revenue, if you know approximately how much money you will be spending, you will be able to plan your business growth.)
- What you can fall back on during lean times. (Watch this one! If you have nothing to fall back on, you are operating without a safety net. When there is an unexpected lull in your business, you need to know if—and how—you will ride it out until the next contract is signed.)

- The expected life cycle of your business. Do you want to run the business until you retire? What will you do then—sell it, turn it over to a family member, or phase it out? Whatever you want to accomplish with your business should be documented and implemented as part of your business plan.

Plan with the End in Sight

Do you have a will? Most people do not—they are unwilling to think about a time when they will no longer be alive. For many of the same reasons, most people can't bear to plan what will happen if their business fails. What will you do if all your plans fail? I've owned enough businesses to know that, despite your best efforts, any business can fail. Planning for the "worst-case scenario" is an important part of your business plan.

Years ago I was trying to purchase a restaurant business with a partner and needed a loan to do so. An advisor from SCORE (Service Corps of Retired Executives from the U.S. Small Business Administration) kept asking me what the worst-case scenario was for this proposed restaurant. I was starting to get annoyed by this man's determination to poke a hole in my seemingly perfect business plan. The advisor and I went back and forth—him trying to make me consider potential disasters and me trying to convince him there was no way the business could fail. For every possible demise he could envision, I had a solution.

The advisor finally leaned back and asked me again if I felt that there was nothing that could bring this business down. Could I envision anything that wasn't covered by insurance or by my positive attitude, or couldn't be saved by my long line of skilled people? "Nothing will bring this business down," I confidently restated. "This business is stable, has been planned from top to bottom to be successful . . . it won't fail."

The advisor then showed me a newspaper clipping about a restaurant that had recently failed. He asked, "What would you do if, through no fault of your own, a food handling employee contracted hepatitis and spread it to several regular customers before the health department stepped in and made a public spectacle of closing the business?" Suddenly my enthusiasm was shot down. I knew that no affordable insurance would cover much more than a few days of lost business. To reopen a restaurant after such an event would be suicide. As the owner of the restaurant in the article had discovered, no matter how much you do or say, customers will not return after a case of food poisoning.

Once I was forced to admit that even my "infallible concept" could fail, it was time to plan how to protect myself and my assets from disaster. I was then much more receptive to setting up the business with safeguards to protect me.

I didn't get the loan, but I got a lesson that was much more valuable. The business that I was so confident about did close several months after opening. I had not detected that my main financial partner had prior problems with the IRS and had been using our restaurant revenues to pay off other debts. Fortunately I had taken measures to protect my assets and myself. After a nerve-wracking inquiry in front of a group of IRS agents, I was able to use my records and business plan to show that I was not a participant in my partner's schemes. My partner, however, had to answer for his own actions.

That experience was many years ago, and the lesson stayed with me. Several years after my conversation with the advisor, I was planning to open another business—this time a sandwich shop—in the center of a major downtown district. I had done my homework and researched the potential for the site. Although I was confident that the business would be successful, I protected myself for that worst-case scenario. The business was incorporated and well insured. I made certain that the business was run "by the book." The business was already making a good profit the second week after it opened.

My wife had asked me what the probability was for failure of this business and I had replied, "The only way I can see this business failing, other than a food poisoning, would be if the entire city collapsed around it . . . and what's the chance of that ever happening?" That was in the early 1990s. A year later, the economy took a major hit, and that particular downtown district took an even harder hit. After two more years of realizing that my and my wife's investment and all the new money we were pouring into this venture were not going to rescue it from its worst-case scenario, we, like many others in the area, closed the doors.

Other business owners who have shared stories with me have bemoaned the huge debts they had incurred and the incredible responsibilities with which they had saddled themselves. Some had put their homes and retirement investments on the line. I realized that the only action I had taken differently from these other people was that I planned and financed the business not only to succeed but also with the realization that it might fail. Although it took a few years to recover financially from that venture, I still am grateful to that persistent man from SCORE who pierced my state of innocent enthusiasm and showed me that there is a worst-case scenario for every business.

Worst-Case Scenario

What would be a worst-case scenario for a Web design shop? There are many. The Internet could become a major security risk due to an unforeseen virus. Web sites could become so cumbersome that only large design firms could handle them. Domains could be tied in with an organization or government that created a closed system of licensure. Web sites could become so simple to build that no one used Web design shops anymore. This doesn't mean that you should not go into the business, any more than you would decide never to ride in an automobile because of the remote risk of an accident. As with anything that we do, there are risks. It is a good idea to be aware of as many of those risks as possible, but don't become paralyzed by them.

It might help you draft this part of your business plan if you think of it as a will for your business.

- When (not if) your business dies, who gets the computer? Does the IRS? Does your landlord? Do you?
- What happens to the office space? Is there a long-term lease? If so, what happens when the business dies—is someone required to pay the lease for the remaining years? If so, is that provided for?
- What happens to the clients? Do you have provisions to sell their hosting business to another company if your business dies, or do they have to find their own Internet access?
- Are you protected if a client tries to sue you because your business died and took his Web site with it?

Much like the death of a person, the death of your business can leave plenty of turmoil in its wake. Also much like the death of a person, if you don't plan for those details in advance, they are much more difficult to deal with. Shutting down a business is emotionally draining, with many issues to handle. Like me, you may one day be grateful that someone made you realize your business might not live forever.

Expenses to Plan For

Start-Up Costs

It is difficult to tell exactly what it would cost to start your Web design shop. When I started my business, I already had a scanner and some other tools. I didn't want to invest in a read/write CD-ROM unit at first, and I didn't need to rent an office. Your start-up expenses will most likely be different from mine.

The Start-up Expenses Worksheet shows many of the expenses you may incur. Some estimates are included for your reference, based on my own experience. You may already have some of these items, and may decide that you don't need others right away. You can always buy more equipment as your business gains momentum.

Start-Up Expenses Worksheet

Item	Estimate	Real Cost
Laptop computer	$600–2,000	
Mobile cart for laptop	$30–60	
Printer	$50–150	
Scanner	$50–150	
Read/write CD-DVD	$50–150	
Fax machine	$0–100	
Digital camera (rechargeable batteries, memory)	$50–200	
Cell phone	$100–300	
Professional fees (attorney/accountant)	$500–1,500	
Insurance (liability, property, etc.)	$0–1,200	
Surge protectors	$20–50	
Software (graphics, design)	$50–2,000	
Printing (business cards, letterhead)	$20–200	
Setup of Web server space	$200–1,000	
Phone line installation (two lines)	$35–150	
File cabinet	$20–400	
Office furniture	$0–3,000	
Office supplies (blank CDs, pens, staplers, etc.)	$50–300	
Start-up advertising	$0–1,500	
Licenses/permits	$10–150	
Other:		

Operating Expenses Worksheet

Item	Estimate	Real Cost
Office space (home office may pay rent back to you)	$0–1,500/mo.	
Advertising (estimated as percentage of desired sales)	2–4%	
Web server space (per account, per month)	$10–40/mo.	
Online connection (high-speed connection)	$25–65/mo.	
Local phone service	$35–60/mo.	
Long distance phone service (depending on client location)	$0–500/mo.	
Cell phone	$25–100/mo.	
Electric and other utilities	$0–100/mo.	
Automobile mileage or expenses and parking	$10–50/mo.	
Insurance	$30–200/mo.	
Periodicals	$0–20/mo.	
Bookkeeping/accounting	$20–100/mo.	
Printing and postage	$25–100/mo.	
Your salary (Don't forget this one!)	$1,000–5,000/mo.	
Health insurance	$0–500/mo.	
Personal income tax, FICA, other withholding	$0–??	
Other:		

Operating Costs

Much like the start-up costs, operating costs can be very hard to estimate. I prefer to pay personal visits to many of my clients, so my mileage costs are higher than those of someone who conducts most business by phone, Internet, and courier. The

Operating Expenses Worksheet gives you estimates, but you will need to create your own figures based on experience or by working with your accountant.

For estimating purposes, operating expenses are put into two categories: fixed and variable. Fixed expenses stay steady no matter how busy or slow you are. For example, if you pay rent, it usually stays the same regardless of whether you are having a good month or a bad one. However, if you don't have any business, your cost for printing and copying will usually be lower than if you are cranking out lots of work. If you are setting up many new clients, your Web server charges will be higher than if you have no business.

Other Expenses

In addition to the operating expenses on the worksheet, there are others that are not quite as visible. These are expenses that come up only occasionally. You will need to keep padding available for these expenses.

No matter how much we wish otherwise, all equipment (including laptops!) breaks down eventually. Sometimes it can be repaired; other times you must replace it. Be prepared for equipment failure, and plan what you will do when it happens. Don't be lulled into false security just because your equipment is under warranty; you may need something fixed faster than the manufacturer is willing to do it. For example, my laptop once broke down while still under warranty. Although I could have gotten it fixed for free by shipping it back to the manufacturer, I would have been without it for two to three weeks during a critical contract that I couldn't stall. I chose to void the warranty, open the case, and fix it myself. I'm not happy that I had to do that, but sometimes you must take the path that makes most sense at the time, not the path you planned to take.

Membership dues to organizations such as your local chamber of commerce or networking group generally are paid annually and should be included on your worksheet. But there are also periodic networking social events that you may wish to attend with a stack of business cards in hand.

You should attend at least one large computer or Internet conference or convention each year (more than one if you can afford it and have the time). You can usually get free passes to the exhibitions, which will allow you to see the latest software, gadgets, and ideas. You can either plan in advance for these shows or wait until you see one coming up in your vicinity (or in an area you don't mind taking a business trip to). I usually don't preplan any of the events I attend. Typically when I project that I will be able to attend one, my business takes a major upswing. So, I just wait until I see that there is a good combination of a business lull and convention. I then plan a quick trip and go see what is new.

Do you think you will need some classes to keep up with the ever-changing technology? You might look for information from free online tutorials, but many people can't learn that way. If you need a structured classroom setting to absorb the latest in technology, set some funds aside for classes.

It is a great feeling to have a computer ready to go with all of the latest, greatest software. However, don't forget that periodically most of your software will become outdated. Prepare to spend some money from time to time to upgrade your system.

Pros and Cons of Different Business Structures

When you are planning your business, you must choose what form of business organization you want. Your accountant and attorney will be able to help you decide this. There will be some pros and cons to weigh, based upon your specific needs. My opinions may give you some insight. However, until you get feedback from your team of professionals, you shouldn't assume that one is better than another. Remember that I'm not an attorney and my explanations of business structures are from a layperson and must not be construed as legal advice.

Sole Proprietorship

A sole proprietorship is just what it sounds like—it is you and your business. This is the simplest business structure, and is popular with small businesses starting out. The advantage is that it is very easy to set up and comply with the requirements of the structure. The accounting system that you use with a sole proprietorship is simplified—you take money in and that is your income. You spend money that is necessary for the business and that comes off your income.

To offset the simplicity, there are some major disadvantages. The main disadvantage is that there is no protection for you or your personal property. You have made it clear that you are willing to risk everything for your business. If a disgruntled client feels that he lost millions of dollars when the e-mail stopped flowing for a few hours, he may file a lawsuit. While this is being battled, your house and personal belongings could be in jeopardy. If you have a sudden illness or accident and somehow your business runs up a huge debt, you are personally responsible for that. If a client stiffs you for a bill and you shut down his Web site (please don't do that without your attorney's blessing!) and he sues you for destroying his business, you need to worry about the risk to your personal belongings.

Anyone can sue you for anything. If you have done everything correctly and are careful, they probably won't win, but of course there are no guarantees. You must decide if you are willing to risk all your personal possessions.

Partnership

A partnership is very similar to a sole proprietorship except that, as the name implies, there is more than one person involved. This doesn't necessarily mean that your responsibility is diluted among others—if someone successfully sues the partnership and one person can't pay her portion of the settlement, the others are responsible. You are responsible for the consequences of anything your partner does.

Before you sit down with your attorney to work out an agreement for your partner(s) and yourself, you must make some tough decisions. First, who gets what percentage of the business? It sounds easy—maybe everyone gets an equal share. However, in that case what happens when a decision must be made and nobody agrees? Does everyone have an equal vote? (Sounds like gridlock to me!) Decide now while everyone is on friendly speaking terms because, in the heat of a business decision, no one will be able to decide who breaks the stalemate.

What happens to the profits? Does everyone share equally? Did someone bring in extra equipment? Is there compensation for that? If not, can that person pull the equipment out of the business if he wants to? If so, what happens? Do you have extra talents? Should you get extra compensation for that?

I've seen many businesses where one partner is a rainmaker and another a propeller-head. In setting up the business, they each recognize and appreciate the other's skills, and they agree to split the business proceeds equally. A year later, the rainmaker is out having a great time schmoozing people, buying drinks, getting contracts signed, and getting lots of lavish praise for her business.

The other partner is back at the office working. On some days it's a challenge to keep up with the work being brought in. Not getting any recognition becomes less and less fun. Spending the company's money to buy the rainmaker business dinners starts feeling unfair. The propeller-head begins to wonder why he even needs a rainmaker now that the business is established. The rainmaker, on the other hand, is hearing the propeller-head grumble. She feels that without a steady stream of business, the propeller-head would have nothing to do. "Let him go out and try to sign up customers for a while," she mutters.

You can see how communication is deteriorating. What has changed? The rainmaker is better than ever at bringing in contracts. The propeller-head is keeping the work moving. Both are doing exactly what each of them expected.

Business partnerships are a lot like marriages. Without strong communication, problems will develop and build to dangerous proportions. You may not sign a prenuptial agreement before getting married, but you should work out one for your business partners! This is the time to negotiate for terms that will make everyone happy. Take this opportunity to point out the flaws in yourself and your partners and prepare for any compensation that will be needed to offset those. Decide how and when you will set up meetings to make sure everything is on course. If you don't do these things now, it will be much more difficult to do them when problems arise.

The most important part of your partnership is the issue that is thought about least. What will it take to unravel the partnership when the time comes? If in two weeks you realize that your new partner is crazed with power and you have made the biggest mistake of your career, what will it take to walk away? What will it take a year from now when you realize that your partner is dragging you down into a losing business? What will it take when you realize that your partner has turned into a rat and is signing up clients for your competition? Or that your partner is designing Web sites outside of the business to avoid sharing the profit with you?

If you feel strongly that none of these scenarios could possibly happen to you, then you probably shouldn't be in a partnership. Even though no one likes to think that a thief might break into his home or car, it is better to protect yourself than to assume that—because it probably won't happen—there is no need to put locks on the doors or remove the keys from the car. A bit of precaution now may prevent anxiety or problems later.

Corporation

This is where the protection starts coming in for businesses. If your attorney sets you up as a corporation, you are telling the world that you do not own the business; the corporation owns the business. You are not responsible for the debts of the business; the corporation is. If the corporation runs out of money, you are not responsible; the corporation is. (However, if fraud is involved, that corporate veil becomes useless.) If a client or vendor has a problem, he will take it out on the business, not you.

It took me a long time to understand that when I incorporate, I no longer own my business—I own all the stock in a corporation, and that corporation owns the business! I cannot take any money from the business without getting permission from the corporation (my corporation!). I can't make major decisions for the business unless the corporation gives me authority to do so. Therefore, I must step into my role as director of the corporation and give myself written authority to pay myself or make major decisions.

When my business was set up as a corporation, I always felt there was a certain amount of schizophrenia in being an owner of one. I was a stockholder of a corporation that hired me to run the corporation's business so that my corporation could gain a profit from the business so that I could receive my 100 percent share of the corporate profits! Moreover, all of this is without my owning the business! That made for much head-scratching. Of course, since the corporation owned the business, it was responsible for any problems that arose. As an officer in the corporation, I was somewhat shielded from the actions of the corporation (with, of course, certain exceptions, such as fraudulent activities).

The biggest advantage of setting up a corporation is the personal protection it affords you. If you own a house, for example, a corporation will protect it from being taken away from you in the event of a business mishap. Also, you will not be personally responsible for long-term leases if your business closes. Note that in this latter example, most banks and vendors will try to get you to personally sign documents (such as loan agreements and credit applications) rather than having you sign as an officer of the corporation. Ask your attorney how to sign such documents. For example you might want to sign with your signature, followed by your title, then the corporate name (i.e., Jim Smith, President, XYZ, Inc). That makes it clear you are signing on behalf of the corporation. Banks and landlords know that they have better recourse if you sign personally—any financial obligation will stay with you if the corporation dissolves. Therefore, you should always try to sign as an officer of your corporation. If a corporate signature is not permitted, you must decide whether or not you are willing to be personally responsible for any loans, leases, or other expenses.

A corporation is a great way to build a larger organization without jeopardizing the existing structure. Once you (the "board of directors") have set up the guidelines and rules for the corporation, they stay in place regardless of the size of the corporation until the directors (that's you) vote to change them. Another advantage of a corporation is the ease with which ownership can be transferred. Since it is a clearly delineated entity, it is much easier to transfer all or part ownership to others through the sale or transfer of stock than it would be for a sole proprietorship or partnership. Also, there are often tax benefits to having a corporation. Your accountant can review these with you.

All of these benefits sound good until you realize that with that protection comes much responsibility. As a director in the corporation, you must make sure you don't take shortcuts. If you sign documents without indicating that you are signing as president of XYZ, Inc., it will be difficult to prove that you weren't signing personally. If you take money out of the corporation without securing a loan from the corporation to yourself, you may have trouble proving that you take the corporation seriously. If you don't take the bylaws of the corporation seriously and follow them, you may someday find that a legal problem ends with the opposing attorney "piercing your corporate veil" and going after you personally.

Another disadvantage of corporations is that running them is very complex. Anything you want to do for your business must be supported by the corporation. In general, if there is no precedent for a business decision, you must go to the corporation and get approval in writing (from yourself) to make that decision. Combined with the need to document everything comes the need to set up the accounting that separates everything.

The tax filing responsibility is significant. In addition to filing taxes for yourself, now the corporation (you) must file taxes for the business that it owns as well. Under the current tax law you cannot take an advance from your business account to pay for something. You must borrow the money, which means drawing up official loan papers, establishing a reasonable interest rate to pay the corporation, and documenting repayment. For taxes, first the Web design shop must complete a year-end accountability statement. Then, the profits or losses and depreciation go into the corporation, which must complete a year-end accountability statement. The corporation then pays tax on its profits. If you received any earnings or dividends from the corporation, you must include that in your tax reports.

Subchapter S Corporation

This is a greatly simplified version of a corporation, although you have some of the same paperwork. You have the protection offered to a corporation, but for year-end filings your taxes are simplified. This may be a disadvantage for tax sheltering purposes, but it makes the accounting and filing much easier. Talk with your accountant to see which type of corporation is better for you.

Limited Liability Partnership (LLP)

Just as the name implies, this is a partnership with limits to the liability. This protects partners in much the same way as a corporation. States have differing regulations on LLPs, so be sure to consult with your attorney and accountant to find out what the specifics are.

Limited Liability Company (LLC)

With an LLC, the member(s) of a company declare that they are putting a limit on their liability. (Note that they are members, not owners.) Much like a corporation, if certain guidelines aren't adhered to and you treat the LLC like a sole proprietorship, you may find yourself unprotected from the limited liability. Get the advice of your attorney, maintain clear records, and treat the business appropriately to protect your personal assets from being intertwined with the business's assets.

Based on the advice of my attorney and accountant, and on the regulations for the state of Connecticut (where my business is located), I decided to change my status from a sole proprietor to an LLC. There were some things I had to get used to, such as no longer being "Jim Smith, Owner" of my company. Now I am "Jim Smith, Member" of my LLC. And on my IRS forms, I must declare myself as a "disregarded entity." It doesn't seem as impressive to me, but that is a small price for protecting my personal assets. Unlike a Subchapter S corporation, I don't have corporate paperwork to file and my taxes are handled more like those of a sole proprietor. (If you decide to become an LLC and don't want to be known as a "member," you can become a "managing director.")

Employees, Subcontractors, or Partners

Whether during the start-up phase or after your business is running, at some point you will need to decide whether to hire employees, engage subcontractors, or structure your business to accommodate one or more partners. At Blarneystone, LLC (my Web design shop), I contemplated a partnership with another designer but found out that he was an even weaker rainmaker than I was. I didn't want a partner with the same strengths as me—my business would benefit only if my partner had skills I was lacking. I decided not to bring in a partner. Periodically I get a contract that requires more scripting and programming than I can handle. I subcontract out that work. With that strategy, I find that I can take care of the clients I have and, even with my dubious sales skills, I have a steady flow of clients. Occasionally I lose someone who can't wait a week or two until I'm free to start his or her project. However, most of the time, as long as I treat potential clients with respect, I either get their business after they've shopped around or get business that they've recommended.

When and if you discover that you need the help of one or more skilled workers, you can choose from several setups. Each has advantages and drawbacks.

Employees

At some point in the development of your business, you may discover the need for some assistance—from clerical support to programmers. A temporary agency may be able to find you a suitable employee. If they do, you pay a premium for that employee, but you are spared from having to pay the taxes and the benefits for the individual. Temp agencies are very good at helping find support staff, but you may not be able to find a top-notch Web designer or programmer through an agency.

If you hire someone as an employee yourself, you will become very intimate with numerous regulations, taxes, insurance, and benefits issues. You will need to get an EIN (Employer Identification Number) from the federal government and the equivalent from your state government. You must withhold federal income tax from the employee's wages. In addition, you must contribute to Social Security, Medicare, and unemployment insurance funds. Depending on the state in which your business is located, you may need to withhold state income tax and make other contributions as well. Along with withholding the money, you must file paperwork and make timely payments to the appropriate agencies. If you fall behind on any of these payments, you will quickly learn why it is so important to make them on time.

This is a lot of work for a Web design shop with one or two employees. I recommend farming this task out to either a reputable payroll company or your accountant. Make sure that however it is handled, it is handled promptly, consistently, and accurately. Remember that no matter who is taking care of this work, you are ultimately responsible.

Many small businesses have decided that it is much simpler to hire subcontractors from time to time for overflow work. You bring in a subcontractor for an assignment and pay him a set amount of money, and when the job is over, he is gone. He takes care of his own taxes, insurance, benefits, and other expenses. (But check with your insurance company for liability and hazard insurance.) This is a great alternative for some Web design shop owners, but there are still pitfalls to watch out for.

Subcontractors

Any time I get a Web design job, I am considered a contractor. My signed contract stipulates that I'm not an employee of the company but rather a work-for-hire for a specific task. It states that my work ends with the completion of that task. If I hire someone on a project basis to help me with a contract, I subcontract her to do a portion of the work. This is why you may hear the term "sub" in reference to workers in this business.

If you're hiring a subcontractor, there is an important consideration you must be aware of. If you hire someone to help you with a job, loan her a PC and software, and pay her by the hour, you have a temporary employee, not a subcontractor. As such, you are expected to file with the IRS, withhold taxes, pay a portion of her Social Security tax, pay for her unemployment insurance, and follow all of the laws specified for employees. You can have your worker sign a paper saying that she is not an employee, but in the eyes of the IRS (and probably your state), she is an employee. You will be responsible for her taxes and possibly for penalties and interest.

The IRS has a publication to help you distinguish between an employee and a subcontractor (www.irs.gov/pub/irs-pdf/p15a.pdf). Many variables help make that determination. The rule of thumb is that the more "independent" a contractor is and the more she can show that your contract is one of many she handles, the less trouble you will have. The Checklist for Subcontractors gives some common questions to help distinguish subcontractors from employees. This is more of a cumulative indicator than a clearly defined set of rules, so it may not be a problem if your sub meets some of the criteria more fully than others.

Partners

Partners can be a very good or very bad way to get the help you need in your Web design shop. You and your partner are in it through thick and thin. On the negative side, if the business has a slow spell and there is not enough revenue to support both of you, there may be some finger pointing and accusations. If you treat your partner like an employee or a subcontractor, resentment may build. You must work together with your partner in order to be successful—if one of you starts planning behind the other's back, it won't work. If the trust between you falters, the business will suffer.

Checklist for Subcontractors

1. *Does the person have his own tools?*
   If someone has his own PC and software, it helps to indicate that he is a subcontractor rather than a temporary employee.

2. *Is the individual working at your office or can he work elsewhere?*
   If you supply him with a desk and require him to work at your office, or specify the hours he must work, he might not be an independent contractor.

3. *Does this person have a specific, clearly defined task with a beginning and an end?*
   If you are paying someone by the hour to help you get through a contract, he might be considered an employee rather than a subcontractor. A subcontractor generally completes the contract and is paid a set fee. If he completes the job in half the time he had estimated, he makes a big profit. If it takes him twice as long, he sustains a loss. (Subcontractors do occasionally work on an hourly basis, and if this is the case with someone you hire, make sure enough of the other criteria are met so your worker isn't viewed as an employee.)

4. *How much guidance and direction are you giving?*
   If you tell a worker that he is to create a database to interface with the Web site you are designing, and if you allow him to figure out how it will function, you have contracted him for that task. If you give him specifics on how the database should function or instruct him on how to build it, you may be using him as an employee.

5. *Are you paying the individual's expenses?*
   If you pay for his gas, photocopies, phone calls, and other expenses, he may be viewed as an employee. If you want someone to be considered a subcontractor, offer a contract that states that he pays all out-of-pocket expenses.

6. *Does the individual work for others under contract as well?*
   If you are the only one he works for, be careful. It doesn't hurt to encourage a contractor to get other contracts from time to time to keep this issue clear. (And for your

own protection as a contractor, if you are contracting with a large corporation and find they are keeping you very happy with contracts, you should still take small outside contracts from time to time. If the company objects to your doing this, explain the reason [and suggest that they speak with their human resources people]. They don't want to be stuck with a contractor/employee dispute any more than you do.)

However, on the positive side, if there is good communication between you and your partner, you can plan to build on each other's strengths to make the business much more vibrant than is possible with most employer/employee relationships.

This may seem like common sense, but it is important enough to warrant a reminder. When setting up a partnership, both partners must be treated fairly in order for the partnership to work. If you find someone who desperately needs work, you could use leverage to get some good terms from that person as a partner. The person might appreciate being partner for a while. However, eventually that person will no longer be desperate, and he will begin to realize that the partnership is stacked in your favor. Negotiation with a partner to get the best deal for just yourself serves a short-term benefit. Make sure that you strike a deal that is fair for both of you.

Several times I have been tempted to create a partnership with an individual who has strength in areas that I don't. I've considered getting someone with programming expertise to partner with me. I've been tempted to partner with rainmakers who love to sell. Each time, I've decided that I prefer to bring in skilled individuals as subcontractors instead. In the past, I have been in business partnerships that were successful, and I have been in ones that led to strife and disillusionment. Because of my experience, I would rather use subcontractors or employees when possible.

When you take on a partner, you have made an agreement to work with that person for a long time—presumably for the life of the business. It is usually very costly and difficult to terminate that agreement. In contrast, if you are not satisfied with an employee's performance, you can fire that person. If you have hired a subcontractor whose work is unsatisfactory, you can choose not to use that contractor again. (If it is a long-term contract, you can either require that person to meet the terms of the contract or remove her from the contract.)

Bringing in a partner can be very rewarding and a wonderful way to help your business grow. But it must be done with great care, under the watchful eye of a good attorney to represent both individuals, and it must be done with all expectations spelled out clearly in the beginning.

Assembling Your Team

As you develop your Web design business, you will wonder how any one person can set up and run a business alone. Most don't. Without meaning to detract from the recognition given to small business owners for their hard work, I've observed that behind most great individuals is an equally great support network. To maximize the chances for your Web business to succeed, assemble the best team possible.

Accountants and Attorneys as Team Players

Through experience I've learned to view my attorney and accountant as members of my team—not as experts who extol their wisdom for me to follow without question. For years, I hired the most prominent attorney and CPA firm that I could (barely) afford for my businesses. These learned figures would set up my businesses the way they "should be" set up. I felt that my opinions and questions about the complex process either would be lost on these superior beings or would lead to a larger bill since I was complicating matters. One powerful attorney was so wrapped up at the state capitol influencing political opinions that a simple question about incorporating my business was delayed for weeks. Also, instead of working with the senior accountant in the esteemed accounting firm, I was paying precious money to work with the junior partners (and not in a timely manner). The giant accounting firm was not the best choice to serve the relatively insignificant (in their opinion) needs of my small business. It's obvious now—I was paying a lot of money without getting my needs met. This memory embarrasses me, but sharing it with you may help you avoid my costly mistakes.

For your Web design shop, you don't need political influence and you don't need the top trial lawyer in the state. You don't need the most expensive lawyer to tell you what type of business structure you should have. You don't need a Fortune 500 accounting firm to recommend what accounts to include in your software program.

What you do need is small business advice. You need members on your team! You need a small business lawyer who will take a bit of time to get to know you and your situation. You need an accountant who understands your personal financial situation and can advise you on ways to lower your taxable income. You need professional team members you can call to clear up something that is puzzling you. You need to be able to give them a heads-up when a potential problem is brewing so they can guide you. (Don't feel compelled to wait until a problem becomes a lawsuit before bringing in your attorney. That's an expensive business decision—and one of the reasons you have your team is to help you prevent those expensive situations!)

When starting your Web design business, you may be tempted to try to save some money by forgoing an attorney and/or accountant. This is not a wise business decision, for a variety of reasons. Much of the information in this book comes with a caveat that you should consult with your attorney or accountant first. Don't rely solely on Internet newsgroups for business advice. Newsgroups can be a great sounding board, but subscribers aren't all lawyers and accountants. Blindly taking the advice of anyone who is not a trained professional can get you sued. If you think it is expensive to have an attorney help you design a contract, think of the money you'll pay one to defend you in a lawsuit! The cliché about being "penny wise and pound foolish" is very relevant for those who avoid getting advice from professionals. (And so is the expression "pay me now or pay me later.")

So now you know you need an accountant and attorney, and you know the importance of finding the ones that are right for your team. How, you may ask, do I find these wonderful people for my team? Ask other business owners for recommendations, then talk to potential candidates to see if there is a good fit. Don't skip that screening step—it's important. The first time someone suggested I interview attorneys before hiring one, I was surprised; I had never considered interviewing an attorney or accountant the way I would a designer or programmer. I also never considered firing one for not meeting my business needs. I now know better. If you are uncomfortable about this, remember that it is a normal part of business. Just as one of your potential clients might interview you to see if there is a good fit, you should do the same with all your team members. Draw up a list of questions to ask your professionals. Listen not only for the answers, but also to see if there is a level of friendly and comfortable interaction. If you feel intimidated, don't ignore the feeling—your instincts are telling you someone is not right for your team.

Questions for Interviewing an Attorney

"What is your primary field of practice?"
If the answer is "everything," run the other way! An attorney who knows that you are there as a small business owner should be able to give you a feel for her areas of expertise and whether they fit with your needs.

"How do you base your fees?"
You need to know what your attorney charges. You also need to know if your attorney charges for each phone call or conversation and what you can expect those charges to be. Some attorneys start the clock anytime you call, whether it is for legal advice or just to provide some follow-up information they requested. Others will tell you before they start the clock running. Some will encourage you to contact them at no charge to alert them to a potential problem; others charge for that. Establish these charges in advance so there are no surprises.

"Do you currently represent any Web design businesses or related businesses?"
Your attorney may not be working with any Web design shops, but the "related businesses" part of this question may give you some insight as to how the attorney perceives your business. A good follow-up question is how he or she sees the related business as being similar to yours. Don't be afraid to probe a bit here. This is not about getting the answers "right" as much as it is a measure of whether you and your future attorney will be able to communicate in a friendly yet professional manner.

"What is your level of experience with electronic law?"
This is an open-ended question. Don't help by following with questions that can be answered with a simple "yes" or "no." You want details from the attorney here, not a simple indication that he or she knows about electronic law. Ask how much experience the attorney has, and in what areas. Ask how recent that experience is.

It's always helpful to start an interview by giving the candidate some background about yourself and your business. Then ask the list of questions you've prepared. You can wrap up the interview by asking if there's anything the candidate would like to ask you.

In the checklist "Questions for Interviewing an Attorney," sample questions are provided for use when interviewing an attorney for your Web design business. Comments on how you might interpret the attorney's responses are also provided. I do the same for accountants in the checklist "Questions for Interviewing an Accountant."

The sample questions I've given you are pointed questions to help take your potential team members off the pedestal on which you may have placed them. After you've interviewed two or three candidates, you should find that some are very candid and supportive and that they appreciate your interest in their profession. Others will view your questions as an invasion of their professional image and will continue to try to intimidate you. It took me many mistakes to learn that I want to hire professionals for their ability to interact with me as a respected and knowledgeable member of my team as much as for their technical know-how.

Opinion Leaders

I have a friend who knows a lot more than I do about stereo equipment. If I'm looking for a stereo, I get information from several sources, then go to my guru and ask him what he thinks of my research. Even though I ultimately make my own decision, his opinion weighs heavily in my choice. Similarly, every type of business has a small group of people who emerge as opinion leaders to whom others turn for information.

If you can figure out who the opinion leaders are for your business, treat them well and let them know how much you appreciate their assistance in finding you new customers. Usually if an opinion leader refers a potential client to me, it is almost a guaranteed sale. Here's someone who needs my services and who found out from a trusted source that I'm the best person around to meet those needs!

One of the best ways to find opinion leaders is through networking groups. Consider joining your local chamber of commerce if you haven't done so already. Some opinion leaders may be among the members, and you can get to know them in a low-key social setting.

If you have a local chapter of the networking group BNI (Business Network International) in your area, explore it as a source of opinion leaders and referrals. (See chapter 8 for more information on this organization.)

Questions for Interviewing an Accountant

"Do you primarily handle small businesses or larger ones?"
This question should get a dialogue going that will tell you if the accountant is used to dealing with smaller start-up businesses or prefers working for larger companies.

"Do you work alone or have a staff of accountants? Do you recommend that for someone like me?"
This two-part question will give you a feel for the structure that your accountant uses. If he or she is part of a larger group, you should ask why and decide if you are comfortable with that arrangement. Also, ask if you will deal with other partners frequently, or mostly with the accountant you are interviewing. If this accountant works solo, find out why. My accountant works alone except for an assistant who answers the phone and does much of his support work. I enjoy the fact that I can call and ask my accountant a quick question, knowing that he is familiar with my books and I won't have to give him a lot of background information first.

"How do you charge for your work?"
An accountant once told me that he had an advantage over many other professionals because, with access to his clients' books, he knew who could afford him and who couldn't! Many accountants base their fees for small start-up businesses at the low end of their scale since they want to be there when the business grows. Although some accountants have a set price schedule that they adhere to, a non-specific answer to a question about charges may not be a bad thing.

"Do you have any flexibility in your fees during my start-up?"
If you like a certain accountant and have a good rapport with her, but feel that during your start-up phase you can't afford the fees she quoted, talk about it. If the accountant can't or won't work with you with the anticipation of future growth, you may wish to keep looking. Accountants are not in business to speculate over your growth any more than you would take on Web customers for that same reason. However, using the same analogy, if you feel you will ultimately make more money from a Web client by accepting a bit less now, that makes good business sense.

Customer Magnets

Like opinion leaders, customer magnets are people who can draw clients to your business. There are two main types of customer magnets: cheerleaders and inter-related businesses. Cheerleaders usually have a personal reason for drawing clients to you. A cheerleader may be a relative, friend, church or civic group member, or just someone who values the work you do and wants to "tell the world" about your shop. Interrelated businesses usually have a business motive for sending clients to you.

Cheerleaders

Have you ever known someone who is so charismatic or bubbly that you just wish you could buy something from him? This is an example of a customer magnet. If you locate people like this and get them excited about your service, they are very vocal and influential and are eager to tell everyone they know about your business! Sometimes in their enthusiasm they may overstate your business, so be on the lookout for that. You may be able to counter this tendency by giving them details about your business and services that will help them focus their enthusiasm.

Notes about Opinion Leaders

- You might be tempted to offer a deal to an opinion leader, but most cannot be bought. If someone offered my friend a free stereo, he might or might not take the stereo. But he would continue to offer his honest opinion about the best equipment around.

- Opinion leaders are not always right. My friend might unknowingly give me incorrect information about a stereo. Still, he knows more than I do, and I would be more likely to believe him than I would an electronics store salesperson. In a similar vein, you may find that potential clients are being swayed to a lesser Web design shop by an opinion leader. Unless you can find out who is influencing their decisions and convince that opinion leader that yours is the superior shop, you may continue to lose business.

- Sometimes you can sell your services to an opinion leader through your potential client. If your potential client says that a friend recommended the XYZ Design Shop, offer to talk directly with that friend. If that doesn't work, give your potential client a list of criteria for comparing services (for example, whether sites they design include key words; whether those sites can be found in the search engines; whether they have cross-browser compatibility). Be sure to show how your sites are superior. Remember that you are doing a secondhand sale here so the more concrete examples you can give, the better. Your potential client will likely run back to his opinion leader and show him what you've presented. You have a chance of not only swaying your potential client but also getting the opinion leader's attention.

- While it is wonderful to have an opinion leader on your side, it does not always work that way. You may find that everyone that you are trying to sell to has been swayed by an opinion leader who doesn't like you or your services. If you can't change that, try to team up with other opinion leaders who are on your side. Put some distance between yourself and a troublesome opinion leader—some day that person may not be as influential, and you will be able to attract clients who were formerly reluctant.

Don't overlook a spouse or close friend as a potential cheerleader. The best cheerleader I have for my business is my wife. Many times when we are in a conversation at a social gathering, she will see an opportunity to mention that I design Web sites. If she is the least bit encouraged by a favorable response from her listener, she shamelessly plugs my services and capabilities in ways that I could never do.

My wife is a respected professional (but not in the computer field) in a major corporation and she has a variety of interests. She has many business contacts who are not computer savvy. What better cheerleader could one ask for! She can interact in a nongeeky manner with people who see her as a nonthreatening computer novice. (Although she views herself as a computer novice, I periodically remind her that she knows more than most of the people she talks with.) I am always glad to take the time to answer her questions about the Internet and the intricacies of designing Web sites because I know that someday she will use those details to promote my business. I advise you not to shrug off questions from your spouse and close friends. Put them on your team and treat them like gold—they can be your best cheerleaders.

Interrelated Businesses

Take a minute to think about businesses whose services complement your own and who deal with the same client mix you do. Many of their clients are potential clients for you. And many of your clients are potential clients for them as well.

Most Internet service providers have neither time nor interest in developing Web sites. If their customers ask them about doing some Web design work, they refer those people to a Web design shop. Why not put your name in front of these potential customer magnets? The better you treat their clients, the more referrals you may get.

There's one important point to mention here: If you host Web sites, do not take a client away from his current host if he was recommended to you by that host. This may seem obvious to you, but I have heard stories about it happening. (Of course, I feel that my hosting service is much better than the local ones. However, if I put my name in the hands of a local hosting service, I'm accepting their level of service as adequate. If I don't feel they offer good hosting, I don't want them passing my name around anyway.) Tread very carefully if one of your referrals wants to switch to your hosting services; otherwise, you may not get any more referrals.

Look around for other interrelated businesses that might be good customer magnets. High-speed DSL companies offer to host customers' Web sites, and some of those clients need a site designer. And what about small business advertising agencies that don't have an in-house Web team? Some of their clients will want to build Web sites to advertise their businesses. What about small business loan officers, attorneys, and accountants? If the issue of promoting their services over the Internet comes up, offer to do their Web work. What about your local computer repair shop or your computer sales shop? Small business owners who come in to purchase or repair a computer may strike up a conversation about getting their business on the Internet. If you have any connections there, see if someone will be a customer magnet for you.

You may come up with other ideas for interrelated businesses that can be customer magnets. Talk to these people and if they are interested, add them to your team. Keep them posted as your business expands. Thank them profusely for any referrals. Tell them the outcome of any referrals they made. If a referral doesn't work out, tell your customer magnet why while lavishing praise for getting the referral for you anyway. This will encourage her and help her zero in on future referrals. Remember that, since this person is on your team, you should also try to help her business whenever possible.

Subcontractors or Competitors?

Many people starting out in the Web design business initially work as subcontractors—it's a low-risk way to learn the business before striking out on one's own. Be careful that the subcontractors you hire are not going to become your competitors later. A written contract can prevent some abuse, but it is also good to make sure your subcontractors are on your team. If you have read chapter 1, you know what skills you can use help with. If you want to subcontract this work out, it will be better to have some people with those skills on your team rather than sporadically calling names on a list. What is the difference? Some Web design shops treat subcontractors as dime-a-dozen workers, there to do a job, get paid, and leave. Their responsibility to a subcontractor, and vice versa, doesn't extend beyond the job at hand. However, if you have a select group of team members whose skills complement yours, you can call on them over and over. They will appreciate the repeat business, and may even refer work to you if it requires skills they lack and you have. Treat your subs like a team and they will be more likely to act like team members toward your clients. Most importantly, once you have assembled a group of colleagues you trust and respect, you'll be best equipped for reaching out confidently to clients.

04 Starting Your Web Design Business

The old adage about first impressions being lasting ones suggests that the first step in reaching out to clients should be a step back to consider your business image objectively. How do you want to be perceived by your potential clients? Is there a style or image you want to project? Maybe you want your business to be known as a high-tech design shop, or a full-service Web design shop with the capability and resources to handle a full range of business needs. Perhaps you'd like to be seen as an Internet consultant with a broad spectrum of knowledge. Or, do you want to be known as a quiet, busy designer who has little glitter but much substance? Or a family person with warmth and sensitivity to the community or to a particular cause? All of these, and many more, are very valid images to develop your business project.

Establishing Your Image

It may help you to write down some statements that you feel describe your business or your focus. For example, in my business, I enjoy teaching and consulting. I also like creative design work. Lastly, I want to enhance others' experience when they are using computers and the Internet. From these statements you can conclude that I should probably conduct some seminars on Internet-related topics. I should focus on designing Web sites for businesses with limited or little Internet experience. Perhaps I should even write books on Internet topics!

Once you have created your vision for your business, you need to position your business to make that perception a reality. Of course, the way to do that depends greatly on what you decide you want for your business. In my own case, I knew I needed to do more than simply advertise my design skills. I decided to teach Internet classes for corporations. I began offering free seminars to groups from whom there was a chance of gaining business. I signed up to teach adult education classes and became a member of the board of directors for a local computer user group. These activities let me position my business as a reliable and trusted guide through the Internet abyss. Although I have many savvy Web design customers, I still enjoy helping Internet newcomers. It's gratifying to me when my clients realize that their customers are using their Web site and that it is a helpful resource.

It is not difficult to envision the type of Web design shop you want to have. But you may find it is challenging to keep that focus. There may be times when your contracts are slim and you will be tempted to change course. There may be compelling reasons to change your course. Analyze them carefully before chasing every tempting offer. You must decide whether a change will reinforce the image you want to project, harm it, or have no impact at all. If the change conflicts with the way you want people to view your business, you should decide whether you want to modify your vision of the business, take the offer and try to minimize the damages, or pass up the offer.

Here's one example from my own business. I decided not to host any pornographic Web sites. These Web sites don't fit my vision of my business for two reasons. First, they don't enhance my image as a trusted small business consultant, and second, they are outside of the scope of the equipment I normally work with. This is not a morality issue as much as it is one of server overload. Porn sites tend to have very heavy traffic, and some overzealous individuals feel compelled to destroy the sites at any cost. I chose to avoid the risks of server overload and hackers. But hosting pornographic sites can be lucrative and many have capitalized on this. It's all a matter of how you want to position your business.

Your Credibility

The topics discussed so far in this section deal with issues that you control: your vision, the steps you take to develop your image, and the ways in which you can protect your image from being diluted. There is another part of this formula that you don't control as much as your clients do—your credibility. Your credibility is based upon others' perception of your reliability, your actions, and your focus. If your credibility is destroyed, only other people will decide when and if it should be repaired. Others control this capricious aspect of your business, although you are the one who establishes it at the outset.

You don't need a sermon on being reliable, trustworthy, and honest. To varying degrees, we all know that we need these positive traits to succeed in business. Your credibility depends on how you stay true to your business's vision and how you consistently show you are a reliable, trustworthy, and honest business person. Credibility is not yours to keep; it is the label that others have the privilege of granting. Safeguard it and you will reap the reward.

Setting Your Rates

The most difficult question when setting up your Web design shop is, "What should I charge?" The reason it is a difficult question is not that it is a Web designer's secret. It is simply because there are so many variables. A pack of gum has an established price. A house has other comparables to help establish a reasonable price. We are in a wild and woolly market without well-established guidelines. Each person lives or dies by what he or she thinks his or her services are worth. If you aim too low, you don't make the profit you could, and that might diminish your value. If you aim too high, you price yourself out of the market. Web design is not a clear, well-traveled path. It is unmapped, uncertain, and filled with opportunities as well as obstacles. The money is good if you enjoy the work and are willing to overcome the obstacles.

To establish some guidelines for your rates, you should ask yourself some questions such as "How much am I worth?" and "What will my market bear?" and even, "How much do I want to earn?"

What Are You Worth?

If you ask ten different people what you're worth, you may get ten different answers. Many of your friends would tell you that you're wonderful and that you should demand an equally wonderful hourly wage. Others might fear that you will be lucky to get minimum wage. Your competitors may try to get you to either lowball your price or overinflate your rates to price yourself out of the market. With all of this "help," no wonder it can be difficult to figure out what you should charge.

You will need to establish what you could get if you were to use your skills in a permanent, full-time staff position. This is the time to do some sleuthing. Go online to some of the job boards (for example, look at www.monster.com, www .careerbuilder.com, and www.dice.com) and see what jobs are available. Look at the salaries being offered for jobs that you feel you are qualified for. But remember: You're not doing this research for an ego boost; you want the facts. So, if you are in a small town in the Midwest, don't focus on the high-end jobs in Silicon Valley. The closer you can get to real comparables, the less likely you will be going without any contracts due to overpricing yourself—or making little or no profit due to under pricing yourself.

For example, I live and work in Connecticut. When I priced my skills for jobs in Connecticut within a reasonable travel range, I found I could probably get a staff job that paid $50,000 to $75,000. If I had stronger programming skills, I could get much more. If I didn't have such strong experience in HTML, I would get less. If I were willing to commute more than an hour during rush hour, I would be in a region where I could command more. The reality is that I feel I could get a job in the $50,000 to $75,000 range without difficulty.

If I divide that salary by the number of hours a full-time staffer works per year, I come up with an hourly rate of about $25 to $35. Is that what I should charge? No! That is what I'm "worth" to an employer—that plus lots of benefits, including insurance, vacation, and paid holidays. A corporation takes care of a great many expenses that are not immediately apparent to most people who are trying to set their rates.

Calculating Employer Considerations

When I work for an employer, I can usually get on-the-job training. I have the benefit of the company's Web security department and its networking gurus. I can get all the office supplies I need to do my work. My computer and the often-expensive software are supplied by the corporation. In addition to health, life, and disability insurance, the corporation pays a matching portion of FICA and Medicare charges.

When I work for myself, I don't have those benefits unless I calculate them into my formula. Without the corporation's deep pockets, if I have a question about a networking issue, I usually pay for the answer out of my own pocket. If I need a book on JavaScript or a new software package, I pay for that myself. If I want to take a vacation, I can't ask my clients to spring for my vacation and continue mailing me checks until I get back; that must come out of my revenues. If I want health insurance, that can be a major expense that I must cover. (Fortunately for me, my wife's employer offers a reasonable health insurance plan for spouses. If you have a spouse who works outside the home, look into whether his or her benefits can cover you.) I invoice clients for all the work I do, and collect from them—there is no accounting department to take care of that. And when a client doesn't pay me, it's not a big, impersonal corporate write-off—it is a direct hit to my wallet!

As you can see, if I worked for myself for the same gross salary I would get from a corporation, I would lose money every time I signed a contract. Corporate employees may be envious seeing an independent contractor being paid double or triple what they are, but in reality there are many expenses that help make this a level playing field. Once you've established the hourly rate you'd get in a full-time, corporate staff job, you need to create a formula for your business overhead. For my own overhead, I mark up my market value by 35 to 40 percent. Therefore, if I earned $35 per hour working in a corporation, I would need to charge more than $50 per hour as an independent contractor, to be on the same ending pay scale. (This is based on a forty-hour work week, not including any unbillable time.)

As most contractors realize, billable time is not the same as time spent working. I can't directly charge my clients for new software, nor the time I spend learning it. Neither can I charge for the time I spend keeping my accounting updated. My billable time is probably no more than half of the time I work—and in fact, often billable time is much less than that. Given that, my initial hypothetical $35 hourly wage that grew to over $50 needs to be adjusted again. Since I can bill for less than half the time I work, I must double that $50.

You have seen how, using some real numbers, we can come up with my worth. Obviously, those same numbers won't work for you. You may not have a spouse who supplies you with health care benefits. When starting out, you will need to work more hours per week marketing yourself (and those are unbillable hours). You may need to make some payments on a computer or software. The best way to determine your own rates is to work out a formula with your accountant. Your accountant should be accustomed to helping small business owners establish their overhead and rates. He or she will also be familiar with your region's taxes and income-matching items such as FICA.

Of course, there are some other factors to consider when setting your rates. These include how much you want to earn, how much the market will bear, and what your competitors charge.

What Will the Market Bear?
I can say that I want to earn $100 per hour, but my clients may not be willing to pay me that much. There are several ways to find out if they will. First, I can check with my competitors. As I mentioned earlier, they may or may not give me an accurate answer. Most Web designers don't like to admit it if they are getting a low hourly rate, so

consider the possibility of exaggeration. A better way might be to look at those designers' Web sites. Many Web designers post their hourly rates on their sites. Again, this may not mean that they get that amount, just as the sticker price on a car doesn't necessarily reflect the final selling price. If you have some friends in small businesses who have recently hired Web designers, ask what they found to be a reasonable hourly rate.

The most reliable method of finding out what the market will bear is through trial and error. The first few times you go out to talk to potential clients, you will probably be using this method to some degree anyway. If a client asks what you charge to update a Web site, tell him your hourly rate. If he screams, you might be too high. If he smiles and jumps on the deal, you might be too low.

These aren't completely accurate indicators, but after a few clients scream, you will start to get the message that your rates are higher than your market will bear. If your clients start questioning your experience and wondering why you are giving them such a great deal, you might consider raising your rates a bit so you don't devalue your services.

It's a little harder to interpret the actions of potential clients who decide to hire someone else. Sometimes it's because your rates are too high. Sometimes it's because your competitor has more experience than you do. And sometimes an opinion leader has endorsed one of your competitors. You may want to politely follow up with the people who didn't hire you. If both you and they are comfortable with this, you can get useful feedback (and maybe even change a potential client's mind).

Taking Advantage of Low Bids

Shortly after I began my Web design business, I underbid on a job but had a chance to rectify it. I had intentionally bid a little low, to increase my chance of getting the contract. The client's response was, "Wow! You are willing to do all this and it will only cost me this amount of money?" My first response (after silent regret upon realizing that I could have bid higher) was to explain that there were a few extra charges—one for search engine placement and another for an additional task. That eased my pain a little bit for grossly under-estimating my fee out of inexperience.

Because I was still a bargain to this client, I had to justify my low bid somehow. Otherwise he might have assumed that I was inexperienced (which was true, but which I preferred to downplay). So I explained to him that I was intentionally giving him a great deal because his was a high-profile company. I said that I hoped that, once he saw how good my work was, he would tell multitudes of others about the great job

I did. He was comfortable thinking of me as a shrewd business person wanting to use his company as a stepping-stone. He knew that I wasn't going to do a cheap job on his Web site, but rather was planning to give it the royal treatment so I could use it as a showpiece. Of course, I gave him the same great service that I gave everyone, but it did turn a potentially uncomfortable situation into an opportunity for both of us.

How Much Do You Want to Earn?

If all of these calculations to establish your rate overwhelm you, there is a shortcut—but it may not be as accurate. You can work backward from your desired income. Each year, you decide what you want to earn. You determine what your expenses will be, and add this to the first figure. Include what it will cost for software, hardware, books, supplies, insurance, taxes, and everything else. The sum of those numbers is what you will need to earn in a year. Once you have that annual number, divide it by the number of weeks you plan to work, then divide that figure by the hours that you plan to bill for each week. If your figures are correct, that's what you will need to charge per hour to obtain your desired income.

No matter what method you use to calculate your rates, you may have trouble getting the rate you feel you deserve. If you need to earn $100 per hour to match what you could get in a staff job, and the market won't support that rate, should you even consider opening your own Web design shop? Are there any other "hidden" values to doing so? You may have reasons for wanting a Web design shop that are as important as money. Here are some of mine.

- As an employee, I had very little voice in the type of computer or software I could get. I had whatever was the corporate standard. If I wanted a software program to help me with my job, I needed to go through major battles to get it approved. If I put it on my computer without approval, I was violating major corporate rules. With my Web design shop, if I need something in order to do my job, I reach into my pocket and buy it.
- As an employee, if a client became very difficult to work with, I didn't have the authority to drop that client. In my shop, if there is an unworkable problem with a client, I can make the decision to drop that client and lose those dollars.
- As an employee, anything the company bought was written off through the company. Now that I own my business, at tax time I can offset all of

my income with all of my expenses. When I want a computer magazine, I can recover a portion of the cost as a business expense. If I want to go to an Internet conference, I can write off some of it as a business expense. (Caution: Don't fall into the trap of assuming that, because these expenditures are tax write-offs, they don't cost anything!)

- As an employee, someone else took the risk and received the rewards. Many people like it that way, but I want to be responsible for my own blunders as well as my brilliant thinking.

- You may very well decide that, even though it may look like you make less money in your own Web design shop, there can be hidden value that makes it the right choice for you.

Charging by the Hour and by the Job

The ideal situation for me would be to set an hourly rate and charge that for everything I do. That's the easiest and surest way to be compensated accurately. However, that is not always feasible. When a relative newcomer to the Internet wants a Web site set up, she doesn't want to know my hourly rate. She wants to know what it will cost her to get the site up and running. I could tell her that I estimate it would take me about twenty hours at $75 per hour. But the client might be concerned that she is trusting me to deliver a service at an estimated cost, which I won't guarantee. She may instead hire someone who will work at a cheaper rate and who will give her a set price. The quality of the work might not be as good, but at least the client can be sure she's not risking an expensive, runaway project.

I've come to realize that, since clients like this are novices on Internet-related matters, I am the one in control of the project. To get the business, I have to take some of the risk to ensure that the client won't be stuck with a runaway project. I need to determine what the client's needs are and then give him a contract with a set price that we are both comfortable with. I usually charge by the job based on how long I think it will take to complete the project times my hourly rate. If the client requests some add-ons halfway through the project, it is my responsibility to have him sign an agreement authorizing the extra charge. If the project takes me more time than I expected, I absorb the excess costs and, with luck, learn how to prevent that from happening again. If I can finish the site in less time than I estimated, I come out ahead. (That helps make up for the losses I sustain.)

I give a set price for search engine notifications and updates, since I know approximately how long that takes. When I update the content of a Web site I've created, I usually charge by the hour. By the time the client wants me to do those updates, we already have a good business relationship built upon trust. The client knows that there will be no runaway expenses and that she will get a good value for her money. She sends me the information to be updated; I make the changes and bill her.

The only time I insist on doing hourly work for a new client is when I'm taking over an existing Web site and doing the updates. I don't know what the person before me has done to the code. I don't know what shortcuts she may have taken. For those times, I explain the reasons why I can't give the client a set price for the work. I also assure her that, although it probably will take about X hours, I will contact her if I find anything that will change my estimate dramatically. When I host a Web site, my charges are based on a combination of the cost to me plus a reasonable markup, which is tempered by what the market will bear.

Coping with Shops That Charge Less (or More) Than You Do

You will have no problem finding some Web designers who charge more than you do and others who charge less. The prices are all over the place. Once you've determined your rate, don't let the others sway you. Sometimes I'm tempted to raise my rates because "everyone else is charging more." Other times I'm tempted to drop my rates because clients are complaining that others' rates are much lower. I used to revise my rates based on the feedback I was hearing at a given time. I have since decided that in a competitive business like Web design, other designers' rates may somewhat influence how I initially set my rates. However, other designers don't set those rates—my customers and I do. I recommend that you adopt my philosophy and set rates that you feel are fair and competitive. After this, stick to those rates as well as you can.

If a client points out that one of your competitors charges less than you do, try to point out the features you offer that others don't. Be careful not to get defensive—remember that your client is giving you an opportunity to explain why your services are worth the extra money. If he wasn't interested in your services, he would simply switch to your competitor.

Avoid saying negative things about your competitors unless you know your potential client very well. If you try to downgrade a competitor's reputation, you will probably take your own reputation down with it. Talk in general terms about "other Web designers in the business." I find it safest to talk in a way that educates a potential client. I might say, "Some Web designers may design your pages to look good on a single browser and tell your customers that if they don't use that browser, it's the customer's loss. I design Web sites to look good on a broad range of computers—including Macs, PCs, older machines as well as newer ones, slow modems as well as high-speed connections." You can see that I am not denigrating a particular competitor. If a client does decide to look elsewhere, at least he will know how to judge other designers' work. If he doesn't like what he sees, he may be back.

On the other hand, if you are dealing with a client who has received some bids that are much higher than yours, she too may be reluctant to hire you. It can be just as difficult to sell to a client who thinks your price is low as to one who thinks it's high. She may wonder why your services are so cheap. Is it the quality of your work? Is it because there will be some important details that you omit? Is it because you don't know what you're doing and the Web site will reflect that? You must address these concerns if you expect a client to hire you.

Once I had a client query me on my quote after he received high bids from two large design shops. I smiled and told him that those firms have a full staff to pay even when they have slow periods, so they have to make up for it by charging higher rates. I reassured him that, because I have subcontractors to take up any overload, I can keep my rates within reason. I also told him that instead of having to equip several people with computers and software, I have only my own equipment and expenses. I then pointed out to the client that he wouldn't be dealing with a variety of people who would tell other people what needed to be done. He would be dealing directly with the designer creating his Web site—me. That eliminated any concerns about my prices being lower than someone else's.

Turning a Suggestion to Do "Speculative" Work into a Sale

Early in the life of your business, someone will probably suggest that you build a "sample" site for him, or create a draft or a few pages of his Web site. He will assure you that as long as it looks good, you will be paid for the work after you've "proven yourself." During lean times, you also may be tempted to create a site for someone and then try to sell it to him or her. Or, a potential client may approach you with the idea that if you design a free or low-cost Web site for him, because of his high-profile business, you will get many more great-paying jobs from others. Each of these tactics is a part of speculative Web design work.

When you start out, it is good business sense for you to design a few discounted or free Web sites for deserving nonprofit groups or for businesses you want to use to showcase your work. This isn't speculative work; it's part of your marketing strategy. It would, however, be speculative if you designed a Web site for an organization in a gamble that you'd get future business or good PR from that effort.

Here is how I determine if I'm about to do speculative work. Speculative work is risky. I spend my time and hope to come out ahead. Doing free work in exchange for some sales tools is not a gamble. I know I need to give away some money (time) in the beginning to get the sales tools I need—I can accept this because I know what I will get in return. However, I'm not as willing to give away money to a company just to speculate that they might bring me some new business some day.

You are offering a service that has value to your potential client. You are viewed as an expert. You are offering to use your valuable time and expertise to create a great Web site for someone. However, if you decide to spend your time with no assurance of getting any money, your time is no longer valuable. Unlike a refrigerator or house that is made in advance because it can be sold to someone, you have created something with the understanding that it will *not* be sold to anyone else. You have told the client that your time is so undervalued that you are willing to use some of it in hopes that you will get something in return. This is not a very good bargaining position.

If you are being asked to do a Web site "on spec," this is where your portfolio is useful. (The Web sites in your portfolio can even be the free ones you've done to showcase your work.) Explain to your potential client that, although you enjoy your work, you try not to work for free. If the client needs proof of the quality of your work, show him your portfolio. If he questions your ability to do the job, analyze your presentation and determine why he feels you wouldn't be competent. Then give him the information he needs to be reassured of your competency. If he says that he needs a draft of the Web site to take back to his boss, you are talking to the wrong person. Offer to set up an appointment to give a presentation (sales pitch) to his boss.

If you feel you have adequately responded to your potential client's concerns, yet you still aren't getting the sale, you should wonder (not out loud!) whether this person is sincere about hiring you. Although most potential clients are sincere and interested in working out a deal, you may run into someone who is just not willing, or able, to hire you. If you have given your best presentation and answered all of his concerns, and he still insists that you work on spec, it is probably time to walk away. Thank him for his time and for considering using your services.

You've just planted some ideas in this client's head that may need some time to develop. He now knows that you are a professional and you are confident in your work. It now is up to him to decide whether he is able and willing to remove the obstacles and hire you. I'd love to say that he will probably call you back tomorrow, but don't hold your breath. The few clients who do call you back generally do so because they are ready to hire you as a professional Web designer. Those are the ones who will treat you with the respect you deserve.

How to Give Yourself a Raise in Pay

You might periodically want to adjust your hourly rate to "give yourself a raise." I've found that I worry and fret about how my clients will handle me pushing my hourly rate up by $5 or $10. I finally brace myself for an onslaught of complaints and give myself the well-deserved raise. Naturally, my fear of the negative reaction is far greater than the actual reaction from my clients. Most don't even notice that my rate is different until I point it out to them.

You may find, as I did, that you have some longtime customers who have been faithfully staying with you since the very early times. They were with you back when you started and it was as much a fun hobby as it was a small business. They never asked for much, and you'd make changes to their Web sites for little or no money. Now you need to establish your rates with these clients without shocking them with a huge jump from a small fee to the current market rates.

My way of dealing with that was a bit unconventional, but it worked for me. One such client e-mailed me and wanted me to make a few changes to his Web site. I started my time clock and made the changes. I created an invoice for the time I spent, times my normal rate, which equaled the total charge. I then discounted it 100 percent. With the invoice, I included a "coupon" for an hour of work in the future at 50 percent off as thanks for being a longtime client. Although I gave away some work, I was able to make that client feel special as one of my most loyal customers from the early days when I was starting out. Yet at the same time, he knew that he was "becoming" a paying client. I still don't charge him my full rate, but he understands that he is a paying customer.

I've also got another client from my early days whom I used to charge very low rates. I still charge him a discounted rate. I bill him at my current $75 per hour rate and on his invoice I discount it so he knows he's a very special client (and never forget that those start-up clients are very special clients!).

Business Contracts

When starting out, many Web designers feel they don't need signed contracts. They have a variety of rationalizations.

- "I know the person that I'm doing work for, so I don't need a contract."
- "I'm not going to let the client have the work until I get paid, so I don't need a contract."
- "Asking someone to sign a contract shows that I don't trust him or her."
- "Contract or no contract, someone is only as good as his or her word."
- "I'm afraid I'll scare clients off if I insist they sign a contract."

When I started my Web design business, I felt uncomfortable requiring clients to sign contracts. After working to persuade a client to hire me, and demonstrating that I'm reliable and friendly and helpful, I felt like I was destroying our fun fest with that contract. I hated having to shove an eight-page legal document in front of a client and demand her signature. Even though I knew I was doing the right thing, I felt the tension mounting as she scanned the sections about what I would do if she didn't pay, and what I wouldn't let her do, and all the things that weren't included. Although I didn't want to make light of the contract and tell the client to just sign it without reading it, I also hated how it seemed to douse a perfectly good mood that I'd set up. I finally realized that it wasn't the contract; it was my presentation that was the problem.

In the section on character traits in chapter 1, I said that the better you can be at switching between your roles, the more successful you will be. Contract presentation is a great example of my rainmaker trait drumming up business, followed by the suit presenting the contract. I may also need to put on my propeller hat or ponytail for some last-minute programming or design clarification to smooth the way for the suit to complete the contract presentation. I finally realized that the reason I was uncomfortable about contracts was because I was forcing my sales persona to present the contract. I should have been creating a natural and comfortable progression from selling to contract agreement (and from rainmaker to suit). In the next section I will tell you how I learned to handle this progression, then scrutinize portions of the contracts that I use. You can decide what will help you the most.

Using a Contract as a Selling Tool

A contract can be either a deal killer or a normal part of your business. Much of that depends on how you view contracts. I'd start my presentations by telling potential clients all the wonderful things I could do for them to get their interest, and then I'd suddenly bring out this dreaded contract. My attorney had created this document. He and I had reviewed it together so that I would understand it. We had talked about what parts of it I felt were most important, and why certain sections were there. We had tweaked it and shaped it until I felt it met my needs and he felt it adequately protected my interests. I knew my contract was a good document, with terms that protected both my clients and myself. However, instead of introducing the contract with this background, I'd drop it in front of a potential client and ask him to look at it and sign it.

Some clients would tell me that they'd look at it when they had a chance and get back to me with any questions. Other clients probably sensed my discomfort and would thumb through the document and reluctantly sign it, trusting that I wasn't going to take advantage of them. One day a potential client asked me to go through the contract with him. I started out dreading the ordeal, but soon realized that this was a great opportunity. I had begun wading through the contract with somber explanations while my client tried to lighten the mood with his comments. Finally, I relaxed a bit and found that I could say in plain English, "This section warrants that I actually have the qualifications to do the job right" and "That section assures that we will both work together to complete the Web site in a timely manner." I could even state, with a smile, "This section is for any scoundrel who would dare not to pay me!" I ended my review by reminding the client that I'm a Web designer, not an attorney, and then I read the last paragraph of the contract that states, "This CONTRACT constitutes the sole agreement." I told my client that he should believe the contract rather than anything I said. He laughed, said he never believes anything anyone says anyway, and immediately signed the contract! I was surprised and delighted at how easy and natural that had been. Even though I had stumbled over a few sections that I had never quite understood, I went away feeling that I had discovered a new sales tool—my contract!

A few years (and many contracts) later, I am thoroughly familiar with everything about my contracts, and I feel very comfortable discussing them with clients. Some clients appreciate going through the contract line by line, while others skim through it and appear impatient if I start talking too much. It is no longer a mood dampener in my presentations. If a potential client asks about nondisclosure, or copyright issues, or extra costs for tasks or expenses not included, I pull out the contract and show her the section that addresses her concern. I work sections of the contract into the discussion wherever appropriate. This way, the contract is a natural part of our business agreement, not the tension-filled finish to an otherwise pleasant discussion.

Creating a Contract

I am not an attorney, and don't claim to be passing out legal advice—that is your attorney's job. I'm happy to share my experiences and some of the reasons I have put certain terms in my own contracts, but you and your attorney must decide what is best for you. Notice that I talk about deciding what is best for you. Your attorney shouldn't be working without your input—after all, you hired him or her to be on your team of experts.

In creating my contract, my attorney interjected what he felt should be there and then we would translate that into lay terms. He had to keep reminding me that a contract is *not* a marketing tool, but a contract. I kept reminding him that, although I didn't want to mislead clients, I didn't want to scare them away with legalese either. Together we gathered the needed information, he explained where I was leaving myself open and how to watch for potential problems, and we were able to develop a contract that both of us felt satisfied with.

Elements of a Contract

Start by writing down what you think may be important in a contract. Have a section for items that remain the same in each contract and another section for items that are variable (client name and address, starting date, etc.). Try to keep all the variables together. By doing this, you can create a standard contract that allows you to fill in the blanks. This is helpful if you are in a meeting with a decision maker who wants to sign up and write a check immediately. Simply fill in the top section, review the remainder of the contract, sign and date the contract and have your client do the same, and you get the initial payment. I learned the value of this the hard way. I used to gather information and then create each contract on my computer. Then I realized that I was losing too many opportunities where the client was prepared to sign up but the contract wasn't done. Now, when a client is ready, so am I.

Key Terms in a Contract

Creating a contract specific to your Web design shop and the services you expect to provide is an important part of your setup process. You will want to design a document that covers as closely as possible all the variables of a typical arrangement. That boilerplate document can be modified if needed, but it should address as many standard issues as you usually encounter. The most common of these are described below, and I will go through some of the information that I use in my contract. An example of a contract for a Web design business appears in appendix B.

Contact Information

The beginning of my contract is where I put contact information and other details I will need to begin the setup process. This includes details for inputting the new client into my bookkeeping system and to register the client's domain name.

Definition of Terms

In this section, I define my company name using a single word so I don't have to list it in full each time I refer to it. I do the same with the client name, using a fill-in line. Anything that you refer to in your contract can be defined in this section for brevity. (For example, it is easier to say *contract* throughout rather than *this agreement and its attachments, Web Site Design Worksheet, and Payment Schedule*.) Be sure to check with your attorney to make sure that the terms and definitions you select are usable in the contract.

Authorization

It is important that you have written permission to access your client's Web site and that you have approval to get the job done.

Warranties

This section assures your client that you are indeed capable of performing the services that you have agreed to do and that you will do so without violating any laws. This also contains a section that protects you and the client concerning the IRS questioning your status as a contractor. The client is affirming here that you are in control of the procedures and the methods without his interference.

This section also assures that the client has the power to authorize this agreement and will supply you with the necessary materials to get the job done.

Tips for Using Contracts

- If a potential client tells you she doesn't work with contracts, pack up, shake hands, and walk away. (If this person doesn't want to be "confined" by a contract, she may also decide she doesn't want to be confined by payments or by stipulations that protect you—and herself.)

- Don't assume that you don't need a contract if you are paid in advance. There are other issues besides payment. If someone sues your client for using copyrighted material and he points the finger at you, do you have any proof that he was supposed to check that? The client may think that he paid you to research all copyright issues. A contract is easier than a court battle to prove otherwise!

- If you are doing work for someone high up in a big company, get everything in writing. The reality is that big companies have major personnel shifts frequently. The person you worked for this month may not be there next month when it comes time to be paid. Large companies have been known to become faceless just when you thought you had an ally who would "go to bat" for you. Not many allies will jeopardize a good job to make sure that you are paid!

- Contracts are not "just for people who don't trust each other." I can't expect every client to remember everything I tell him. A client may not understand some of what I say—it's a lot of new information and new terms to grasp. Any of these issues can lead to confusion or misunderstandings without a contract. (For example, in my zeal to show a client all the wonderful features of her new Web site, I may not make it clear enough that she is not permitted to send any junk e-mail, or spam, from my Web server.) A contract is considered the appropriate venue to make sure everything is covered.

- A contract can be modified to meet a specific need. If your contract specifies final payment to be within two weeks of completion of the design work and a potential client needs four weeks to pay you, you must decide if that's acceptable. For me, if that is the only clause standing in the way of an agreement, and if I can wait the extra two weeks, I modify the contract. I simply cross out the "two weeks" and put in "four weeks." Then I initial the change and have the client initial it. (Of course, while the client still has the pen, I'll turn to the last page to get a signature there as well!)

Standard Web Site Products

This section is where your attorney will count on you to come up with the information. He or she will simply verify that the format is compatible and accurate. In this section you can explain how you define a "standard Web site design." It doesn't mean that a design job can't vary from this definition; that is what the "Web Site Design Worksheet" will spell out. If your client wants extra pages or doesn't want you to use any graphics, for instance, you can define those in the attached worksheet.

If you list something in this section, you are guaranteeing that you will deliver on it, so make sure you understand what you have here. This is not a section for sales pitches or flowery "best service in the world" language. Be very concise and straightforward about what you will offer. Remember, you can always throw in some additional features that aren't spelled out here, but once something is in your contract, you are obligated to deliver even if it cuts into your profit.

I want to point out the need for a clause in which you limit your client to two revisions. I put this in after working with a client for three months on revisions. He would send me some updates and tell me to go ahead and make the changes. I would do that, and a week later, I'd get a few more. Every time I assumed the site was complete, I'd get a few more revisions. At that time nothing in my agreement prevented endless revisions. Apparently my definition of a finished Web site wasn't as clear as I thought it was. You should be sure to let clients know that if their Web site needs more than two redrafts, it will cost extra. Most clients are eager to get their Web site up and running and are getting anxious by the time we have completed a couple of drafts anyway. This clause just gives the protection needed for those rare occasions when the quest for perfection gets out of hand.

To make this work for me, I now explain to a client in the beginning that he and I will work together to get the site the way I think he wants it. When I've done that, I send him an e-mail telling him that it is ready for his approval. If he finds major changes, I encourage him to list all of them at once and send it to me so I can get his site the way he wants. Once I feel that the site is just the way he wanted it, I send him another e-mail telling him that the draft is ready for his approval. In theory, these are his two drafts.

Realistically, I've never charged extra if a client wants another one or two drafts. I just remind her (if it seems to be a problem) that I want to make sure I get it right this time since we've already done our two drafts per the contract and I don't want her to have to pay extra. This gives her a heads up that she needs to be clear and get all the pieces together.

If, in negotiating a contract, your client ever balks at the two drafts, ask him how many drafts he thinks would be reasonable. If he says three or four, cross the two off and put the new number and initial it. No big deal. What you want to avoid is the open-ended situation where the information comes dribbling in. If you find yourself in that situation anyway, you can always gently remind the client that you are worried because you don't want him to have to pay extra for the extra drafts if it can be avoided. This way, the two of you are working together to solve that problem rather than your wondering when it will all end!

Another tip: When going over a contract, if a client balks at the two drafts clause (or any other) *do not* brush it off and tell her not to worry about that clause because you never enforce it. That can create a bonanza for her attorney on lots of different clauses if it ever came to be shown that you weren't planning on enforcing some of the parts of your contract. Take whatever clause is creating a problem and see if you can mutually work out an agreement (that's all part of negotiating). Make the change, initial it, and have the client do likewise. If you want to soften it a bit, tell her that your horrible attorney makes you do things that way. Then she has no doubt that you take your contractual agreement with her seriously.

In this section I also tell my client I won't guarantee a certain rating in the search engines. I have referred to this clause several times with clients who assume that if I am registering them with the search engines, I must be able to assure them a high spot. I point out to these clients that I don't have any control over the search engines. All I can do is design the Web site to attract search engines and then notify them that it is out there. Making sure your clients understand this can save some bad feelings later.

Web Site Hosting Services
If you offer hosting services, you need to define what you consider to be the standards for your Web site hosting. Explain how you will handle the registration of a domain name. It is important for you to state that just because a domain name is available during an initial discussion, there's no guarantee that it will be available when you try to register it. Some fierce battles have been fought over domain names, and you need to make sure you are not stuck in the middle of one of those. Any other stipulations you have are listed here as well—one example is my policy prohibiting

spam. (This is actually a rule from the hosting company I use; I am just reinforcing it in my contract.) Rather than individually listing all the features of my hosting, such as daily tape backups, e-mail forwarding, auto-responders, etc., I keep this information in an electronic form and refer to that Web address in my contract.

I added another line to this section after changing a procedure in my hosting renewal policy. When I began offering hosting services, I told my clients that they would be hosted from quarter to quarter and they could quit at any time. This created a lot of administrative work for me, and it forced my clients to make a decision each quarter either to renew with me or switch to one of my competitors. I changed my policy to state that unless I hear otherwise, the contract is automatically renewed each quarter. Invoicing is automated, and my retention rate is higher now.

Maintenance

Unless you include a maintenance agreement with each contract, I suggest you create it as a separate contract from this one. Some clients who initially decline a maintenance agreement, later decide they want one. If yours is a separate document, you can offer it when clients are ready. My contract states that I will make minor changes at no additional cost, but I define what a minor change is, and give a finite time period for making the free minor changes.

Some day you will probably have a client who edits a few sentences of his Web page that has some scripts buried in it, then expects you to fix the ensuing mess. You should make it clear that you will only do so for an additional cost based on your hourly rate. This is similar to a service contract on a computer that states that if you attempt to fix the machine yourself and then request repairs, the work will cost extra.

Payment Terms

I have a standard payment policy, which is spelled out in the "Payment Terms" section of my contract. I get all expenses that I will need to initially pay out (for example, the domain name registration and the hosting fees) upon signing the contract. I also get half of the design charges at that time. And before I upload the final, approved site, I get my final payment. This usually gives the client and me an equal incentive to complete the project.

Completion Date

The "Completion Date" section explains what is needed to meet that date. Some other Web designers' contracts include specific dates here. I find that most of my clients don't have a realistic idea of how long it will take them to gather information for me to proceed. So as long as they are "working expeditiously" to that end, I know I can do my part as well. If a client can't produce the necessary documents for me, waving a contract in her face will not create a very pleasant working relationship.

Once I had a client who wanted me to agree to penalties if I caused delays and we missed the deadline for getting his site online. I agreed to that—as long as the same penalties would be applied to him if he didn't get the documentation to me when promised. I assured this client that I could meet my deadlines if he met his. This way the appropriate person would stand to lose if the site did not debut on time. The client decided to leave the contract unchanged and work with me to ensure that the site was delivered on time. (It was.)

Assignment of Project

I use an "Assignment of Project" section to let clients know that I will hire subcontractors if needed to meet deadlines. I assure them that I am still ultimately responsible for their site, and that since my reputation is on the line, they can be assured of the very highest quality of work.

Copyrights and Trademarks

There are many copyright and trademark battles being fought over the Internet. Always point out to clients that anything they put on their Web site or have you put on their Web site is their responsibility. They must make sure that all copyright issues have been addressed. Many times clients assume that if they get a paragraph or picture from another Web site that doesn't say it is copyrighted, they can use it. I refer them to several resources on copyrights on the Internet, including the U.S. government's Library of Congress Web site. Although I make it clear that I'm not responsible for copyright violations on a client's Web site, I don't want to have to pay my attorneys to prove that in court. If there is any doubt, I send a warning message reminding my client that she will need to defend any copyright battles herself.

Electronic copyright laws are still not clearly defined, and they are in a state of flux. It is important that you and your attorney discuss copyright issues and decide how to word this section of your contract to protect yourself from inadvertently becoming entangled in a nasty copyright battle. Remember that anything you place on the Internet is available for everyone to scrutinize. If something isn't yours, make sure you get approval to use it.

Limited Liability

The "Limited Liability" section is where you remind your clients that you are not willing to be held liable for any problems with their design work on their Web site. They are not allowed to put anything on their site that will create problems for you or for themselves. If they do, they are on their own.

This is one of those sections that the attorneys enjoy writing about and discussing and we mere mortals should avoid. When I read it, I think it says, "I'm not responsible for anything . . . but if I am responsible anyway (I thought I wasn't?), it is only for the amount that I received plus attorney fees." That is why I made sure to tell you at the beginning of the section on contracts that I'm not an attorney and am not giving legal advice. My opinions are as a Web designer, not as a lawyer. Your lawyer can explain liability much better than I can.

Indemnification

A section on "Indemnification" clarifies that the client will not hold you liable for problems arising from your services. This may sound redundant, and you may feel that stating this point repeatedly is overkill for a standard Web site designer. However, the e-commerce business has special security issues, and loss of potential revenue is a serious risk. It's good business sense to have your attorney spell out the limitations you are willing to accept.

Laws Affecting Electronic Commerce

Again, I include a section that stipulates that in matters of e-commerce, the client is willing to be responsible for complying with such laws and will defend me against any lawsuits or other headaches.

Copyright to Web Pages

Some designers state in their contracts that the site copyright will be transferred to the client once final payment is made. Other designers keep ownership of their material and let the client use it. I state that I own the copyright to the site during the building of the Web site. When I get the final payment, the site copyright goes to my client but that copyright covers only those elements for which I hold the rights. If there is a magazine photo that a client told me was OK to put on the Web site, I don't own the rights to that photo and therefore I cannot transfer the copyright to the client. Those rights remain with the original rights holder.

This means that the client is responsible for obtaining copyright permission for anything he uses. If I put a MapQuest map on his site, I don't want him to come to me six months from now and insist that I "sold" him that map. If a client pushes and wants to own everything I put on his site, I very carefully spell out each item that is included, since I don't have problems with his owning my work.

However, if I use a subcontractor or use a free copyrighted script from another source, that has to be negotiated individually. One of my subcontractors gladly gives up rights to his work, while others insist on huge piles of money for such agreements. (They never get the huge piles of money, but I always give that offer to the client as an option!) I have one subcontractor who has an ongoing relationship with a client who insisted on owning the work on the Web site. The client's lawyer worded the copyright clause such that any "original work designed for that Web site" was turned over to that client. After a chat with my attorney, I suggested to that subcontractor that if he was going to use any script or program that he wanted to own the copyright to, he should just make sure to use it on another public Web site first and declare ownership of the copyright to it. That way it couldn't be considered "original work" designed for the client's Web site because it was used elsewhere first.

So, to be safe and to simplify things, I keep an arm's length from copyrighted materials and let my client be responsible for those battles. If she wants me to state that my materials be assigned to her, no problem. She just has to understand what is mine to give.

I also insert a line in the contract that allows me to use bits of a client's Web site in my portfolio if I so desire.

Authorship Credit

I tell my clients that I am proud of my work and would like to include a small line at the bottom of their site telling the world that I designed it. I explain that either of us can remove this credit line at any time for any reason. That way, if a client changes his Web site to the point where it doesn't reflect well on me, I can ask him to remove my credit line.

Nondisclosure

A nondisclosure statement shouldn't be necessary in a perfect world, but putting it in the contract assures your clients that any private information they disclose to you will go no further. I've had clients who were planning to move or expand, and they needed to know that any information we discussed would remain confidential.

Arbitration

An arbitration clause defines the means for settling disputes. You and your attorney should discuss the specifics of this clause.

Payment of Fees

This section explains what happens when payments are delinquent or when they don't come at all. It is necessary to define this. Otherwise, you may be obligated to keep a Web site on your server while you try to extract payment from a client.

Entire Understanding

As the title states, this clause declares that this contract is the entire understanding. Anything else my client thought we had agreed upon that is not included either must be added or doesn't apply.

Web Site Design Worksheet Attachment

As a separate attachment, I have a design worksheet, and I will use it to design the site. On this sheet I include work that I will be doing for the client. This doesn't include everything I will do since most of that is stated in the Standard Web Site Products and Web Site Hosting Services sections of the main contract. Anything that is not part of a standard Web site, however, is included here, such as an additional agreement between the client and myself to create hundreds of links on an extensive links page. Also, anything that is a clarification of the standard Web site goes here, such as a description of each individual Web page included in the site. It is the only part of my contract that is not boilerplate and doesn't look like an official document.

Payment Schedule Attachment

I lay out the payment schedule in two sections. The first is the total amount that the client will need to pay for the project and for Web hosting during the first quarter. If there are extra charges that I don't offer as part of my package such as domain name registration, I would put an asterisk to a footnote about it. This will notify my client that, although he won't need to pay me for this expense, it is a necessary expense in order to complete the process. I then itemize all charges. In the second section, I give the payment schedule. This shows what is due upon signing the contract. It also shows what and when additional payments must be paid.

Signatures

Last but not least, under the Entire Understanding section are the spaces for signatures. With the client's name and yours in ink on the line, you're ready to begin the creative work—a well-earned part of a well-planned process.

Accounting and Record Keeping

Even before you have your first paying client and have begun to receive income for your hard work, you will need to establish methods for keeping track of the money and paperwork tied to your business. There are many software packages available to help you get organized and keep your inbox manageable. Based on your personal preferences, however, you will have to decide which accounting and filing systems will work best for you.

Accounting Methods for a Web Design Shop

There are two main accounting systems you might use for your Web site business: the cash method and the accrual method. You and your accountant will need to decide on one or the other, based on a variety of factors.

Cash Accounting

The cash method of accounting is the way most people keep track of their personal finances—money you receive is income and money you spend is expenses. This is the easiest system to understand and usually the easiest to use. If you buy some software and don't pay for it until the invoice comes a month later, it is not an expense at the time you get it, but rather when you pay for it. If you get a new client who pays you in advance for work that you will be doing next month, it is an expense for that person when you get the money—not when you do the work.

Accrual Accounting

The accrual method of accounting is more complex, but there may be some tax benefits. The accrual method simply says that just because you got some money, that doesn't mean that you did any work for it yet. Also, just because you paid an invoice doesn't mean that you got the goods yet. Furthermore, just because you got some goods doesn't mean that you paid for them. With the accrual method, cash is just one of many factors to track. Any financial activity that occurs, whether cash is exchanged or not, is a financial transaction. You also track such things as your accounts receivable (money people owe you), your accounts payable (money you owe others), your assets (value within your business), and your liabilities (loans, equity, payable sales tax).

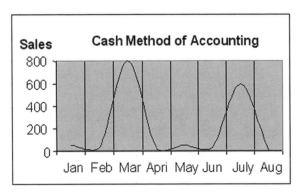

Figure 1

A benefit of the accrual method comes when you need to find out how the business is doing. By using the cash method, as depicted in figure 1, you are able to see your cash flow over a period of time. The peaks and valleys represent when you have been paid for a job, but not when you are working. Even though several jobs were being done in January and February, I wasn't paid for them until March. Thus January and February have barely measurable sales figures. March, on the other hand, was not a busy month, but since I was paid for the two previous months' work, it looks spectacular. I then worked through August primarily on a long-term contract. A large payment for that came in March, a small payment arrived in May, and the remaining money was paid in July. The chart, however, appears as if business was slow in April, May, and June. It is good to know your cash flow so you can adjust for these kinds of peaks and valleys. Nevertheless, remember that this method does not give the complete picture of how your business is doing.

If we use the accrual method of accounting (figure 2) for the same time frame, we can see that the business was not idle for most of the year as suggested in figure 1. Although we saw in that chart that the cash came in chunks, we can tell from the

Figure 2

accrual method that the business was relatively steady, with a slight peak in the beginning of the year and dips in April and July. The same income numbers are used as in the cash method, but by allocating income and expenses based upon the times that the business incurred them, rather than when payment was received, we get a more realistic idea of how the business is doing.

Here's another example of how the accuracy of the accrual method can help you. Using the cash method, businesses that are financially strapped and not paying their bills can look like they're doing all right. Some income is coming through and very little money is going out. But by using the accrual method, I have a clearer picture not only of my income and payments, but also of what bills I am getting and unable to pay, and how much money I am awaiting from clients who are late in paying me. Sometimes I don't like the picture that is painted, but that dose of reality is necessary. It allows me to plan whether I need to prospect for more clients or shake down some of my late payers. Without the numbers to use as a guide, it is too easy to second-guess or justify those valleys.

Maintaining Your Books

There are two methods that I recommend for maintaining your books. I call these the shoe box method and the PC accounting method. The shoe box method of accounting is just what it sounds like—you get a shoe box, throw everything in it, and let someone else figure out what each piece of paper is and what should be done with it! The PC accounting method is for people who have a bit of experience with small business accounting and are willing to use commercial packages such as QuickBooks, Peach Tree, or Money to track the business. With either method I strongly recommend that you use a Certified Public Accountant (CPA) or a very good, dependable accountant for your year-end books. This should be someone you feel comfortable calling upon periodically for recommendations and answers to your questions.

Shoebox Accounting

Years ago, an accountant taught me the shoe box method of accounting. She rescued my business from complete destruction due to a lack of accounting. Since at that young age I had virtually no knowledge of or experience in keeping books, I was a good candidate for the shoe box method. This accountant actually brought me an old, marked-up shoe box and put it on a shelf beside my desk. Whenever I got a receipt for a purchase, I put it in the sacred shoe box. Each day when I ran the cash register totals, I simply tossed the daily tape into the shoe box. I had a staff of employees, so she had me sign up with a payroll company to take care of all the tax forms and related documents I was drowning in. The payroll company adopted the accountant's shoe box method, placing a box marked "Payroll" next to the accountant's original shoe box. Anything that dealt with payroll went into the payroll shoe box, just as anything that was related to accounting went into the accountant's original shoe box. Anything I was uncertain about went in the accountant's shoe box for her to figure out.

Once a week my accountant sent a staff person to my business to empty the shoe box. Once a month, the staff person also picked up my checkbook and reconciled it, then returned it a few days later. A couple of weeks after the end of each month, I got an envelope back from the accountant with all of my receipts, invoices, bills, unidentified scraps of paper, and whatever else I had thrown in the shoe box. I also got a statement telling me how the business had done.

My accountant worked with me for a couple of months to help me translate what my receivables meant and what assets were. After that, I was able to focus on my business rather than the perplexing procedures and jargon of an accountant. When I had bills to pay, I'd write out the checks for the bills. If I got anything I wasn't sure of, I'd attach a note and throw it in the shoe box. I was able to run my business without having to learn everything about accounting. Anyone without a strong background in small business accounting would benefit from this system. (Read further in this chapter for advice on how to find a good accountant.)

Accounting Software

These days, I use QuickBooks to maintain my records. (I admit, however, that I'm tempted from time to time to return to the simplicity of the shoe box method.) If you are familiar with most general bookkeeping tasks and don't mind maintaining your own records, most of the popular computerized accounting software should work well for your Web design shop. Here are some helpful tips for using those programs:

- When you set up your business using the software, if a Web design business is not an option for business type, choose either a graphic design business or a consultant business. This will set up the accounts so that you can bill by the hour.
- If you are going to have payrolled employees, use an advanced software package such as QuickBooks Pro. (You might not need the Pro version if you supplement your bookkeeping system with a payroll company that creates all of the tax forms.)
- Some programs like QuickBooks Pro have a feature that allows you to track your time for clients and bill for portions of a project. I chose to keep track of my billable time with another software program, called TraxTime.
- You will be asked whether your fiscal year is a calendar year. Unless your accountant has compelling reasons otherwise, it is best to choose the calendar year as your business year. That means that when everyone else is bemoaning the current tax season, you will be moaning with them (not too much, I hope!). It is best to be in sync with the calendar year for a variety of reasons. In fact, if it is close to April 15 and you need to delay a Web Site deadline by a couple of days to finish filing your taxes, your client will probably be pretty sympathetic.
- Take the time to become very familiar with a shortcut that QuickBooks calls memorized transactions. (This feature has different names in other accounting software programs.) With this, you can create an invoice for a client, take a "snapshot" of it, and use that same template for future invoices. When you have a client whom you bill quarterly for hosting, create one of these templates and configure it to remind yourself on a quarterly basis. Each time you go into QuickBooks you will get a reminder of any invoices that need to be created and sent. Make a quick modification to the "hosting

from/to" dates in your invoice, print it, and send it. As you get more recurring invoices to create, this feature will become invaluable.

- If your invoices grow to the point that you are spending a lot of time creating, mailing, and tracking invoices, you might want to consider an online invoicing service. I now use FreshBooks (www.freshbooks.com) for all my invoicing and QuickBooks for everything else. For around $35 per month, FreshBooks automates all of my invoicing. Clients get invoiced automatically via email, and they can pay by credit card online or mail me a check. If they don't pay on time, they automatically get my polite reminder. Then fifteen days later they get a second notice. If they still don't pay, they get a stern notice of their past-due bill. The positive impact it has on my ability to get paid in a timely fashion with minimal intervention has made it well worthwhile for my business.

- Don't let your accounts receivable get out of hand. Most accounting software has the means to track how late your clients are, and you should become familiar with those reports. Particularly with smaller amounts, it is easy to let invoices ride instead of following up with a client with whom you've worked hard to develop a good relationship. Don't fall into this trap! I have been fortunate that most of my clients pay on time, but the few who are slow can take more bookkeeping time than all of the punctual ones combined. Using FreshBooks helps with the reminders but you still need to know when to give a personal nudge.

- Even if you keep on top of your accounts receivable, you may occasionally need to write off a bad debt. By keeping close tabs on your accounts, it probably won't be a large debt. In any event, learn the steps to write off unpaid invoices in your software. (Please note this crucial advice: Many Web designers assume that if a client doesn't pay up, they can simply shut down the client's site. Beware of doing this without talking with your attorney. Your contract may give you permission to shut down a site, but if an angry client with an aggressive attorney decides that you caused the loss of thousands of dollars—or worse, the demise of his business—you may need to pay your attorney much more than the hosting fees to defend you.)

- For any regularly recurring bills that I get, I also set up a memorized transaction. For example, each quarter my business credit card is billed for each client's hosting cost. If I depend on the hosting company to never make mistakes in its billing, I'm asking for problems. Therefore, I create an automatic charge to my credit card account. Now each month when I reconcile my credit card statement with my accounting records, I can tell easily if there are extra or missing charges from my hosting company.

- Sales tax is different for each state. Make sure you understand what is taxable in your state. To find out, see if there is information on the official Web site for the state you are in. Print the document for your records if you find it there. Or if you have or know an accountant, check with her. Do not ask another Web designer; he or she may not know. I did some subcontracting for a local Web designer who was, at the time, much bigger than I was. He was charging sales tax, and when he'd give me my subcontracted earnings, it was minus the sales tax! I told him that there was no sales tax on Web design. He insisted that there was and that he had always charged his clients tax. I took my money from him minus the 6 percent he held back for taxes. I later rechecked with my accountant and then the state revenue department and confirmed that he was not supposed to be charging tax. By that time he was no longer in business, so I couldn't even find him to tell him he was wrong!

  If you find you are required to charge tax, apply for the necessary tax ID and start collecting and paying immediately so you have a record of compliance. It's not too much of a pain to complete the sales tax paperwork once you've gone through it once or twice, and being up on the tax laws will present an air of responsibility to your clients. Nothing looks as unprofessional as you will when you nervously squirm after a potential client asks you why you aren't charging sales tax when you aren't really sure what the correct answer is. So make sure you know what your tax responsibilities are.

- Back up your work. Even though you are regularly backing up your entire computer, it is a good idea to do a separate backup of your accounting file to a USB flash drive or a network each time you do your books. If ever your hard drive crashes or your accounting data are corrupted, you will be glad you took the few minutes necessary to save your most recent work. As a computer whiz, you don't want to go to each of your clients and admit that because you didn't back up your work often enough, you lost your accounting information for the month and need to find out how much they owe you!

Using a Bookkeeper

For my Web design business, I actually use a combination of QuickBooks, Fresh-Books, and a part-time bookkeeper. I used QuickBooks to set up my bookkeeping system. However, I had trouble maintaining the books on an ongoing basis, so I opted to hire a bookkeeper for approximately an hour every other week. It took some searching to find the right person. I needed someone who knew a bit about QuickBooks and didn't mind moonlighting for just a few hours a month. I wanted a person who worked through an agency or other company so I wouldn't need to set up a payroll system. And finally, I needed someone that I could trust to maintain my confidential records.

To find someone like this, try asking your accountant for recommendations. You don't want your high-paid accountant to do the work himself, but he might have someone on staff who wouldn't mind the extra task. Another option is to speak with some temporary agencies, especially if they are nearby, but be very clear that this is a small account with very limited hours. If you don't have a payroll, make sure you adhere to the guidelines for contract workers.

Remember that the couple of hours per month your bookkeeper works probably benefit you more than they do the bookkeeper or the agency. Once you find a person who meets your criteria, be prepared to take over for him or her periodically when vacations and other activities come up. Treat the person kindly in the hope that you won't need to take over too often.

My bookkeeper and I work in tandem. I put all of my deposit slips in the file cabinet drawer that now serves as my "shoe box." I include a note that specifies which client matches each deposit. I put a copy of each new contract in the drawer so that my bookkeeper can set up the new account(s) in FreshBooks. I include details for any payments that have been received. I also include receipts for payments and purchases I've made, noting whether they were paid by check, cash, or credit card. When my checking account and credit card statements arrive each month, those are placed in the file drawer, too.

My bookkeeper inputs all of the information from the file drawer and files away the papers as necessary. She creates invoices in FreshBooks from my time report to be emailed out.

I have read that when a business owner does the routine bookkeeping, it takes hours because each item is a reminder to check on something else. That is definitely true for me—I am frequently sidetracked and it seems to take forever to complete the routine books. When someone else does the books, she is focused on the task, so it is done quickly and efficiently. This frees me to devote my attention to the business itself.

Keeping Records in a Virtual Office

Keeping records is difficult enough when you spend all or most of your time in your home office. Keeping records in a virtual office is an even greater challenge. After I figured out that I couldn't carry everything I needed when working outside of my home office, I created a strategy for doing the next-best thing. Here's what worked for me, and what might help you.

Even though I love automating my business using my laptop and desktop computers, I admit that the paperless office is not yet here. Contracts are still printed on paper and filed in manila folders. Whatever else (if anything) goes into the folder depends on the client and the project. I still need to store hard copy and photos from some clients, as well as printouts of Web pages in progress, with handwritten notations. Most of the inactive folders are kept at my home office. However, any folder for active projects stays in my mobile file case, which I carry on my two-wheel cart.

Talk about a portable office! I can put my office in the trunk of the car or the back of the van and go to an appointment. I usually leave the file box in the car or van and take just the laptop to clients' offices. If I'm traveling and at a motel or in an office where I'm going to do some work, I grab the cart with file box and laptop together (hoisting them separately and then strapping them together if I'm feeling puny that day). Then I'm ready to wheel my "office" to its new location for some work.

I keep a resealable file envelope in my laptop case for receipts, bills, and other accounting-related paperwork. This way I can easily find my records when it's time to dump them into my shoe box/file drawer. My QuickBooks software is loaded on my laptop so I can refer to it when I'm on the road. (Most accounting software licenses allow you to install a copy on a desktop computer as well as a laptop, provided that you are the only person using it. Since I use my laptop for most tasks, QuickBooks is not loaded on my desktop, but it's nice to have that option.)

Contact Managers

There are many good information management software programs to help you keep track of your contacts. Some are part of a comprehensive "office-management" package that includes an e-mail program. Others are stand-alone products. I use Microsoft Outlook, which is an integrated system. Outlook's task section reminds me of things I need to do. The notes section stores all those bits and pieces of information when I can't figure out where else to put them. Outlook's e-mail program allows me to easily drag an e-mail into the calendar function to list a meeting or drag it to my task folder to set up a reminder. (Some people are uncomfortable using integrated systems, however, because of the perceived risk of viruses.) Google has a full suite of apps that are worth checking out that can take care of all those tasks.

In addition to using Outlook, I used to carry around a daily planner. I'd swap information back and forth between the planner and Outlook as often as I could. But much of the time either my planner or Outlook was out of date. I finally got a smartphone, and that solved the problem. When setting up an appointment, I no longer have to wait until my laptop boots up to find out if a particular day is open. I look at my smartphone and get an instant answer. Every fifteen minutes all the changes I've made to either my laptop or my smartphone are synchronized automatically! There are many types of smartphones with a dazzling array of capabilities.

06 Making Web Sites with an Impact

You probably have many creative ideas for beginning the most enjoyable work of your Web design business, but don't be shy about adding to your collection. There are many fine books and online resources on using HTML (HyperText Markup Language) to design a Web site. (See the sidebar for some recommended HTML resources.) It is beyond the scope of this book to reiterate all that information. This chapter assumes that you have a basic knowledge of HTML and have put together a Web site for yourself or for a friend. We will examine what makes certain Web sites better than others and analyze Web sites in various stages of development. Throughout, I will share with you tips and tricks that I've learned through experience.

Essentials of a Business Web Site

The best Web sites are not necessarily the best-looking Web sites. Rather, they are the Web sites that accomplish what the business wants them to. If your client shows you a Web site that glitters and shimmers but doesn't accomplish what the client wants, it is not a good Web site. It is easy to agree with your client and design his Web site to have the same look and feel as one he likes. However, as the expert in this business, you need to make sure the client understands that, while the "bells and whistles" may seem impressive, they may also cut out any customers who don't have the latest computers and software. You must be willing to diplomatically tell your client why his ideas won't translate well to the Internet. You must also be willing to explain the possible disadvantages of a Web site that is based solely upon visual stimulation instead of reliable and appealing design principles. You can start by asking your client if he is willing to lose 10 to 20 percent of his potential customers by forsaking stable HTML principles. This is the time to reassure your client that a "good" Web site doesn't need to look dull and unattractive—it just needs to follow some conventions that will make it available to a broad audience.

Mike Kear, owner of AFP Web Development in Australia, uses this scenario to illustrate the disadvantage of using an inexperienced designer to set up a business Web site:

> A reputable Web development company goes to bid for a complex site. Their bid is based on the number of people they'll need to do a good job, the professional skills required, and the cost to cover its overhead with something left over. Then the IT manager says, "That seems expensive. I know a kid who can do it for much less than that," and then gives it to the chairman's nephew or someone, who might well be technically adept enough to produce a Web site, but has no clue as to all the other things he has to know. Such as how to find out from the company why their customers buy their products, or, enough knowledge of typography to know not to have a zillion different fonts. The inexperienced designer is so desperate to impress his first client with how clever he is, the site ends up being a showcase for his talents rather than the client's business—it is covered with animated gifs, flash, etc., that has no purpose for the site. (This is not bashing animations or flash, they have their place ONLY IF the purpose of the site requires them.)
>
> Or the young designer doesn't realize that "state" is a U.S. phenomenon and many countries don't have states, or, for that matter, zip codes. Nor does the kid realize that the phone number format used in the USA is only used there and in Canada. I even had a major international company require my social security number before it would let me download some shareware. But, being an Australian, I don't have a social security number.
>
> Being technically adept is not enough....A technically stunning site that ignores many really important things will end up as a site that doesn't work.

In general, a good business Web site should appear quickly on a screen. It should be consistently easy for novices as well as experienced users to navigate. The site should be attractive when viewed with any of the major Web browsers and should look good on a variety of screen sizes and configurations. Users should be able to quickly find what they're looking for on the site.

> **HTML Resources**
>
> **HTML for Beginners**—A very thorough primer on HTML for those either getting started or needing a refresher. There are also forums on related topics at this site. www.htmlcodetutorial.com
>
> **The Easiest HTML Guide for Beginners**—A step-by-step guide to putting a Web site together. This is very basic, but it is a good way to get started. www.tips-tricks.com /begin.asp
>
> **The Bare Bones Guide to HTML**—A good site to easily find a tag—this is one to keep handy. www.werbach.com/barebones/
>
> **W3C's Home Page for HTML**—W3C (World Wide Web Consortium) is the organization that works on and publishes the standards for HTML. This is an authoritative Web site as well as a good resource to seek out information on cross-browser usage of HTML tags. (Note: This URL is case sensitive.) www.w3.org/MarkUp/Guide/

Fast Loading

Many Web designers have powerful computers with fast Internet connections. They forget that a few people still use slow modems to connect to the Internet. When I'm in my office, I have access to a high-speed DSL line. However, when I'm on the road, I'm at the mercy of a client's phone service or the local hotel's overloaded Internet system. That is when I really appreciate Web sites that download quickly.

There are many design techniques for reducing download time. Following are four I use often:

1. Using HTML text near the top of the page to distract the eye from slow-loading graphics
2. Compressing and reducing graphics files as much as possible without destroying the quality
3. Using thumbnails to link to larger photos
4. Avoiding excessive nested tables or use CSS instead of tables

Let's look at each of these techniques.

Using HTML text to distract the eye

Text and straight HTML codes load very quickly. Giant graphics do not. If you have a client who wants a large graphic on his home page, try to dissuade him from that notion. Explain that a customer with a slow connection will need to wait a long time to see the page. (You will have to point out that several seconds is a long time to wait on the Web.) Remind your client that the customer will see only a portion of the home page initially—only what will fit on his monitor without scrolling. If nothing is visible because that large graphic hasn't loaded, a browsing customer will not wait. He will bounce back out and go to the competitor's Web site.

If you absolutely must put large graphics on a home page, try to incorporate some HTML text above or around the graphics. In figure 1, the graphics at the top of the home page are surrounded by text. When a viewer looks at this site, his eyes have some text to read while the graphics are loading. This text can include the company name as well as a slogan, or some information about the company, or the address and contact information.

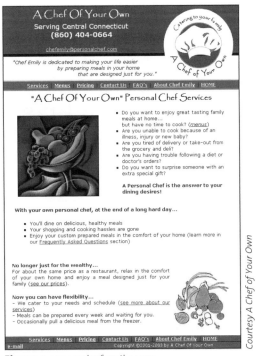

Courtesy A Chef of Your Own

Figure 1 www.chefemily.com

Compressing and reducing graphics files

The second technique for faster loading of graphics is to compress the graphics files. I have seen many examples of graphics that were not compressed enough and therefore loaded very slowly. If you are going to create Web sites, you must have a program such as PhotoShop, Fireworks, Elements, GIMP, or PaintShop Pro to help you manipulate graphics. With any of the good graphic design programs, you can usually reduce the size of a graphics file to one-tenth of the original size (sometimes even less) without any noticeable reduction in quality. While you are manipulating the file in your graphics program, make sure the ending height and width is the size you need for your Web site. I've seen Web sites that required me to download a huge thirty-inch-wide graphic that is going to be viewed in a two-inch box. Make sure you don't make viewers waste time downloading a giant file if it will only be viewed in a small space.

The three main graphics file formats for Web sites are gif (pronounced *Jiffy* without the "Y" or *gift* without the "T"), jpg (pronounced *jay-peg*), and png. A general rule of thumb is to use gif or png files for logos and files with very few colors and when you need a transparent background.

Use jpg or png files for photographs, but be careful when compressing an image. If you reduce the size of a jpg file too much, it will start to distort or wrinkle—particularly in large areas of the same color, such as the background of a photograph. Until you get a feel for that threshold, it might be better to create several compressions of your jpgs to see the smallest you can go with the least distortion.

As you reduce the file size for gif files, you will reduce the number of colors. As you reduce the number of colors, you will reduce the chance that the picture will look the way it should in a variety of browsers—bands of colors or dithering are likely to show up. If you aren't familiar with these terms, go to one of the many excellent Web sites on graphics or pick up a book on Web graphics. Otherwise, you may embarrass yourself when someone views a Web site on a different browser than the one you use.

Web-safe Colors

There's one consideration when you're reducing the file size (and consequently the number of colors) of a gif: the issue of "Web-safe colors." I learned about this one the hard way. When I first began designing Web pages for customers, I created a site I was extremely proud of. Because I was still relatively new to Web design, I spent a lot of time on the project and included a personal visit to the client's office to show off the finished product. I was ushered into the client's conference room for the final rollout and to get my well-deserved pat on the back. My contact in that company even invited the organization's CEO to the "unveiling" on a large-screen monitor. I navigated my clients through their new Web site to the sound of oohhhhhh's and aaaahhhh's. As my final flourish, I opened a page with a background of soft blue ocean water (to represent their theme). But instead of soft blue, this page had a hideous purple background that made the black text almost illegible! After much embarrassment and many lame excuses for the page that was supposed to be the highlight of this site, I assured my clients that I would fix the problem.

I then belatedly learned that browsers don't all use exactly the same colors. If the color that looks good in one browser isn't used by the other browser, it picks one that it thinks is close. Since most of my soft blue colors weren't available in other browsers, the browser used for my grand presentation picked the purples that almost sank my budding career! If you aren't familiar with "Web-safe colors," be sure to learn about them. Your graphics program or a graphic design Web site is a good place to start. Once you understand how to stay within the safe colors, you will be able to reduce the size and colors of a gif file yet be confident that the graphic will look good in any major browser.

Using thumbnails to link to larger photos

There may be times when you want to use a full-size graphic to show some detail that would be lost otherwise. To do this without increasing the page's loading time, create a thumbnail (smaller picture) for each picture. It allows the page to load quickly, yet the viewer can select any thumbnail to see an enlarged (and slow-loading) version of that picture. Each thumbnail should be large enough to give an idea of what the image is, but as small as possible so the page loads quickly. I have seen some sites that use the HTML code to reduce the size of the main picture in order to make thumbnails. When this is done, the thumbnails are actually large pictures that are downloaded before being reduced. That defeats the purpose of thumbnails, which is to reduce the initial download time.

Avoiding excessive nested tables

For many designers, the placement of div elements with cascading style sheets is used instead of tables for layouts. This is the preferred method. However, if you are working with an older Web Site that uses tables to lay out an entire Web page, then nests a table inside one of the cells, then adds others inside the nested table's cells, it will slow down the loading of that page regardless of what else you've done to speed it up. This is because the items in each nested table won't be visible until all of the tables have been loaded.

If there are nested tables being loaded, and your overall table extends beyond the bottom edge of the browser window, the whole page may be blank until the entire file loads. Your viewer may well assume that the site is down. He will have browsed on to another site before your lovely configuration of tables finishes loading. Try to arrange your Web site so the area of the page that is first viewed is not in a table that is nested several layers deep. Or better yet, use cascading style sheets (CSS) to lay out the sections of those older Web pages and completely avoid nested tables.

Easy Navigation

Many newcomers to the Internet feel like idiots because they get lost navigating a Web site. However, for the most part, problems in viewing a Web site are not the fault of the novice but rather the designer. Unless you know that your audience is made up entirely of experienced Web users (I seldom run into a situation like that), make sure your navigation tools are easy and user-friendly. It may be trendy to get rid of the underline that signifies a hypertext link, but your user may not recognize the words as links without it. Similarly, if you use graphics for links or don't make your navigation buttons look obviously like buttons, your viewer may not know that your Web site goes beyond the home page.

You've probably seen many Web sites that use a consistent navigation bar on the left side of every page in the site. This is done so a visitor can understand how to navigate through the site. If you put the navigation bar across the top of the page, the bar may be cut off on the right side, losing some buttons. If you put the navigation bar only on the bottom, it may not be visible at all unless the viewer scrolls down the page. Even then, he's forced to go to the bottom of each page to navigate through your Web site. If you put the navigation bar on the right side, you must be careful that your page doesn't have any fixed-width elements or large graphics that might push it out of view beyond the right edge of the browser window.

In figure 2 there is a navigation bar on the home page. If you go to this basic site online (www.attorneyoconnor.com) you'll see that the same navigation bar is consistent throughout the Web site. On any page within the Web site, you know how to

Figure 2 www.attorneyoconnor.com

get to any other page. The same principle applies to larger sites as well. No matter how complex the Web site is, you should be able to organize the topics and subtopics to make navigation easy.

No Web designer has ever told me that a Web site he or she designed is difficult to navigate. To a designer, almost any Web site is relatively easy to traverse. However, I suggest that you acid-test your sites from time to time. Find a beginner, put her in front of the computer, and give her the URL for the home page of one of your sites. Ask her to give you the fax number for the company, or a department head's name, or something that isn't on the home page and may not be immediately available. Then stand back and watch. The most difficult challenge is to keep your mouth closed! Don't give tips; don't offer help; don't flinch, wince, or groan. Just watch and learn from her mistakes or comments. (Don't respond, just listen.)

If your "guinea pig" finds the item she was searching for, ask for something else in another section. Don't help her get back to the home page or to another section. Just watch! You may be surprised. For instance, maybe you had assumed that everyone would look for a map and directions to the business in your About Us page, but your tester mistakenly went right to the Site Map page to look for them.

Be sure your site has a consistent look and feel. If you are doing a partial redesign, do a quick facelift for all the other pages. Look again at figure 2. Each page in this

Web site displays the same faint watermark behind the text and the same headers. Besides giving consistency to the site, reusing the same picture in the header of each page speeds load time. After a graphic has been loaded one time, it remains in the browser's cache (its memory). This means that the graphic in the header doesn't need to be reloaded when a user jumps to another page in the site.

Cross-Platform Compatibility

Most Web surfers have probably seen a site with a notice stating that the site should be viewed with a certain browser and a certain screen resolution. I feel that such disclaimers are an indication of a poorly designed Web site or a lack of consideration for the audience. The marvel of the Internet is that it was designed to be cross-platform-compatible—meaning that visitors can view Web sites with a variety of computers and software.

Someone using a Macintosh may have a different font size on the screen from a PC user. A Firefox user may have a different screen margin than an Internet Explorer user or a Chrome user. Someone who is visually impaired and is using a screen reader may "see" the Web site through audio equipment rather than a visual screen. Someone who has a new computer with a high-resolution monitor may see finer details than someone with a limited budget and an older computer. Someone with a smartphone may be looking for information while on the road. Each of these people could be potential customers for your client. Your goal should be to make that Web site look great on as many configurations as possible. When you are learning how to design Web sites, it may seem impossible to make a site that will satisfy such a diverse group. This is one of the elements that differentiate effective Web sites from those that chase away customers.

If you tell the world that the only customers that you want are ones who have Internet Explorer version 8.0 or greater and a screen resolution of 1024 x 768, you are telling everyone else to go elsewhere or change their computers to match your wishes. This will alienate some of your viewers, and the ones you don't drive away may have a bad browsing experience anyway. Maybe you've encountered this yourself. If you have ever needed to use a scroll bar on the bottom of a page to read across that page and then scroll back to the start of the next line, you have been a victim of poor Web site design.

Of course, you need to draw the line somewhere about what you will and won't be designing for. Almost any site I design gives a good viewing experience to anyone with any version of Netscape or Internet Explorer above version 4, as well as some of the other browsers. I try to make the sites compatible for viewing on a range of screen widths from 640 to 1024 pixels. (Although visitors can generally have a good viewing experience with other configurations outside of this, I usually can't justify charging my clients to make adjustments specifically for others—unless there is a business need to do so.)

When I create a Web site, I keep in mind that a portion of my viewers may be people with disabilities. I always try to make my sites accessible to this audience. One way I do this is by labeling all graphics with the tag ALT= parameter. (Of course, any site I design whose primary audience will be people with disabilities is totally accessible.) Most government-related Web sites are expected to be accessible to people with disabilities. If you are designing good Web sites, you may be surprised at how easy it is to bring the sites into compliance for use by visitors with disabilities. For more information on the Web Accessibility Initiative, go to www.w3.org/WAI/.

There are many books and online resources to help you design cross-platform-compatible Web sites. At the end of chapter 8, I list some resources you can use as starting points in your research. In addition, here are a few quick tips I've learned:

1. Avoid using HTML windows called frames. They are dated and should be replaced with cascading style sheets.
2. If you design a site on a computer with 800 x 600 resolution, be sure to view that site using 1024 x 768 resolution as well.
3. Fire up an old 486 computer and see how your site looks on this older machine with older software.

For maximum cross-platform compatibility, watch out for any graphics that are too wide for lower screen resolution. Resize graphics if necessary so that they fit on the smallest screen you are designing for. If you make a large graphic on top or bottom for a logo or banner ad, it will set the width for the rest of the Web site. If that graphic is larger than the screen on low resolution, any tables may also stretch out to that size, forcing your visitors to scroll back and forth to read information on your site.

If you must create tables or styles with fixed widths, be sure to make them narrow enough to fit on the smallest screen you are designing for. Even better, create them using a percentage rather than fixed size. If you make a table that is 80 percent of the screen width, it will be 80 percent of any screen, not just the one you are currently working with. I use the Web Developer add-on for Firefox which has an option to resize my screen to various sizes. If your client tells you not to worry about people using older computers with a screen resolution of less than 800 x 600, remind her that visitors with high-resolution screens don't usually fill the entire screen with a browser window. They may be viewing your Web site in a small window on an updated computer.

Software Compatibility

In addition to hardware issues such as screen resolution, you should be designing your Web sites for a variety of software as well. Unless you have a lot of Microsoft stock, I don't recommend creating a Web site for Internet Explorer without also checking how it looks in Firefox and Safari. Of course, that applies to any popular browser and version. No matter what browser you have loaded on your computer, you should always view your creations in a variety of versions as well as in other browsers. I have a paid subscription to BrowserCam, but there are some others, like the free http://browsershots.org, that will allow you to view screenshots of your work in various browsers.

Flash can greatly enhance a visitor's experience. However, the same compatibility caveat applies here: Not everyone is using the latest plug-ins and browser versions. If you feel compelled to use design features that are not available to all viewers, consider using a feature sniffer as well. This is a script that works invisibly to discover whether the visitor has a computer that is able to utilize a given feature. If not, it presents a "plain vanilla" version of the Web page. This is far more courteous than just telling the visitor where to go to get the needed plug-in. If you don't want to create a separate Web site to cater to those without the trendy features, then don't use those features. Otherwise, your client will lose customers and you will not be serving that client properly.

Readability

A Web site generally should be designed so that it is easy to skim through it to find pertinent information. The best way to do this is by organizing information into brief bullet points. If you receive some text for a client's site that is formatted as complete sentences and full paragraphs, try to reduce the key facts to bullet points if your client will let you.

The Web site in figure 2 starts with a couple of introductory sentences. Then brief, focused bullet points describe the attorney's main practice. The visitor can determine at a glance the scope of the business. If he wants more details about the attorney's background and areas of practice, he can use the navigation buttons on the left.

There are a few business exceptions to this rule. If the main goal of a Web site is to impart detailed information about a specific topic, it is not unusual for the information to be distributed across the entire site and to be narrative rather than abbreviated. Easy navigation is even more important in such a site because you're compensating for the lack of quick, easy-to-scan bits of information.

The Web site shown in figure 3 is very different from the one in figure 2. The figure 3 Web site doesn't need to be reduced exclusively to bullet points. The attorney here is offering information for people who want to expose an employer for stealing from the United States government. Although the ultimate goal is certainly for the attorney to gain business, the Web site is principally offered as an informational vehicle. It is expected that a visitor to this site will want detailed information about how to "blow the whistle," what can happen if you do, and why you might choose to do so.

Even though a lot of information is imparted on this Web site, it is still readable. The graphics intermingled with the text give the eye a rest, as do occasional bullet points.

Figure 3 www.whistleblowerlawyer.com

Standard Web Site Elements

There are some basic pages that are common to most small to midsize business Web sites. These sites usually have a home page and at least one products or services page. They also have a page of contact information, and sometimes a map and directions. A Frequently Asked Questions (FAQ) page answers common questions about the company. Also, there is usually a page about the company—its history, its mission and vision statements, the key people in the organization, and other topics people may find of interest. Other pages, such as links to related Web sites, may be included as well.

Home Page

A home page can be thought of as a magazine cover and table of contents. A magazine cover should convince you to start exploring. It should have some enticements to catch your eye, but only enough to make a quick impact. The table of contents should tell you enough to make you want to start reading.

Similarly, a home page should also have just enough information to catch your eye and your interest. It should have leads into the other sections for visitors who are interested in the topics. In the home page shown in figure 4, there is just enough detail for visitors to scan. From here they can go directly to the information they want.

The same page style is carried throughout the remainder of the Web site. This eliminates any confusion as to whether a visitor is still at the site.

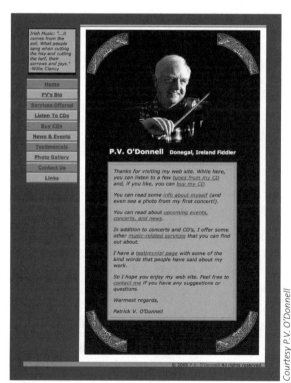

Figure 4 www.pvodonnell.com

Company Information Page

Every business Web site should include a company information page. The Internet can sometimes feel like a very shadowy and nameless medium for communications. It is important to remove your client from that murky image and put his company in the spotlight. The company information page is a good tool for cementing a company's identity and reinforcing credibility.

Figure 5 shows a company information page for a one-person business. We learn that this company has been making historical percussion instruments since 1989, and we find out specifically which instruments the craftsman makes.

We also learn about the person who creates the instruments—his performance background, his university studies, and the impressive list of venues and credentials he has. This Web page takes the craftsman from behind the scenes and shines a light on his impressive talents.

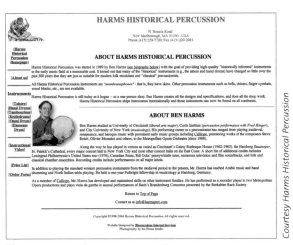

Courtesy Harms Historical Percussion

Figure 5 www.harmsperc.com/

Frequently Asked Questions Page

The Frequently Asked Questions (FAQ) page is one of the Internet's best inventions. As newsgroups (forums) and mailing lists evolved, people found that certain questions were asked over and over. The moderators realized that the most effective way to handle these repeated questions is to point newcomers to the FAQ page. This gave the new visitors a way to get up to speed without wasting everyone else's time.

Web sites, too, make good use of FAQ pages. Look at figure 6 for one example. This nonprofit organization asked the receptionist and other employees what customers frequently asked about. They said many people asked what the "CW" in the company name (CW Resources) stood for. Since "CW" is an abbreviation with a story behind it, this was a question with a long answer.

With the FAQ page you have the time and space to give thorough answers. You also have the opportunity to do a bit of selling for the company. Many people would love to know what makes your client's product better than others. A FAQ is a great place to make that distinction.

FAQs can include all of those important bits of information people want to know that don't fit elsewhere. If you have more than eight to ten questions, break them into categories and put an index at the top of the page with links to each. Or, list all the questions at the top and link each question to its answer below. (If you make either of these choices, be sure to put a link back to the top of the page after each answer.)

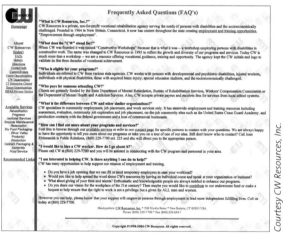

Figure 6 www.cwresources.org/faq.htm

Map and Directions Page

A map and directions to a bricks and mortar location is a big help to someone who wants to visit. It is much easier for a busy receptionist to refer a caller to a map and directions page on the Internet (if the caller has Internet access) than to give out directions.

Figure 7 shows directions to a special needs clinic for children. There are step-by-step directions starting from a major interstate, including local landmarks. In addition, there's a map of the area with the clinic shown.

The maps and directions in this Web site were created internally. However, some clients request maps and directions supplied by online companies such as Google Local (http://maps.google.com) or MapQuest (www.mapquest.com). Some companies allow your clients to use their maps on the clients' Web sites as long as their logo is displayed. (There are some other stipulations to be aware of as well. For example, clients may not put a map on flyers or other advertising media without permission.) Other companies will allow you to link to their maps but not to put their map on your client's Web page. Whether your client prefers Google's maps, Map-Quest, or another service, it's not difficult to set up a map or a link. Go to the map service's Web site, configure a map the way you want it to appear, use the labels and size that you want, and then find the section on their site that explains how to use the map or link on a Web site. There will be an assortment of ways to link to the map depending on which service you use, including a display of the map and a text link.

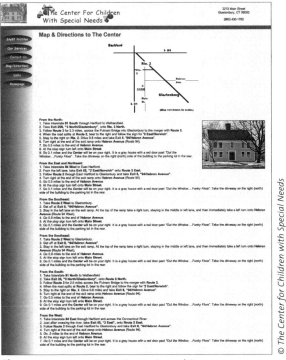

Figure 7 www.autism-ct.com/map.htm

Copy the HTML code that they offer and paste it into the client's Web site. Make sure all links back to the map service are functioning and that the map looks the way you expected it to. That is all there is to it.

Products or Services Page

You will probably need to include at least one page of products or services on your client's site. Many times you will need more than one page for products. E-commerce Web sites, for instance, may have hundreds of products, all interfaced with a database delivery script. In the example in figure 8, the company displays many different products by using thumbnail graphics that function as links. If a site has more than several dozen products, it may be easier to create a database of products with accompanying descriptions. With a service-oriented business, there is usually a page describing the services. Prices may be included on a products or services Web page, or there may be a link to such a list.

Figure 8 www.skiboards.com/index.php?main
–page=index&cPath=2

Courtesy Skiboards.com Skiboards Superstore, Inc.

Related Links Page

To increase traffic to a Web site, it can be a good idea to include links to other related Web sites. In the example in figure 9, the page of links is designed to entice associated businesses to bookmark the site and return. For this particular Web site, the client decided on links to resources including mortgage rates and news, PMI information, real estate Web sites, and the U.S. Department of Housing and Urban Development. Most clients who have been using the Internet for a while can help you put a list of links together, but if a client draws a blank, you may wish to help find some appropriate links. New links can be added from time to time as your client discovers new Web sites or gets requests from visitors.

Figure 9 www.trinityappraisal.com/link.htm

Contact Page

The contact page is a list of ways to contact the company. At a minimum, this should include the phone number(s), fax number(s), and any e-mail and surface mail addresses.

The example in figure 10 shows their contact information even though it appears at the top of each page as well. There is also a link to a Yahoo! map to their model home and office as well as a link to directions. An online form makes it easier for interested individuals to request more information. If the form asks for their e-mail address (and it should!), put a small note below the Submit button reassuring visitors that their privacy will not be violated. Check with your client to approve of any statement you make to that nature though.

Figure 10 www.patlinenterprises.com/contactus.htm

Of course every company has its own specific needs. If you try to create one Web site to fit all needs, you won't be working in the best interests of your client. Use the types of pages we've discussed as a starting point, but allow your client to suggest other pages that might be appropriate. Whether a Jobs Available or Testimonials page is needed, be prepared to offer your services to create a Web site that showcases this unique customer. That is why the client is hiring you instead of using a preformatted template for a Web site design.

Building a Web Site

Gathering Information

Once a client signs a contract, you need to get as much information as possible before beginning your work. When I begin, I request the text that will go into the Frequently Asked Questions page, as well as any of the general information that I didn't get in the initial interview. This might include the client's target market, her goals for the Web site, and any concepts or images that need to be portrayed within the Web site. If I need to, I can start the site design while waiting for information to come in, but it is much more efficient to have everything I need before starting my work.

Building a Foundation

There are some basic tasks that I do with all Web sites. I've learned to complete most of these tasks in a group rather than try to remember them as I go. Generally by the time I'm ready to design a Web site, I have established a domain name and reserved a block of space on a Web server for the client's site. I have a standard cover page that I use as a temporary home page. It announces the upcoming Web site.

Then, behind the scenes, I create the Web site in a directory named "draft." This gives the client the opportunity to view the progress of the Web site at any time, from any location. Unless there is a business reason to do so, I usually don't password protect that draft directory. It is available for anyone to view. That way the client can simply invite friends and associates to offer feedback.

The "draft site" that I use to develop the new Web site is actually a subdirectory of the main site named "draft." When I'm building a new site and you go to the main home page, you will see a not-so-attractive generic "coming soon" page. I don't want that page to be too attractive or the client won't be in a rush to have me change it. However, if you go to the "draft" directory, you will actually see the site being built. That way, my client can not only look at it to see what I've done so far, she can also contact friends and associates and ask them to look at it for more opinions.

I create the FTP path and configuration and set up the tools I need on my computer to begin building the site.

Creating a Layout and an Image

When I'm building a Web site, I spend most of my time determining the layout of the site. You, too, should try to create a look and feel that captures the image the business wishes to project. Is this going to be a Web site with a professional appearance? Will it have a whimsical look? Is the goal to get in, get information, and get back out? Or to linger and enjoy the site (and the advertisements)? Since you probably will have unique goals for each Web site, you should spend a lot of time working on each site's look and feel.

During this phase, you can create backgrounds if needed. You can come up with a style sheet that will maintain the look of the site from page to page. I decide the best way to navigate through the site. I incorporate the logo and the headers and footers into the design. Once I've assembled all the elements, I have the layout for the Web site.

Creating a Structure

Once I have my layout, I use it to create the structure of files I will need. I do this in a directory on my computer called "c:\websites\clientname\draft\" and I start with the index.htm file as my home page. As you can see in figure 11, I create each of these files ahead of time so I have the file structure in place before starting. It is easier for me to link to the various files in the site if this structure is in place. When creating this structure, I use all lowercase letters and end each HTML file name with ".htm" rather than ".html." I am pointing out my file-naming methods not because this is the "correct" way to name files but because I've learned that it is easier

```
Beginning Structure of Directories and Files

.../Draft/
        robot.txt
        index.htm
        faq.htm
        map.htm
        contact.htm
.../Draft/Images/
        logo.gif
```

Figure 11

to be consistent (all lowercase, all "htm" extensions, etc.). I also create a directory called "c:\websites\clientname\draft\images\" in which to put all of my graphics files for the Web site. I create a text file called robot.txt and put it in the root of the new Web site. In this file, I put the following two lines:

User-agent: *
Disallow: /draft/

When search engine robots or spiders come to the Web site, the first thing they do is look for a robot.txt file in the root directory. The first line of my file tells them that the information in my robot.txt is relevant to all user-agents or robots rather than just select ones. It then requests that the robot skip listing the draft directory with the search engines. Otherwise, when I upload the site to the Internet, the search engines will still be listing the draft directory as the Web site location.

During this phase I also scan any photos and use my graphics program to clean up any graphics files and make them "Web site ready." This includes resizing images and saving them as either jpg, png, or gif files.

Putting It All Together

Once I have created the Web site's structure, I can start inserting the client's information into the template to create my Web pages. I correct any spelling and grammar errors I see as I go along. Depending on how thorough my client has been, sometimes I copy and paste sections into the various HTML files that I'm building. Usually, however, I work with sketched concepts, company brochures, scribbled notes, newsletters, and other bits and pieces. I compile the information into Web pages for the client's first draft.

As I complete files, I upload them to the draft site. I usually don't upload pages until they are complete. Otherwise, even though we all know that this is a draft, clients still contact me to let me know that a certain page just stops midway through, or has a chunk of dummy text right in the middle. Waiting until individual pages are complete before uploading them prevents most of this confusion.

Frequently in this stage of the design process, you will think of something that will make the layout more powerful or more interesting. Make sure that whatever program you use for site building has an easy way to update your layout and then propagate it to the entire site. This is one reason I like using cascading style sheets (CSS) for my Web sites. Once I find a little tweak that will improve the look of a site, CSS allows me to include it globally with minimal repetition or backpedaling.

Correcting and Coming to Agreement

When I finish assembling the Web site, it is time to look at the entire site and make sure it achieves the goals the client and I have set. I run my spell-checker through the entire site to pick up any errors I've overlooked. I test links and forms to make sure they all work. Once I feel the Web site is ready to go, I contact my client and ask him to do a walk-through. I tell the client to make a list of any changes that are needed. (If he wants major modifications, we set up a time to go over them together.) Once the changes have been made and the client is satisfied, the site is almost ready to go live.

I make sure each page has META tags such as the title, description, and key words. I make a final inspection to make sure all the HTML code is clean and no empty tags are lingering. I validate the code and clean up any last-minute issues. I check the draft directories to see if there are any orphaned files—that is, any files with no connection or purpose.

Finally, with the blessing of the client (and payment for the balance of the design work!), it is time to move the site out of its draft mode and onto the Internet.

Last-Minute Sweep-Up for a Grand Opening

When I move all the files from the draft site out to the root directory on the Internet, there is still a bit of testing to do. I make a final inspection of each page carefully to check for typos or other blunders. I check every link to make sure none was skewed during the move.

I use Dreamweaver and the links are updated when the files get moved. With Dreamweaver or a similar program, you should be able to simply highlight the files in the draft site, click on "Move," and paste them into the root directory.

If you move the files down from draft to the root (home page) directory and the links still point to the draft directory, you may be using "absolute links" (for example, http://www.newsite.com/draft/images/graphic.gif) rather than "relative links" (images/graphic.gif). If that is the case, do a "Find and Replace" in your software program to change all the absolute links to relative links.

Then check the entire site with a link-checking program such as Xenu's Link Sleuth™. This is a "charityware" program, which means the author suggests that a nominal payment be made to one of its preferred charities. This software and more information on it can be found at http://home.snafu.de/tilman/xenulink.html. By using relative links rather than absolute links, you can move a site from one area to another without having to revise each link. It is outside of the scope of this book to devote a chapter to relative versus absolute links, but if you find you are having difficulties with links when moving an entire Web site, do a search in your favorite HTML reference book or go online and look up "absolute links" and "relative links."

It is better if you can make the final test of the Web site on a computer other than the one that you used to create the site. A couple of times, instead of referencing a graphics file from the images directory on the Web site, I have accidentally referenced it from my computer. Therefore, when I look at the Web site using my computer, the image looks fine—the file is on my C: drive. But when someone tries to view the page on another computer, the HTML file can't find the image. You wouldn't even know this unless and until someone complains.

If there is a form on the Web site, I set it so the results come to my e-mail address. Then I test it completely to assure myself that it is working properly. After I confirm that the form works, I switch it to the client's e-mail address so that the form results are sent to the client. I then run one last test of the form. Last but not least, I contact the client with congratulations and the announcement that the Web site is on the Internet.

Tips and Tricks I've Learned along the Way

■ **Offload completed files.** While I'm building a site, I keep its graphics on my hard drive. When the work is complete, I move all of the site's files from my hard drive onto a writable CD-ROM disk. It is very easy to fill up your hard drive if you don't regularly offload files.

■ **Speed it up.** If a client complains that his Web site is slow, yet you know that you have it on a fast server and haven't had any problems, give him a few opportunities to test his connection. Ask him to go to http://reviews.cnet.com/7004-7254_7-0.html and test his Internet speed. In addition to the speed test, this site provides a lot of information on troubleshooting speed problems. (Naturally, knowledge and information can backfire for you if you are trying to hide the fact that your servers are running slowly. This is why I always keep my clients hooked up to high-speed commercial servers.)

■ **Get the facts about search engines.** If you have a client who is thirsty for vast amounts of information about search engines, or you feel he has been completely misled on this subject in the past, send him to Google's search engine optimization (SEO) site at www.google.com/support/webmasters/bin/answer.py?hl=en&answer=35291. This is a reliable and comprehensive Web site.

■ **Deal with hoaxes.** Prepare yourself for an onslaught of questions about viruses and hoaxes on the Internet. My clients used to send me all of the "sky is falling" warnings they got. Most of the warnings were hoaxes that have been around for years. Telling them these hoaxes are garbage and asking them not to pass along any more didn't make good business sense. Ignoring worried clients wasn't the answer either. So I created a standard e-mail response. In it, I refer clients to some of the good hoax Web sites, such as www.snopes.com, so that they can determine if a warning is legitimate without contacting me each time.

■ **Charge by the site.** I used to charge by the page for Web site design because I could calculate costs easily that way. Then I realized that cost-conscious clients would try to cram as much as they could into a page. If I gave them a limit as to how much could go on a page, they'd try to fill each page to the limit. This may have been economical for the clients, but it was poor Web site design. Web pages were no longer separate sections of information; instead, everything was crammed into as few pages as possible. Now I charge by the site, not by the page. I no longer have clients worried that I'm fleecing them when I encourage them to divide material among several pages.

- **Use licensed software.** If you use unlicensed copies of software from friends, you should stop doing so. Don't worry, I'm not preaching morality here; there are two sound business reasons for making sure all of your software is properly licensed. First, if you are demonstrating a Web site to a client and a warning screen pops up telling you that your trial version of software is outdated, it doesn't make a very good impression on the client. Second, if you have a pirated version, it's more difficult to get upgrades when you need them. You must either wait for your friend to get the upgrade so you can install it, or try to buy the upgrade and make it work on your computer. As a professional you should be legitimate and responsible in your use of licensed software.

Polish and Shine

I keep an eye on the site for a few days to make sure everything looks good. Any typos or tweaks are taken care of immediately. After a few days, I go back to the site, get the key words and other information (e.g., company name, address, description), and register the Web site with the various search engines. From time to time, I look in to confirm that everything still looks fresh, and I test the site with search engines as time permits to confirm that it is being listed.

07

Attracting Customers

Although first impressions may go a long way in helping you jump-start your business, it's a well-deserved—and honestly earned—reputation that will ensure long-term success. To establish a good reputation and attract customers, you'll begin with a strong image and a clear vision statement, but then you'll need to back those up with some top-quality design work.

Establishing a Good Reputation

How do you demonstrate your expertise if you haven't yet been hired for a job? If you don't already have some Web site samples that illustrate your design skills, you may need to do some pro bono work. Your portfolio is your best sales tool, and it's worth doing some unpaid work to build it. So how do you go about finding organizations to donate your services to? And how do you avoid being taken advantage of? Here are some tips to help you.

- When you do free work, try to select a high-profile organization such as a local branch of the United Way, the American Red Cross, or a community service organization.
- Don't get overzealous in your design for a group and make it into a nonpaying lifetime career. Offer to do a Web site that won't require extensive modifications and updates (unless the organization wants to hire you to do those).
- Don't be fooled into designing a free site for a business that promises to promote your services to its friends. I've never heard of these resulting in more business. Your goal is to get Web sites that you can add to your portfolio so that you can build your business. Don't depend on getting business from someone who is unwilling to pay you herself.

- Don't let a business hook you into designing a cheap or free Web site with the understanding that it is a preliminary Web site pending approval for a much bigger and better one for which you will be paid. If you do a great job for little or no money, the company may be happy with that site and never hire you to do a second site. Conversely, if you do a lower-quality site with the understanding that it is a "quick fix" until funding comes through, you will probably be viewed as the designer who does cheap-quality work and shouldn't be hired for the "real" Web site.

- Avoid speculative work. In other words, don't design a Web site for a company and then try to sell it to them. If they are interested in a Web site, your portfolio should sell your services. Also, if you go to them with the work done, they know you are desperate and have nothing better to do; otherwise you wouldn't be designing sites on spec. It would be like mowing a neighbor's lawn and then asking him if he wants to pay you for it.

- If you agree to do a free site so you can use it for your portfolio, ask the organization not to tell people that you are doing the work for free. Try to find a cheerleader within the organization who will speak highly of your talents, and use that person as a reference.

- Don't make your sample sites look like free sites; people will assume they are representative of your best work. Don't offer to do a free site unless you are willing to make it a showpiece for your business.

- Ongoing free work should not dilute your value as long as you set up clear ground rules in advance. Even today, I offer free services as the Webmaster for a large local computer users group. That is my "pet project." I also choose one deserving group each year that needs a Web site set up and has someone else willing to maintain it after getting some guidance. I create the site, upload it, then turn it over to the person responsible for its upkeep. (I offer occasional phone support or troubleshooting when needed.) If I did more free work than that, I wouldn't have time for my paying customers.

Offering your services for free is a charitable activity, but there has to be some reward besides the satisfaction that comes from doing a good deed. Some of the free Web sites you create may actually lead to paying work within that organization if handled professionally and responsibly.

The other way that free work can pay off is in outside contacts. I wouldn't create a site solely with the expectation of getting a useful contact, but occasionally it does happen. If you need to build your portfolio anyway, try to flush out any valuable contacts the organization can provide.

Seminars as a Selling Tool

In addition to designing sites for free, you can build your business without diminishing your value by offering limited advice and low-cost or free seminars to business people. Neither of these has provided me with a great deal of business, but they've enhanced my image, which I can use to turn a reluctant client into a sale.

Once I had a potential client who had been told that there were thousands of search engines with which he really needed to register his site. I tried to explain to him that fewer than ten of the search engines provide well over 90 percent of the search activity. My discussion was sounding a lot like a sales pitch.

I realized that the person who had influenced this potential client had done a good job of confusing him. I told the potential client that in two weeks I was giving a free seminar on using search engines on the Internet. I invited him to attend. He immediately went from a resistant, arms-crossed position to being attentive and receptive. He started asking questions of me and began treating me as the expert with the answers. He hired me without even going to my seminar—he felt that he was getting the inside information piped right into his office. Instead of being another person trying to persuade him, I had instantly become the Internet authority that others turn to.

I encourage all my clients and potential clients to attend my seminars. This gives them the opportunity to see me in a leadership role, giving advice and answering questions in an open and nonthreatening environment. Although I'm always afraid someone will ask me a question that I have no idea how to answer, it seldom happens. When it does, I can usually handle it gracefully, without devaluing my position. People understand that I don't know everything about the Internet and that I'm only there to share what I do know.

Many of the people who attend my seminars are there for the general information and do not directly buy services from me. However, their perception of me as a responsive, knowledgeable person encourages others to inquire about my services. Much like the ripples of water created by a pebble, the impressions of the small group that I directly encounter spread out to larger and larger areas.

I typically offer my seminars to local chamber of commerce groups as well as Rotary groups and other business groups. When approaching someone involved in one of these groups, I tell him that I conduct educational presentations to business groups on Internet-related topics. A few may already have an Internet guru in their group, but many do not. I create a one-page handout with some follow-up information to give out. I make sure my business name, e-mail, phone, Web site, etc., are in the letterhead on the handout.

Seminar Handouts

I have included here a sample handout similar to one that I used with a Rotary group seminar. I have my name and contact information at the top of the page just below the title. I put some related information that the seminar attendees could use later, for example, some popular search engines. I then gave a couple of brief bulleted lists that tied in with my discussion, to help the attendees recall some of the highlights of the seminar. At the bottom of the one-page handout I try to leave room for comments and notes. Once an attendee puts a note about my talk on the paper, it is likely that it will not be left behind after the seminar.

If you decide to try this, don't be afraid to tell the business group that in addition to designing Web sites, you also enjoy sharing Internet information with other business groups if they know of any other groups (most business people belong to more than one group).

I'm not the best at promoting my seminars. For that reason, I try to tie them in with another function or group. Our local computer user group offers seminars, and frequently they invite me to give the larger presentations, which they promote and push. Although you could charge a few dollars to attendees, I've found that if I'm responsible for paying room rental and other expenses, my portion of the take doesn't add up to much. That is why I prefer to offer free seminars for business groups. I'm in it to get customers, not seminar fees.

As Dave Taylor said in his book, *The Complete Idiot's Guide to Growing Your Business with Google* (www.findability.info), "There is no such thing as a free lunch when you're growing your business online. Retail shop owners know this intuitively, that you can build the most beautiful store in town, but if no one knows about it, you'll go out of business before you start earning a profit." Dave drives the point home when he says, ". . . philanthropy doesn't grow a business and doesn't pay the mortgage." Sharing your knowledge and expertise with the community establishes your business and can drive a substantial amount of traffic to your Web site. So don't keep your skills and knowledge a secret. Focus on doing some giving in order to gain.

How to Get That First "Real" Client

Much like selling fund-raising candy as a kid, you probably will get a certain amount of business based upon personal contacts. However, there will come a day when you meet with your first "real" client. You won't be able to count on family connections to make the sale. For the first time, you will have a client asking what other work you've done. You will find yourself needing to convince this person that you are the right designer for the job. Here are a few tips to help you through that.

Do not overinflate your capabilities. If the client asks if you have a lot of experience, and you don't have much, don't be afraid to admit it. Immediately tell this potential client the many reasons why you are still the best person for the contract. You are eager to do the work. You will be there dependably to help the client through the process. You have several Web sites that you have created for other groups. Show your portfolio, but don't overinflate your role in those Web sites. Naturally, if all the work you've done so far has been unpaid, you don't need to announce that. (Many business people may suspect that anyway. Remember, they may have made their start the same way.)

Once you've decided what you'd charge to create this potential client's site, you must be prepared for the response you get to that price. I still get some clients who jump for joy at the great price and others who think I'm gouging them (for that exact same price). When you are starting out, it's important to realize that just because someone comments about the price, that doesn't mean that she knows what is fair.

How should you react if you quote a price that you think is reasonable to do the design work and the client gets excited and indicates it to be much lower than he expected? Keep a "poker face" and explain that you want to give him a good price to create a real showpiece so you can show it off to others as well. Point out that you will also appreciate any leads that the client can give.

On the other hand, if the client indicates that the price seems a bit steep, don't panic. Ask what his impression is based on. If he says a friend has offered to create the site for much less, try to get a dialogue going about the price. What does that price include? Does it include contacting search engines? Does the person know how to design the site for different browsers and different screen sizes? Usually a few questions will reveal that the client isn't very impressed with the other person—otherwise you wouldn't be sitting there. If you can figure out what the client is assuming is reasonable and why, you may be able to salvage the sale. Either way, you are gathering information and experience for future sales, so don't be afraid to ask a few questions. Remember that the answers you get are the client's opinion and not necessarily based on the level of experience that you bring. If you feel the client is being unreasonable, thank him and tell him that you will still be interested in helping him if the situation changes. As with any business discussion, it is usually very unproductive to argue with a potential client.

"No" Does Not Always Equal Rejection

If your sales pitch is rejected, take a few minutes to analyze everything that happened. Ponder the feedback you've received to see if there is something you should change before your next appointment. Take some deep breaths; you've taken some giant steps forward and it is time to learn from them and keep moving ahead.

You probably will not close the deal with most clients the first time you sit down with them. Make your presentation, try to give good responses to any issues they bring up, and ask as many questions as you can. Some of these questions will deal with the client's time frame. If he has a big marketing blitz coming up, he may be anxious to get the Web site up and running. You can tell him that, at this time, you can start on the project immediately and give it your full attention.

On the other hand, if a client indicates that he is in the initial planning stages, don't worry if you don't get a commitment right away. I have many clients who are "almost ready" to get a Web site. The more I push, the farther away they get. I have learned that most of these people will make a decision later. I simply make my presentation, give the client every possible reason to use my services instead of someone else's, and ask if he would prefer that I contact him or if he'd rather call me when he's ready. I find that there are usually pressing business reasons for delaying the decision. If I can exit gracefully while giving the image of a caring professional designer willing to wait until the client is ready, I usually get a call back (sometimes months later) to "talk" some more. Invariably, when the client wants to talk further, he has resolved all the issues and is ready to commit to a Web site.

How to Turn Skeptical Leads into Happy Customers

I do not consider myself a great business rainmaker or salesperson. I would be happy if I had someone else to go out and haul in buckets full of contracts for me. However, until I find someone magical like that, I am responsible for getting my own contracts. You may be in the same situation. The key to getting signed contracts is getting leads, and I will cover that in chapter 8. But for now, let's examine what I do after I have a lead. This includes laying the groundwork, making an initial contact, giving a presentation, and closing the sale.

Groundwork

As soon as I get a lead on a business that may benefit from my services, I start doing my homework. I look to see if the business has an existing Web site. If it does, I analyze that site to see how I could improve it. I then search the Internet for tidbits on that company or the person I will be contacting. Many of my initial contacts are impressed when I mention an accomplishment their company has made that was listed on someone else's Web site.

If I know enough about the client's business, I try to view some related Web sites, especially those of local competitors. It can be a real revelation for a business person to discover that her closest competitor has a great Web site up and running. I bookmark some examples of good Web sites in the client's field, as well as a few examples of bad sites. I don't dwell on the bad sites, but it can be useful to point out some of the drawbacks of having someone inexperienced design a Web site.

If the client doesn't have a domain name, I try to find an appropriate one. I look up the obvious choices first, just to make sure they aren't available. I make notes as I explore the possibilities. If I find a few likely candidates, I make a list. If nothing strikes me, I make a note that the client and I will need to work on this detail.

Making Contact

After I've done my homework, I call the lead and introduce myself. I give a brief reason for my call and say who (if anyone) recommended that I call. I then ask if the client has a few minutes to talk. It is important to ask if he has time to talk. I used to assume that, because the other person is very busy, I should try to give as much information as possible. I would go right into my pitch to try to avoid wasting the other person's time. It took me awhile to realize that if I called in the middle of a meeting or as the person was heading out the door, my introduction sounded more like pressure sales than an attempt to save the other person's time. Once the client slipped a word in to stop my sales pitch, I seldom got a second chance.

If the client isn't free to talk, I ask for a better time for a follow-up call. If I get a specific time, I write it on my calendar. It becomes a top priority. It means the client is interested in what I have to say. If I get a vague "call back in a couple of weeks" answer, I put it on my calendar but assume it may not be a strong lead.

When I do make contact by phone with a client, I start by prequalifying him. It may sound like I'm selling myself, but at the same time I am deciding whether the client needs my services. I ask about his current Web site (if he has one). If he has a site that I was unable to locate, I make a note to myself that he needs help with the search engine listings. I talk about the client's needs and ask if he feels a Web site could benefit his business. (I don't disagree at this time if he says he sees no value to it. That might shut out any further details that could help me decide if the client does in fact need a Web site.) If the client doesn't yet have a Web site, I ask if he has a domain name. If he doesn't, he may not even understand the question.

This brings up an important point. You never want a potential client to feel intimidated by your knowledge. If you sense that he does, adapt your presentation accordingly. For example, when I ask if the client has a domain name and there is silence on the other end of the line, I quickly explain that a domain name is a "Web name"—a dot-com or dot-net name, for example—like www.blarneystone.com or www.cbs.com. For any question that you ask a client, try to remember that he may not understand what you're talking about. As a business leader, the client may feel that he should know all about the Internet. If you can't make him comfortable asking you questions, he may decide to put off making a hiring decision. I try not to wait until someone stops me and asks what I'm talking about—I prefer to anticipate when I've gone over his head and give him the help he needs. It's safer to oversimplify matters than to try to impress a client with your knowledge and risk alienating him.

After you've had a few minutes to talk with a lead, you can assess whether there is any interest on his part and whether you want to pursue the sale. It may seem rather odd that you'd need to consider whether to make this person a client. You've worked so hard to find a lead and talk with him, and now you need to stop and decide if you really want him? Naturally, the hungrier you are and the more time you have available, the less selective you may become. However, I've discovered that if a client is dragging his feet and making the initial contact into an ordeal, our interactions will probably stay this way till the end of the project. It is better to thank this person for his time and invite him to contact you if he does decide to move forward.

Judith C. Kallos, CEO and Director of Internet Development, Internet Studio, Inc., offers these thoughts for initiating contact with a potential client:

> Before the contract is signed, give clients the time they need to feel comfortable with your style and how you operate your company. Some clients should get more time than others. After all, isn't business all about people and relationships? I know those whom I will be able to work with as well as those I can make successful. I also can tell in the first phone call, or if they walk in without an appointment, in the first five minutes, if they are the "type" of people I can work with. I base my decision on how they communicate with me, the demands they make, and the questions they ask.

I had one lead tell me that he saw no value to the Internet and could think of no reason to get a Web site. I gave him some examples of his competitors who were on the Web, but that only made him more argumentative. I gave him several reasons he should consider going on the Internet—improving customer service, making his company more visible, linking to other sites to bring in new customers, and more. I knew a Web site would benefit him, but everything I suggested was vehemently rejected. It was apparent to me that this person viewed me as an "evil techie" who was trying to drag him kicking and screaming to a level of technology where he didn't want to be. I thanked this man for his time and told him to call me if he did decide to get a Web site. Since I had spent so much time researching that type of company before calling him, I decided to call one of his competitors. That person was much more interested in increasing his company's visibility. I usually don't make cold calls, but in this case I had done my homework and I knew that the Internet would be a good selling tool for someone in that business.

If I decide that I would like to work with a lead and he's expressed an interest in my services, I set up another appointment. If the client's office is within driving range, I offer to meet him there with my laptop. Otherwise, we can schedule a phone call.

The Presentation

When you meet with a client, you should have all your tools ready. I have my laptop with the battery charged and ready for a couple of hours of use. My browser is loaded and set to the site where I will begin. My laptop is in suspend mode so there won't be a long wait for the boot-up process. And, although finding a wireless signal to view Web sites during a presentation can interrupt even my smoothest presentation, I always have my wireless card ready to help make a sale.

Examples of good and bad Web sites should be stored on your hard drive. There are several software programs that enable you to save Web sites. My favorite is HTTrack (www.httrack.com). This is a free (GNU General Public License) software that creates a full copy of a Web site on your hard drive. Do not use it on large Web sites, but for a few dozen pages, it can quickly create a copy. If you make a copy of a site to show, unplug your Internet and test your copy ahead of time so you know what you are capturing and how to smoothly refer to the sites. Murphy's Law will take its toll plenty of times even when you are prepared. Don't assume you can use the client's computer or assume you'll be able to connect to the Internet for your

TIP

If you have several Web pages that you wish to review, use PowerPoint for your presentation. First, open a new file for PowerPoint. Then create a copy of the browser's screen you want to capture (shift-PrintScreen) and paste it into the first PowerPoint slide. You may need to use your mouse to stretch the image to full screen size. Repeat this for as many screens you want to save as slides and save the file as a PowerPoint show (pps) on your desktop for easy access.

demonstration. That will be the one time that the client has a bad connection or your wireless system will falter. (Of course, neither of these would be your fault, but you are the one who looks bad.)

If the sites I want to demonstrate are individual pages, I can capture screens and use PowerPoint. With a PowerPoint presentation, I can show a potential client other Web sites that are related to that business. It gives me a chance to start a dialogue about what he or she likes and dislikes, and most business people appreciate that I took the time to do my homework about related businesses.

In other words, if the client owns a candle shop, for example, go online and find some nearby competitors and put screen prints of them in your PowerPoint show ("See, Barb's Candles down the street is online and is able to show some of her products to a market that you need to be able to reach!"). Show a site or two that are bad examples ("See, this candle shop in California has no way to contact the store, and this other one looks very cheap and homemade."). Don't dwell on the negative ones, though. Also show several good examples ("This candle shop in Oregon has a lot of features that I will be incorporating into your site" and "You can see that this Web site isn't cluttered, and much like I'll be doing with yours, it is easy to navigate through.").

With your presentation:

1. Don't rigidly stick to a script with PowerPoint. Be ready to skip around if it seems appropriate. If you feel the client may not appreciate the "bad examples," just breeze right by them. "Oh, let me show you an example I think you'll appreciate" <click, click, click> (as you speed past the ones you don't want to show).

2. Be prepared to abandon the PowerPoint presentation if you feel the client wants to ask unrelated questions or is ready to hand over a check! You may spend lots of time putting together the PowerPoint show only to find it was unnecessary backup material. Don't despair—it's the sale you want, not accolades about your PowerPoint presentation!

3. On your way over to your appointment, speculate about the various ways that the client may use to signal that he is ready to sign up. Will he quietly agree with everything you say? Will he suddenly cut you off and ask where to sign the contract? Will he tell you how impressed he is and ask you to drop by tomorrow after he's had a chance to review the information? Will

Seven Steps to a Presentation That Sells

1. Introduce yourself. Even if the client knows you, briefly review your experience and the scope of your business.

2. Encourage the client to ask questions at any time. Assure him that no question is too basic. Then, ask any key questions you haven't addressed in a previous conversation.

3. Ask if the client has a domain name. If not, discuss some options. Discuss the challenge of getting a memorable name, and encourage the client to act quickly if he thinks of a name that isn't already taken.

4. Ask the client for examples of Web sites he likes or dislikes. Ask what influenced his opinion on these particular sites. This will give you clues about what he has in mind for his own site.

5. Show some of your own examples of good and bad sites. Show the source code of a site that looks good but has a poor search engine ranking; point out the META tags. Assure him that when you design sites, you strive to make them not only aesthetically pleasing but also prominent and easy to find.

6. If the client asks about costs, the scope of your services, or a guarantee that you will deliver what you have promised, take this opportunity to bring out your contract. After addressing the specific question, review the rest of the contract if time permits.

7. After completing the contract review, ask if the client would like to sign up now to have you create a Web site. If he says yes, fill out the contract, sign and date it, and ask for the client's signature. Then turn to the last page and tell the client that all you need now is a check so you can start working!

you both be laughing about something when he asks you what he needs to do to get this thing rolling? As you are on your way to visit the client and thinking through some of these possibilities, it will help you get in the right frame of mind and help you prepare for that moment when the client says, "Yes!"—however it is said.

The final tool you need for all meetings is a contract. This may seem obvious to some of you, but the first few times I went out on sales calls, I didn't have a contract.

I figured I'd get the potential client interested and then run back, create a contract with everything filled in per our discussion, and fax it to the client or deliver it in person.

Sending a contract after the presentation sometimes works. However, remember that you are dealing with busy decision makers. Once you have given them a presentation, they often want to make a decision and move on to the next thing. If you don't have everything available for them to make that decision, you may never get another chance to sell to them. I probably lost a couple of sales because I thought that putting a contract in front of a client during the presentation would scare him off.

My lesson about carrying contracts was learned from one memorable client. I had been giving a great presentation to a decision maker for a company that I really wanted as a client. The meeting was going well and the client seemed impressed with my capabilities. About halfway through the presentation, as we were really starting to "click," the client interrupted. He said, "I'm very impressed with you and want to do business with you. I hate to cut you short, but I need to get to a meeting. Can we just quickly take a look at the contract so I can sign it, get my bookkeeper to issue you a check, and get to my meeting on time?" I had everything with me except the most important item—the contract. Since then, I always carry a blank contract for the person who waves a check in my face and wants to buy on the spot!

Closing the Sale

If your presentations are like most of mine, and no one is there waving a check in your face, you will need to learn one of the most important parts of a sales call—closing the sale! For me, this used to be the hardest part of my job. I enjoyed talking about Web sites and designing them, but I always had trouble asking someone to buy one from me. When I first started out and didn't carry a contract with me on my sales calls, I did not close many sales—I wanted to have a good time with the client and didn't want to ruin it by asking for a sale! Seems silly, huh?

Most of us face the same situation to some degree. However, if you are your own sales staff, you must learn how to close the sale. Here are some tips that may help.

- The decision maker has many important tasks to do. Your presentation is probably one of the smaller ones. Don't drag it out for too long. Before you start losing momentum, ask for the sale.

- If you ask for the sale, stop and do not say anything else. Wait until you get a response. If you think the silence is uncomfortable, that is because your presentation is making the client decide. Don't create a distraction during that decision.
- If the client wants to think it over before deciding, you may not have given enough reasons to sign up today. Are there other reasons he should know about?
- If the client hasn't yet registered a domain name, remind him that just because the name he wants is available today, this doesn't necessarily mean it will be available in a week or a month. Acting today would be his best opportunity even if he still wants to wait on the Web site. Once he sees the benefit of securing a domain name with you, he is more likely to proceed with the Web site as well.
- If the client has agreed to use your services, subdue your impulse to express relief or fear. Some Web designers have been so excited that they talked their way out of the sale. If you wipe your brow and say, "Whew, I thought I was never going to get any sales this month," you may find that you won't get any sales for the month. If you try to ease your nervousness by joking, "Gosh, now I had better learn how to put a Web site together," you may not need to. This is a time to be cordial and professional. Thank the client, assure him that he's made the right decision, and don't give him any reason to back out.
- If the client wants to make a deal but doesn't like the price, be prepared to decide whether you will lower that price. I don't reduce my prices unless I also reduce the amount of work I'm offering to do. If there is a legitimate concern about the price, talk about what other designers charge and why your prices are in line. Offer to show some other Webmasters' price lists that are higher than yours. As a professional, you should try to remove obstacles that are hindering a sale, but if you know your prices are fair, don't allow them to fluctuate.
- If the decision maker is unhappy about some aspects of your contract, it is your choice whether or not to permit a change. Your attorney will probably not like this, but you are the one in charge so you should decide. Ask if this is the only term preventing a sale. If it is and you can contact your attorney for a quick opinion, do so. If this change is not the only one, try to combine all changes and then get the okay. I generally make these decisions without

consulting my attorney, but I've been dealing with contracts long enough to know when I'm taking a risk and whether I want to take that risk. You may wish to stay close to your original contract unless you have compelling reasons to modify it.

- To modify a contract, simply make the change in the margin, initial the change, and have your client do the same.
- If you must wait for a bookkeeper to write a check, suggest that both the client and you sign the contract; that way, when the check arrives you can start work without further delay. This sounds better than saying that you won't start working until you get the money.
- Some people feel that if you try to close a sale and someone says no a couple of times, you should try several more times. I feel that if that much resistance occurs initially, difficulties will continue as the site development proceeds. Designing a Web site is a partnership of work. If the other partner is reluctant, it will be hard to extract the necessary information to build the site. It could be wiser to lose the sale.

Seeding the Field

I used to try to get every sale where a potential client seemed even remotely interested in a Web site. It seemed like the harder I tried, the more resistance I met. Of course, while starting out, I needed every contract I could get, and it was frustrating when someone wouldn't make a commitment. I would spend a great deal of time with a potential client—who seemed genuinely interested—but in the end I couldn't make the sale. I would reluctantly move this person's name to the "dead lead" section of my contact list.

As time went on, I discovered something surprising. Months after I gave up on a lead, I would get an unexpected phone call from that lead, saying he was ready to get a Web site! I realized that as long as I stayed in occasional contact with these "dead leads," many of them would eventually become clients. Some of these people told me that an important client asked about their Web site, which made them realize the value of being online. Others said they had attended a trade show, or found out how well a competitor was doing thanks to his Web site. Still others revealed that, because they didn't know very much about the Internet, the ideas that I presented had to grow on them for a while.

This gave me a new way to think of my leads—a way to view them in different stages of growth so I wouldn't be so frustrated by a lack of immediate commitment. I even revamped my method of tracking my leads in my contact list. Cultivating my Web design business was not unlike a farmer seeding a field. Now, if a potential client seems reluctant and wants to wait a while before moving forward, I stop trying to force the sale. I don't consider that person a dead lead, but rather one that needs to grow for a while. If a prospective client is reluctant to sign a contract, I view him as a "seedling" that isn't quite ready yet.

This doesn't mean you should ignore the seedlings. Neither should you pull them out of the ground every day to see if roots are sprouting. Periodically, check whether you can do anything to help a seedling grow. Many of the seedlings do eventually grow into sales if you give them the right nourishment. Some don't. But you don't remove a seedling from your field unless he's told you he is not interested in your services.

When a lead indicates that he might be interested in talking in a few months, put a note on your calendar to follow up. Don't get frustrated that he isn't interested now; you've just planted another seed. It may sprout in two months, or it may take longer. Be happy to know that seedlings are planted for the future.

When a client expresses an interest in a presentation but isn't yet ready to commit, ask when he would like a follow-up call. Promptly mark that on your calendar.

In my business, I try not to question whether every recalcitrant client is planning to take my ideas to someone who will complete the job for less money. Sure, this can happen, but I choose to believe that the nourishment I give a seedling will pay off eventually. I simply wait until it's time to reap my rewards.

Tracking Your Time

There are many ways to keep track of the time you spend with your clients. Whatever method you choose, be sure it is easy for you to start and stop your times. If you use QuickBooks Pro, the built-in timer should meet your needs. There are several other software programs that may also meet your needs.

My timer of choice is TraxTime by Spud City Software. I have mine in my Windows start-up folder so it loads each time my PC starts. It stays minimized until I call on it. I simply choose my current project (or add a new one), and click the large "punch in" button. There is a notepad built in for recording specific tasks that are in progress. When I take a break or quit, I click the big "punch out" button to stop the timer. It's that simple.

When it's time to bill clients, I can generate a report with the time I spent and notes I made about each task. These reports are available in various formats such as a database file, a text file, a printed document, or they can be viewed on screen. I usually preview the report; then, if everything looks okay, I use it to create my invoices for my clients.

Here are some tips to keep in mind for billing clients.

- Many clients are surprised by how much time it takes to create a Web site or do corrections. Good reports combined with a professional time log will alleviate most concerns. The more detailed the time-tracking report, the less likely it is that questions will arise.
- Include your hourly rate in your contracts and perhaps on your Web site. It will dissuade some people from haggling over your rates if they see that your rates are firm and universal.
- When you set your hourly rate, choose the increment of time you will round off to, as well. Early in my career a client asked me in what increment I billed. I stammered momentarily and then quickly told him that I billed in quarter-hour increments. I've since discovered that I prefer to charge by the minute, with a fifteen-minute minimum. It is much easier to make that decision in advance than to change it later.
- This should go without saying, but don't fudge on any of your billings. I've heard of Web designers who decided that, due to some rationalization, certain clients should be charged extra, and who felt the easiest way to do so was by fudging on the time they worked. This is not acceptable. If you find any of your subcontractors or associates doing this, they should find themselves outside your business circle.

Creating a Steady Stream of Work

When to Offer a Deal

Some Web designers refuse to post their rates because they vary those rates depending on how busy they are. I don't recommend this. Make your rates clear and don't waiver from them. Some time ago, I had one long summer where business was particularly slow. I gave one client a discount as an incentive to sign up immediately. That bridged the gap until other work came in. If you need to do that, be certain that the client understands that this is a one-time offer. Ask the client not to discuss the price break with any other potential clients.

Clients rarely complain about my rates. I'm certain that most would try to haggle if they felt that they could get a lower price by doing so. This is why I don't start down that path. If I have no contracts, that is when I can least afford to take a pay cut. Should a similar situation develop in your business, invest that downtime in getting new clients. If you fill each lull with discounted work, the regular paying clients will become fewer and fewer.

Leveling Out the Peaks and Valleys

Most Web designers have lulls in their business. When I started out, I had lulls that lasted for weeks. No signed contracts. No Web site maintenance to do. Nothing! I would try everything I knew to bring in new business during those lulls. Finally, I would get a client to sign a contract. Oh, boy . . . work to do! Then another client would sign a contract. Then another. Suddenly, I had a lot of work to do.

You will probably have the same experience. There will be slow times that make you wonder if you got into the wrong business. Then there will be times when everyone wants work done at the same time. Here are some of the ways to reduce the peaks and valleys of your workload.

When I started, I didn't have a list of potential clients. I pursued every lead I got. If someone was interested, she got my full attention until she either hired me or told me to go away. Over time, I've learned to use lukewarm leads as one of my leveling tools. When there is a lull in my business, I pull out my list of undecideds and start renewing contact with them. As my list has increased, so has my ability to find someone who is ready to sign a contract.

When I started my Web design shop, I felt that I would never be able to get enough business, let alone have so much that I wouldn't be able to handle it. After a while, I started realizing that it might be possible at times to have so much business that it was overwhelming. Of course, having more business than you can handle is as bad as not having enough. Now, anytime I sign a contract, I block out a period of time for developing that Web site. I avoid making promises about time based upon the client's needs. If I have Web sites already in the queue that will take another two weeks, I tell my client. (I assure him that I will register his domain name immediately, though.) I encourage him to begin submitting materials right away so I can be ready to go in two weeks.

If a client has a rush job and can't wait until I'm free, I seldom delay the clients who are already scheduled. I explain to the rushed client that I can't bump someone else. However, if the client is willing to pay a 10 to 20 percent surcharge, I say I can try to bring in a subcontractor to help me get the rush job done. Generally, when there is an extra charge attached, the sense of urgency disappears.

There is a natural leveling effect in having time to pursue business while you're slow and not having time while you're busy. When you need clients, spend time promoting your business. Go to networking gatherings and pass out your cards. Talk to everyone you can to try to bring in more business. Once the business starts coming in, you'll get busy and won't have time to do marketing. After a while, you will recognize when a lull is coming up and you can start to market your business before the lull hits. That goes a long way to bridging the gap.

Another way to bring some consistency to the business is by creating monthly maintenance agreements and hosting plans. Although hosting Web sites isn't that lucrative, it still helps to have that steady cash coming in. If you have a client who needs weekly or monthly updates to his Web site for schedules or specials, you can offer a discounted package for the updates. That way, you know that you will have that bit of consistency within your fluctuating routine.

Agencies

When business is slow, you may be tempted to contact an agency for an assignment. Sometimes agencies have good jobs available. But some agency representatives have gotten a bad reputation for exaggerating the number of contracts available or the compensation being offered, so go in with your eyes open. If you have solid programming or networking skills, you will probably fare better at an agency than someone with only limited HTML skills.

Some of the job descriptions call for a totally unrealistic combination of skills. For a three-month contract job, they ask for someone experienced in UNIX, Linux, C++, Java, Oracle, SQL, MySQL, ASP, Networks, TCP/IP, Visual Interdev, VBA, VBScript, ActiveX, ODBC, and more. There are occasional messages in consulting mailing lists about the most absurd of the ads. Of course, if you knew something about everything listed, your knowledge would probably be very superficial. If by some chance you were an expert in everything requested, there would be no way that a company could afford you for a short-term contract anyway.

If you find a contract that seems to fit your location and most of your skills, you may wish to consider it even though you may be weak in some of the requested skills. I am surprised at the number of ads that are filled by someone with limited knowledge combined with the desire to learn. As someone told me, "I don't know too much about Active Server Pages, but if I get the contract, I'll spend the extra few days necessary to train myself." The fact is that if everyone took on only assignments for which they were thoroughly skilled, there would be little professional development. Like most people, I have taken on tasks that required skills that I was lacking—it is called "tutoring by the seat of the pants!" However, be careful that you don't deceive anyone in order to get a contract.

Finding headhunters and contract brokers is not difficult. Finding good ones can be a bit more challenging, though! If you are networking with other Web designers in your area, keep your ears open for recommendations. Go online and check some of the job boards such as www.monster.com or www.dice.com to see which headhunters and contract brokers are most active. The Web site www.realrates.com, hosted by author Janet Ruhl, is a good resource. There are some listings for contracts, although most are for independent contractors with programming/network skills rather than for Web designers. The Web site also has a tips section and an archived message board; you'll get many tips on dealing with agencies, contracts, insurances, taxes, and much more.

Accepting Subcontract Work

One of the best reasons for networking with other local Web designers is to get and give overflow work. Occasionally a colleague will simply refer a client to you and leave it up to you to take care of him from start to finish. I prefer this to acting as a subcontractor handling only part of a job for another designer. I don't need to worry about any conflicts with the other shop since this is now my client. I can charge what I want, do what the client wants (instead of what the other designer thinks the client wants), and reap any word-of-mouth and future spin-off business from this client.

However, usually a Web design shop will subcontract you to help with a time-critical job or some overflow work. Subcontracting with other Web designers can be either a great way to bridge a work gap or a nightmare. Be sure you have a good subcontractors' agreement before doing any work. Otherwise, if the contractor's client is unhappy with the final product, you may be caught up in the dispute—even if your part of the job was perfect. Your contract must make it clear that you are responsible only to the designer. Also spell out how much money you will get, when you will get it, and what rights you have if you are not paid. This is yet another lesson I learned the hard way.

Contracting Subcontracting Work

I once did some subcontract work without an adequate contract. I had subcontracted for this particular Web designer before, without any problems. He called me in a panic about doing some coding for one of his Fortune 500 clients. Rather than taking the time to put everything in writing, we agreed upon my hourly rate and he e-mailed me the work that night. I put aside a couple of my contracts that weren't a rush and both of us worked for almost a week to update his client's Web site. I wasn't satisfied with the caliber of work he was requesting—the pages were compatible only with Netscape (the browser of choice back then)—but he claimed this was what the client wanted. I put the completed work on a protected directory for his approval. As he approved the work, he took my pages, added his finishing touches, and packaged them with his others.

At the end of a hectic week, the contractor submitted the Web pages to the company for approval and payment. The company decided that his layout wasn't satisfactory and refused to pay him. I offered to help the contractor revise the project, even though I hadn't been responsible for the client's dissatisfaction—I had done exactly what the contractor had requested.

The following week, when I billed the designer for the work I had completed, he told me that he couldn't pay me until he got his money from the company that was withholding payment. I diplomatically reminded him that I had worked for him, not his client, and should be paid regardless. He then admitted that he was broke and therefore had no choice but to wait until he got paid, either by the client in question or another.

I knew at this point that because I was working without a contract, I was dependent on the designer's rapidly declining integrity for payment for my work. I could not go to the Fortune 500 company for payment since I didn't have a written contract to protect me.

Protection of my work under copyright laws would not help me since the client hadn't liked the work and thus didn't plan to use it. As a business person, I would have been at a disadvantage if I took the designer to court and tried to plead my case based on a verbal agreement.

I limped away from that experience and learned to never again work for a Web designer without a written contract. Not only had I not been paid for that job, but I also had stalled a couple of my good clients in the process. My philosophy now is that if you want to do some subcontracting work, it is only a subcontracted job if there is a signed contract! Otherwise, it is an offer to do free work with the hope of some payment at the end.

Don't let that experience dissuade you from ever accepting subcontracted work. It hasn't stopped me—I've subcontracted to work for other designers, with great results. It is a good way to pick up tips and build a networking structure while putting some well-needed cash in your pocket. Don't be afraid to call your associates when you are idle to see if they can use an extra pair of hands. Unless they ask you not to call, they probably will appreciate that you took the time to keep in touch.

08

Thriving and Growing with Your Web Design Shop

Once you've mastered all the techniques and technicalities of doing business in and out of your home-based Web design shop, you will still need to work hard to keep your business growing. Even when you think you've struck a good balance of work and income, you must stay focused on ways to promote your business and gain new clients. You will need to experiment to find out what works for your skill level, your region, and your personality. The idea of cold calling potential clients never appealed to me, but you may enjoy that approach.

Here are some common methods for cultivating business, along with my opinions based on my firsthand experience. My successes—and blunders—will give you some guidance for your own decisions.

Traditional Means of Effective Advertising and Promotion

I have never used a Yellow Pages ad as a marketing tool—so many Web designers have told me it's not worth it. The same is true for newspaper advertisements and direct mail campaigns, to a lesser extent. Your experience might be different, though, particularly if you are an Internet service provider as well as a Web designer. If you want to experiment with either type of ad, give it a test run before committing much of your advertising money.

People who are very price conscious and are comparison shopping are the ones most likely to respond to a Yellow Pages ad or newspaper ad. This is one reason I don't use ads in these media to cultivate business. I am not competing against the lowest-priced Web designers; if I were, I couldn't afford to maintain the level of quality that I like to provide.

Another means of advertising is through local Internet service providers (ISPs) and Web hosting companies that don't offer Web design services in-house. I list my design services only with companies whose hosting services

I'm comfortable recommending. If a call comes in from someone who was referred to me by a local ISP, I do not encourage him to switch from that ISP to my hosting services. Poaching those clients for hosting seems unethical. If at any time the client expresses dismay with his local ISP and asks about my hosting services, then I will inform him, but I try to avoid using heavy-handed sales tactics. I don't make a big effort to create or maintain listings with the ISPs, since I've received only two calls that were directly related to a listing I have with one local ISP. One of the callers was doing some long-range planning; after meeting with him I learned that it would be a year or more before he would be ready to hire a designer. (This was several years ago, and that company still hasn't done anything.) The other call turned into a good client. After beginning to work with him, I learned that he contacted about a dozen people on the ISP's referral list. Out of those, only three responded. I was the only one who followed through on his request for a proposal. Even though I won by default, I like to think he got the best of the list anyway! The point here is that just because there are several people on a contact list doesn't mean that several will respond to a request. Try posting your name, and see what happens.

Tip

To find out when a Web page was last modified, create a bookmark or favorite in your browser. Change the name of the bookmark to "SITE UPDATED" and change the bookmark's URL to the following JavaScript code. This will usually pop up a screen telling you the date the site was updated. (If the site creates pages dynamically—for database work, for example—this tip won't work. What you'll get is the current date.)

```
javascript:Slm72UrP='Last%20modified:\
n';if(frames,length>0){for(Wh6ToE4n=0;Wh6ToE4n<frames.
length;Wh6ToE4n++){void(Slm72UrP+='Frame%20'+Wh6T
oE4n+':'+frames[Wh6ToE4n],document.lastModified+'\
n')}};Slm72UrP+='Document:%20'+document.
lastModified;alert(Slm72UrP)
```

If you'd prefer to copy and paste this, go to www.blarneystone.com/designbusiness/notes.htm to get an electronic copy.

Sleuthing for New Business on the Internet

As you look at Web sites on the Internet, keep your eyes out for ones where you feel you could make a major impact. Go beyond sites that are functional but could use some fine-tuning. Look for those Web sites that have sections "under construction" and sites that look like they haven't been updated in years.

Want to see when a site was last updated? A snippet of code (see sidebar) may allow you to find out. If all the pages seem to have been updated today, chances are the site is dynamic, rather than static (a dynamic site is one where the pages are created by the server on the fly vs. a static site which was usually created with HTML one page at a time). If you find a Web page that is two years old but refers to its data as being current, the company may need some help updating the Web site.

If you stumble across a Web site that you weren't able to find listed in any search engines, check the site's source code for META tags. If there aren't any, evaluate the site. If you feel you could improve it, contact the company and ask who makes the decisions about the Web site. Call that person and offer your services for search engine placement and site modification.

If you want to know about the person or studio that set up a Web site, go to a domain name database, such as http://network-tools.com. In the "WHOIS" section it might give you the contact person(s) for the Web site. But be careful about using this information to market your services. It may be the contact information for the site's Webmaster. That individual may not appreciate your trying to take over his job!

If you find a Web site that is outdated and appears to have been abandoned, don't stop at just that one Web site; look for others! If the defunct Web company put a credit line on the Web site, do a search for that credit line on other sites. You may find several Web sites that were abandoned by that design shop. You might become a "knight in shining armor" for those neglected companies.

If you notice that the Web design shop that neglected one site is keeping others updated, be cautious of the company with the outdated site. It could have been abandoned because the head of that company doesn't place much value on an updated Web site. It could also be because that company didn't pay its bills and would be happy to string you along the same way. If you do decide to take over a neglected site, go into it with your eyes open. You don't want to inherit someone else's headache!

Developing a Network of Referrals

When I was starting my Web design business, people told me over and over that the best way to get business is through referrals and networking. This has certainly proven to be true. More than 90 percent of my business comes from referrals and word of mouth.

If a business person wants to have a Web site designed, he has many options. A neighbor, a relative, or a friend may offer to put something together. Designers may contact the business owner, either by phone, email, or by direct mail. There is also an abundance of instructional software, CDs and DVDs, and online resources available to guide a beginner through the design process.

Often by the time I solicit a client, he has turned down many other offers. What can I possibly offer this business person that others have failed to offer? A great Web site? Others have already promised many bells and whistles. A good price? Others have already promised ridiculously low prices. A list of testimonials? Others have created those as well.

This reminds me of the story of the circus ring full of clowns. No matter what you try to do, if you are standing in the same ring as the clowns, you are going to be thought of as one of the clowns. If you stand there in the traditional playwright's garb and recite Shakespeare among the clowns, you will be viewed as a clown reading Shakespeare. If you dress in business attire and explain the theory of nuclear physics while clowns cavort around you, still you will be viewed as a clown. The more serious you try to be, the more ridiculous you will look. The only solution is to get out of the ring and find a better method for communicating your message.

The best way to get the attention of an overwhelmed business owner is to find an advocate, either in that organization or with connections to it. The advocate must be someone with access to the key decision maker. That is what networking can do for you. Without the ability to find the right person to contact, I'm another clown, waving my arms around trying to convince a client that I'm more serious than the others.

Chambers of Commerce

Check out your local chamber of commerce as a potential source of leads. If there are already several Web designers among the members, ask how active these folks are. I wouldn't necessarily recommend joining a group that already has a dozen Web designers vying for referrals.

However, don't be afraid to join a group that has a few Web designers who are less protective of their turf. You may find yourself the one who is most willing to go the extra mile. After a while, you may find your influence with the group growing while the others stay the same or decline.

Social Organizations

All sorts of social groups—from the Rotary club to a local gardening group—may give you business leads. I am not much of a social butterfly, so I can't speak about the range of organizations, and I don't know which are better than others. You should research that and make your own decisions based on your interests and the area where you live.

Evaluate some of the groups to which you currently belong. Do you belong to a church group? What about a Thursday night poker club? A boating club? A computer users' club? If you don't belong to any organizations, it is time to join some. Even if you don't join for social reasons, you should earmark a portion of your business hours for social meetings. Although you probably shouldn't write off your poker club losses, the dues and expenses from certain other organizations may be legitimate tax write-offs if you use those groups to tap into clients.

I mentioned that a computer users' group is a possible resource for networking. However, keep in mind that most people who join a computer users' group do that to develop the resources to do computer work themselves. I belong to a large computer users' group that has a mixture of do-it-yourselfers and computer professionals. Most of the members are willing to tackle projects like designing a Web site by themselves. However, if they realize that a project is more than they can handle, they are willing to call in a professional for help. Since I'm perceived as one of those professionals, I periodically get the call. I'm also contacted by members whose employers need Web help. Once in a while I need to gently remind someone that the help he's requesting is outside the realm of free advice. Usually, though, it's not a problem for people to differentiate between free advice and work.

Business Networking Organizations

There are groups that are specifically organized to network and exchange business leads. Some are based on carefully developed procedures, some on bartering services, and others on simply supplying one another with business leads. Unless you or someone in your Web design shop has strong selling skills, I suggest that you look into some of these groups.

Business Network International (www.bni.com) is a great resource for referrals. This business and professional networking organization has over 5,500 chapters worldwide (sixty just in my state of Connecticut). Depending on your location, you may have several chapters from which to choose.

I learned about this organization through an online mailing list for an HTML writers group. A Web designer from Canada spoke highly of his BNI chapter and recommended the organization for people around the globe. I e-mailed him for more information. He suggested I try a local chapter for six months to a year. (He cautioned that the first two or three months aren't always a good indicator of how the networking group will pan out; it can take a bit of time to spread your message.)

Indeed, for the first few months, I got just a trickle of business from the group. (Of course, the profit from one good contract easily paid for my annual membership dues, which were around $250.) I now have enough firsthand experience with this group that I'm comfortable recommending them and telling you my opinion of them.

Business Network International has a rule that only one person from any profession is allowed in each chapter. For me, this is one of the biggest advantages of the organization. If you join a chapter, you will have no competition in your group to dilute or scramble your message. You have the opportunity to demonstrate to your group why they should recommend your services over anyone else's.

The chapter I belong to (www.ctbusinessnetworkers.com) has a great mixture of business people, including a financial advisor, a banker, an insurance agent, a realtor, a business lawyer, and a printer. I have the opportunity to give my sales pitch directly to these professionals, many of whom interact with potential clients of mine each day. I also get to find out about their businesses so I can refer clients to them. (There's no better way to get someone's attention than to refer business to him or her.)

How Business Networking Works

Here is how it works. Each chapter has a weekly meeting day and time. You must be willing to commit to showing up every week for meetings. (Combine that with the fact that most meetings occur at 7 a.m., and you have the biggest drawback to the organization!)

Take note: There are some relief valves in place to make that requirement manageable. If you can't make it to a meeting, you are allowed to find someone else to fill in for you. If you have a helper, relative, or other person who will tell everyone how wonderful you are, recruit him or her as a backup. Otherwise, most chapters have a list of substitutes who are on call and eager to sit in for you. If you do miss three meetings within a six-month period without having a substitute, you can be ousted from your coveted seat in the group.

Once you get past the shock of early rising and make the commitment to attend every meeting, the rest isn't too bad. At the beginning of each meeting, we go around the room and each person gives a sixty-second "infomercial" or request for business. For the first few meetings, I just told a bit about myself as a Web designer and asked members to contact me if they knew anyone who needed a Web designer.

After a while, I learned that, although a general plea can work, that sixty-second time slot was an ideal time to ask the group for specific requests. There are about thirty people in our chapter, most of whom have connections all over the region. I target a company I'd like to work for and use a portion of my sixty seconds to ask if any member has a contact within that organization.

The first time I tried asking for a specific connection, I had targeted a local candy company whose Web site was poorly put together and woefully outdated. I knew that I could help them if they were receptive. I asked at a chapter meeting if anyone had a connection with the organization. I discovered that one of our members made weekly deliveries to the company and was in regular contact with the owner. The ending wasn't that exciting, since the owner explained that a close friend was taking care of the Web site and they were very happy with the status quo. (This was in spite of my attempts to show the flaws in the Web site.) But at least I was able to talk with the owner and didn't have to spend any more time pursuing that client.

Training Your Networking Group/Sales Staff

That weekly sixty-second slot is an opportunity to stand in front of my own thirty-person "sales staff" and give them something of substance to help me with. If I train them properly (see following paragraphs) about what to look for as they go about their business, I will get sales out of it. If I am not specific and just tell them to contact me if they come across someone needing a Web site, they may or may not think of it. This group is not simply a huge funnel waiting to direct business my way. Rather, it is a tool that is capable of generating real profits for me if I take the time to sharpen and use it properly.

After the sixty-second sales pitches, we take a few minutes for business details and networking over coffee. Then the group listens to short presentations by two members (one five minutes long and the other, ten). Members give presentations on a rotating basis. This is an opportunity to learn a bit more about various members and their businesses.

When it is my turn to give a short or long presentation, I use it to sharpen the skills of my "sales staff." I tell them what makes my services better than those of other Web designers. I give them tips on how to distinguish potential clients from people simply looking for some free advice. And I instruct them on what to watch for in their travels.

For example, if a member is in an office and the receptionist is giving someone elaborate directions, that may be a good opportunity to ask if the company has directions on its Web site. This might trigger a conversation about their outdated Web site or the one that someone started and never finished. The receptionist might even mention that her boss has been trying to find a dependable person to design or update the site. That little tip that I gave my group might get me in the door to solve a very specific need for a new client.

If you are interested in joining Business Network International, attend a couple of meetings as a guest. This will give you a feel for the people you would be linking up with. This is important because if you join, you will be spending a lot of time with these people.

Picking a Networking Group

There are a couple of details to look out for in the meetings since—in spite of the organization rules—each chapter is a bit different. See if the group is clearly and enthusiastically gathering to exchange business referrals. If you get the feeling that it is simply an early morning coffee klatch, it may not be the right group for you. If you attend a meeting and no one asks you what your business is, you may want to look at other groups. The personality of the group is also an important factor for me. If I'm going to get up at the crack of dawn, I don't want to sit in a meeting with a bunch of dull, sleepy people—I want to conduct business, laugh, share information that can help others, and get some business in return. I was lucky that the first group I looked at easily met all of my criteria. Maybe you will also find such a group. Think of it as interviewing to hire a part-time staff of sales people— if they seem to be eager to help you in exchange for your helping them, hire them!

Online Marketing

Since I'm a Web designer, people seem to expect that the majority of my business originates from my Web site. They are surprised to discover this isn't the case. Don't expect to sit back and watch the orders pour in from your Web site. In fact, if you are telling your clients to expect that to happen with their own Web sites, you may not be treating them honestly. Even the largest Web sites must use additional methods to promote their business. Some use TV, newspapers, and other people's Web sites. Some use word of mouth.

This is an important point, so let me restate it: Your Web site, even with the best search engine rankings, probably will not generate the majority of your business. Now that we have that understanding, let's look at why I have a Web site and why you should, too. Validation! I can have the best Web design shop around, but if I don't have a Web site or I have a poor one, my business will probably not be viewed as a valid business. TV commercials usually are not designed to give you a lot of information about a product. Yet, when we see a product's ads frequently, there is an unspoken validation. Have you ever heard someone say, "I see their ads all the time," as if that means something? A Web site can work the same way to validate a company.

Here's an example of how it works. I once redesigned a Web site for an office complex in Hartford, Connecticut. After the Web site went live, the owner/general manager began to actively use it as a selling tool. He works it into conversation every time someone calls or comes in to look for office space or rent a conference room. He'll say, "If you need directions here, go to the map and directions section of our Web site" or "You can see a picture of that conference room on our Web site" or "There's a price sheet for those services on our Web site." He doesn't say that because he dislikes giving the directions over the phone or can't quote a price off the top of his head. He does it because he knows that when potential customers go to his Web site, if they are interested, they will look around a bit to learn more about his facilities and services. They are no longer talking to some stranger about some potential dump. They can now see his picture and his staff's pictures, along with photos and details about the offices and services. Suddenly the entire operation has some validity to it.

This owner loves to tell a story about a time when he was on the phone with a potential client and mentioned the Web site. He could tell that the person on the other end was looking up his Web site while they talked. He said that once the person had a chance to look at the building and some offices on the Web site, the conversation was no longer made up of wary questions. It suddenly became very easy to set up an appointment for a showing.

This owner's listings are very strong in the various search engines, a situation that does drive traffic to his Web site. Some people will inquire about his offices after finding the Web site. However, if he sat by and waited for people to fill out the contact form, he would have an empty building. Instead, he uses the Web site as one of many means of getting people beyond their initial indecision. He puts his Web address in his Yellow Pages ad. He puts it on his business cards and letterhead.

Informational Web Sites

As a culture, we have been programmed not to ask too many questions, especially those that may lead to stressful interaction. Your Web site can show potential customers the particulars they are uncomfortable asking about. Try to figure out what will attract your clients to you—what bit of information or image will resolve their reluctance. Your Web site should exist as a way for people to get more information about you or your work. It might be embarrassing for a friend—who should already know—to ask me what I do for a living (something about the Internet?), but he can go to my Web site and get enough information to refer me to others.

Your Web site should be a strong representation of the type of work you do. A couple of years ago I told a client that his Web site should be targeted to his market and should achieve very clearly defined goals. He didn't understand and he asked me to use my site to illustrate my point. I suddenly realized that my own Web site was inadequate! I wanted my Web site to introduce me to people and give background, yet it was based on a template from other sites and barely indicated that I design Web sites. I mumbled my way through that experience, then revamped my Web site to fulfill my own expectations.

Here's a summary of the goals I want my Web site to accomplish.

- The site should introduce my business and give some background and history.
- It should introduce me and give some of the details that people might want to know but won't ask. Visitors can learn that I give seminars and lectures periodically, and they can find out about my professional background. There's also a link to my personal site, so people can learn more about my interests.

- The site should contain a page with some of the long-winded technical elements that are included in my hosting packages. I can't remember everything, nor do I expect my clients to, so the details are there for them when and if they need those specifics.
- The site should give an idea of my rates. It is difficult to nail down prices on design, since projects vary greatly. But I can at least give some ranges, which is helpful for people who are concerned about getting in over their heads.
- Finally and most importantly, the site should give the viewer an opportunity to read some testimonials and view links to some of the other Web sites I've created.

Daniel Wedeking, owner of Electronic Surfer Website Maintenance, Inc., offers a commonsense idea for gathering testimonials for your Web site. Daniel suggests:

> If a person writes you a letter saying what a fine job you've done with his project, why don't you just ask him if you can post it on your page? If you don't, you could be losing out on a great opportunity to re-enforce your relationship with your customer. Give him a call, ask him how everything is going and say "oh, by the way, do you mind if I put that letter you wrote me on my Web site?" Not only will you make him feel a part of your team, but also you might get a little extra traffic from his friends and family who will want to see your customer's name online.

Once I started treating my business's Web site as I would a client Web site, it became an effective tool. It accomplishes what I want it to, rather than merely being a static declaration that I'm in business. It portrays an image—friendly yet professional. Treat yourself like a client and find out what image and goals you want for your Web site. Then create the site to meet those goals.

Social Networking

Even though social networking may seem to be a recent phenomenon, it goes back in Internet years to its infancy with online communities such as The Well, which was started in 1985 as a dial-up bulletin board system (BBS). Social networking is, as it sounds, a network or community of people sharing similar interests.

Some of the popular general social networking sites include Facebook, Twitter, MySpace, and LinkedIn. Depending on what Web site you are working on, you may find some smaller networking sites that are more targeted to your client's needs since there are social networks for a wide variety of interests. So whether you are working on a medical site, an educational site, or some other, you can help your client by finding those related sites and then encouraging him to become an active participant.

For your own Web site, you may want to have a presence on LinkedIn and Facebook and others. If you enjoy creating Web sites for musicians, you will want to have a second Web site on MySpace as many musicians gravitate to that one. Set up an account on Twitter and periodically go out and search your town and explore a bit to see what others are discussing. At first it may seem to be very nebulous but after using it for a while you will discover pockets of information of interest to you. Think of what a hero you can be to one of your clients if you match him up with someone looking for his services.

Trade Shows and Home Shows

In establishing a niche market for your business, you can make your hobbies pay off. Whether you are interested in collecting coins or trading Barbie dolls, or enjoy fixing up your home, there are probably some shows and meetings that you can attend. In our area there are home shows, boat shows, flower shows, camping shows, business shows, job shows, and plenty more to choose from.

My wife and I enjoy attending the local home shows. There are several of them within driving distance of us. It costs us $10 each plus a couple of dollars for parking. Before the show, I do my homework. The local newspaper publishes a list of the vendors that will be at the show, and the show promoters display the list on their Web site. I go through and check each of the local companies to see what its Web site looks like. If I can't find one, I make a note of it. If one looks outdated, I note that the company may be delighted to meet someone willing to help. It is important to find out what days and times are the lulls. That is when I like to see the show. I take my business cards with me, and my laptop with several examples of Web sites I've done.

If I'm interested in a vendor's product, I get a conversation going about that. Otherwise, I don't go in under false pretenses. I mention that I design Web sites and hand the vendor a card. If someone shrugs me off, I don't push. There are always plenty of others. If a vendor is eager to talk, I make sure I don't interfere with his sales job. He isn't there to buy from me, so I stay alert to his wishes. Most of the time, we chat for a while and then he wants me to contact him a couple of weeks after the show. Sometimes he is happy to stand around and talk to anyone. Either way, I try to establish whether he is a potential client while he is getting a feel for how it would be to work with me.

These people are willing to pay to promote their business (otherwise they wouldn't be attending the show). They are looking for new business and are frequently interested in learning more about opportunities on the Internet. A direct mailing will cost them thousands of dollars for a one-time impact.

This is your opportunity to attract some new business. If you line up some new clients, the few dollars you spent attending the show was a deal! If you don't get any new business from a show, hopefully you've had a fun time walking around looking at the latest products. The benefit to repeat visits is that once you've lined up a couple of vendors as your clients it is much easier to sell to others. Just mention that you have done a Web site for the vendor the next aisle down and watch the interest level increase.

How to Know It Is Time to Grow

One of the pitfalls of a small business can be the temptation to grow into a large business too quickly. The fallacy is in thinking that if you can make some money with the business you have, all you need to do to make ten times as much money is get ten times as much business! Most owners of large Web design shops long for the days when they didn't have the headaches and responsibilities that come with expansion. They wish that they could get a Web contract and work on it from start to finish themselves. The cliché about the grass being greener on the other side is very true with Web designers looking at how big their shop should be.

A natural pattern of growth can benefit your business and pay you dividends if done in a sensible and methodical way. As your client list becomes longer and people are waiting for you to serve them, it may be time to consider growing a bit to accommodate them. If you prefer the administrative tasks required to operate your business more than the hands-on design work, and you have access to others who want to handle the design work, this may also be a time to look at growing to another level.

I have owned enough businesses to be painfully aware that the temptation to expand should only be undertaken after much study, worry, and deep contemplation.

Ask yourself many questions before embarking on an expansion.

- Are you growing so that you can start making a profit? If you can't make a profit now, most likely you will find yourself owning a larger business that can't make a profit either.
- Are you growing because you like to be in charge or like to be the boss? Most business owners will agree that when you work for yourself, you are "in charge." As you get more people working for you, you relinquish some of that control. The employees are the ones who make the decisions, they are the ones who interact with your clients, and eventually you will realize that they are the ones in charge. You do have the ability to influence them—and threaten them with dismissal if necessary—but unless you are micromanaging them, you are no longer exclusively in charge.
- Are you growing because you want to design more Web sites or write more scripts? As a business owner, you have many responsibilities. As a business owner of a larger company, you will have even more to be responsible for and will likely need to bring in help to complete your tasks.

If you decide to grow beyond a small Web design shop, be sure to include David Siegel's *Secrets of Successful Web Sites: Project Management on the World Wide Web* in your library. Read it from cover to cover, and take special notice of the section that describes Web design businesses of varying sizes. Siegel has a great way of clarifying the issues faced by Web design shops of different sizes.

How to Keep Up with Ever-Changing Technology

Keeping up with the growth of the Internet and Web design is a major part of your job. You need to read and learn constantly to serve your clients well. Here are some of my favorite resources for keeping up with the latest in technology.

Online Resources

Since these are online resources, they aren't guaranteed to always be there. But since most have been around for a while, you can expect they will continue to be available.

www.internet.com

For information on the Internet, www.internet.com is one of the most useful sites I've found. This Web site gives you links to many other sites for Web designers. Just click on the Web developer link for access to WebReference; there you'll find statistics, JavaScript code, jobs for developers, and much more.

www.webmonkey.com, www.webdeveloper.com, www.alistapart.com, and www.communitymx.com

Each of these sites has excellent information for Web designers. Whether you are looking for a tutorial for your favorite graphics program or some programming tips, these Web sites are reliable and informative.

www.projectseven.com

This site is run by a team of Web professionals. Their books and information are excellent. Although the site tends to be Dreamweaver-centric, it also has tutorials and articles applicable to all Web designers. The PVII Web site can help you break out of your rut.

www.w3.org

The World Wide Web Consortium was created in 1994 to develop common protocols for the World Wide Web. For the most part, W3C is vendor-neutral—meaning that they try to stay out of the conflicts between Firefox, Netscape, Internet Explorer, Chrome, and others. If you want your Web site code to be up to standard, the W3C is the standard. There is also a very popular code validator on this Web site. I recommend using it to see how well your code will work with various browsers.

www.wilsonweb.com

Ralph F. Wilson has a Web site that is a treasure chest of useful information on Web marketing and specifically e-commerce. There are thousands of useful, searchable articles and statistics that can be used to help in selling a client on setting up an e-commerce Web site or strengthening a weak one. Wilson has a subscription newsletter and periodically e-mailed list of links to current events and trends. At the time of this writing it cost $50 for a year for everything, but you can also get a lot of free information from this Web site by spending some time looking through the offerings for the freebies. Wilson has evaluations of everything from shopping carts to gateways to promotional tools.

Trade Publications, Books, and Periodicals

There are very few trade publications that Web designers can have mailed to them. I've found several that have come and gone lately. I used to subscribe to a few, but as they closed up shop, I've found it to be just as helpful to bookmark useful Web sites such as www.internet.com that have been around for a while and have a variety of information sources.

You can obtain several books that can help you along the way. One of the most powerful general idea books I've read is *Don't Make Me Think: A Common Sense Approach to Web Usability*, by Steve Krug. This is a small book, easy to read, and interspersed with humor, but the message is very clear: Visitors to your Web site are not there to think or to admire your talents. They are there to get a fax number, or to buy a widget, or to look at an article, or to find out something about your company. If you can't give them what they want without making them ponder which link to use or what page to go to, they may start to think. If they think, they might think it is easier to go elsewhere. Or they may think that they really don't need that widget after all. Often Web sites are designed to be beautiful at the expense of functionality. This book should help you design great Web sites that give visitors what they want, without them even thinking about it.

A book that gives you a great overview of what your client should have is *Webi-fiable* by Tim Priebe. This book was written for someone looking to hire a Web designer. It outlines many of the questions that your client may be asking you. If they don't know what those questions are, this book will give you the jump on it.

Another good book for Web designs is *Creating Cool Web Sites* by Dave Taylor. Dave says, "Cool pages aren't enough . . . Whether you're building a sophisticated commercial Web site or just creating an online spot to call home, good Web site development is about a lot more than just HTML nowadays." His book reflects that philosophy. This book starts with "What Is the Web Anyway?" and walks you through an extensive course on how to design Web sites that are not just cool but also professional.

Dave Taylor also wrote *The Complete Idiot's Guide to Growing Your Business with Google* (www.findability.info). When I read it, I thought it would be the usual book on improving my Web site's position with the search engines. I've done enough of that to know whether someone knows what they are talking about. I was surprised to find that Dave did an end run around the topic. This book is packed with solid information about planning and marketing a business. It is an easy-reading book about how to build your business and how to use that knowledge to build your client's business. And he does manage to work a lot about search engines into his book as well. Does he know what he's talking about? I did the acid test; I typed his name in Google. Out of two-hundred million listings, Dave Taylor was in the top three. Is it magic? Sneaky tricks? No, Dave has an extensive Web site of information called "Ask Dave Taylor" (www.askdavetaylor.com) in which he plies his skills. His book is a great book for beginners and advanced Web designers alike.

A good textbook that helps many Web designers in creating style sheets is *Cascading Style Sheets: The Definitive Guide* by Eric A. Meyer, considered by many to be the CSS guru. This book is not the most current one out there, but for someone starting out and wanting to unravel the mysteries surrounding CSS, this is still the best reference book available. *Eric Meyer on CSS* and *More Eric Meyer on CSS* are his more recent books, but unless you already have a good foundation on style sheets, those might be more in-depth than you want. They are, however, great follow-up books once you feel comfortable with the basics from his *Definitive Guide*.

If you care about design and style in your Web sites, be sure to pick up a copy of Patrick J. Lynch and Sarah Horton's great *Web Style Guide*. This is not an entertaining book for reviewing at your local library's book club meeting. It is a textbook, a manual, and a very focused how-to guide for Web site style. Read it through to get some ideas on how a Web site should be put together. Then keep it on hand as a great reference tool for design ideas. The focus is on Web sites for non-profits and other organizations rather than business but the level of detail will give you plenty of new ideas. This is not a coding book or a programming book; it's a book that looks at a Web site as a complete unit. Lynch has a very strong design background; he worked for many years as design director at Yale University School of Medicine.

Organizations

Check to see if there is a computer users' group in your area. If so, go to some meetings and get involved in the organization. If it helps you get more business, great! If you find that you are giving out free advice and getting little business in return—as is the case with the group I belong to—stay active. These groups need the support of people with computer expertise and will appreciate whatever you can offer. I feel that the local community supports my business and this is one of the ways that I can support the community in return. If I get some business benefit, it's a bonus—I don't depend on my local computer users' group for business. A fringe benefit is that if you are active in the organization, it can occasionally help sway a potential client who is undecided about whether to hire you.

www.iwanet.org

The International Webmasters Association (IWA) is an international organization for Web designers. If you do nothing else, read its Standards of Professional Practices (search the site for "Standards of Professional Practices") and try to shape your business after those principles.

The organization is a good one, with benefits including a members-only discussion group and mailing list, an electronic magazine, job postings, certification programs, a calendar of events, and much more. You can get a trial membership to see if the organization meets your needs.

www.graphicartistsguild.org

The Graphic Artists Guild is an organization that gives graphic artists a central clearinghouse for information and discussion. If your Web design shop focuses more on graphics than programming, this might be a good organization for you to join. It is a good resource for any Web design shop owner—check out the Guild's popular handbook *Pricing and Ethical Guidelines,* and look at its contract analysis and other information relevant to the field.

http://webprofessionals.org

The World Organization of Webmasters (WOW) is also a high-profile educational provider for Web designers. The WOW Web site has useful information and a scale of memberships for students up to professionals and corporations.

Mission and Vision Statements

My mission is to operate XYZ Web Design Shop in such a way as to provide high-quality, Web-related services to small and midsize businesses in a professional manner. My business will be focused on offering one-stop shopping for clients looking for quality Internet services at a fair cost.

My vision for XYZ Web Design Shop is to design and be responsible for eighty to one hundred commercial Web sites. I will add value to—and resell services of—the best commercial servers that are available for small business use. I will contract with an average of three new clients per month as well as provide maintenance service to existing clients at the rate of thirty billable hours per month. I will have access to two or three good sub-contractors, who have strengths in programming, database, and server skills and whom I can call on to help with jobs as necessary.

Personal Evaluation

I am highly proficient in business organization and in layout and design of Web sites. I enjoy discussing business needs with clients. I do not have the desire to create scripts for Web sites much beyond pasting preexisting ones and tweaking them.

I have worked for ABC Corporation at their computer help desk for ten years and have spent the past three years helping them to update and maintain their Web site. I have also worked with various departments training their Web developers in design and layout of a commercial Web site. Prior to my employment at ABC, I worked for seven years for ABBA Manufacturing Company. ABBA has been a manufacturing firm in business since 1898. They are becoming aggressive in marketing to gain more overseas accounts. I have begun discussions with them about their Web site needs.

I moonlighted by creating Web sites for a few small businesses and have done extensive work with a local ballet troupe to create an interactive Web site, which will help them coordinate their events while traveling.

Services and Products

XYZ Web Design Shop will design Web sites and offer to upgrade ones that are outdated. I will also offer a top-grade Web hosting package for clients. Until I get enough clients, I will offer classroom-training events related to the Internet to augment my income and to gain more exposure. Package deals will be available to clients who have frequent update needs, and for those who have irregular Web site maintenance and update work, I will bill on an hourly basis. I will also offer to register domain names for clients, but because the profit margin in doing this is so small, this will be more of a service than a moneymaker.

Business Niche or Image

XYZ Web Design Shop will try to focus on the Internet needs of small businesses. XYZ will offer one-on-one consultations and extensive handholding. It will not focus on the price-sensitive client as much as the client who wants to get extra attention in exchange for a product she is happy with as well as a fair Web design rate. XYZ Web Design Shop will put an emphasis on community involvement and activities. It will also conduct public seminars to raise the awareness of small business owners who may otherwise be overwhelmed by the confusion surrounding the Internet. I will position XYZ Web Design Shop to be a general Internet clearinghouse for information and issues.

What Type of Business?

For the first year of its existence, XYZ Web Design Shop will be a sole proprietor. After that time, I will be able to afford to have an attorney and accountant help me turn it into an LLC. After ten years, it may be reasonable to convert it to a corporation. At that time I would begin to turn the business over to someone else and it would make it easier to sell shares to the person taking it over.

Location of Business

I will establish my office in the basement of my home. It will be centrally located so my clients can come to meetings or consultations (or I can meet them at their offices if they prefer). My basement has a separate entrance leading to the driveway, and I will have a sign pointing to the office.

Employees and Support Staff

XYZ will have no employees. An attorney and accountant will work for XYZ on an hourly basis as needed. I have a neighbor who does bookkeeping who will do my books once a week and I will pay her as a subcontractor. I will also subcontract any overflow business as needed. A member of the Small Business Association's SCORE (Service Corps of Retired Executives) will work with me during my start-up period as a nonpaid advisor and consultant. My brother-in-law will help on the sales front on a subcontract basis, and he will only be paid for signed contracts.

Competitors

The competition in my area is mostly from two large firms with staff Web designers. These businesses are seeking contracts from larger companies that need extensive Web sites that are highly interactive. They will not be attracted to my niche market of smaller businesses with limited funds and undefined needs.

My other competition consists of the numerous individuals who design Web sites on a freelance basis for small companies. Their main selling point is that they charge much less and usually know the owner of the company through some common connection such as a social group.

My main pitch to the small businesses will be that Web design is my livelihood, so I will be available any time they need changes or updates. I have better tools and software than the average moonlighting designer and can give them the features that they request. In addition, as a business owner and someone who works with other business owners, I know how to create a Web site that will generate interest for their customers rather than a simplistic Web site containing basic information.

Advertising and Marketing Plans

XYZ Web Design Shop will be primarily marketed through word-of-mouth resources. I will join my local chamber of commerce and a couple of networking groups in my area. In addition, I will continue to provide computer training at my local high school's adult education program.

I will also try to join a local bartering group to help me get started. Even though I may not get much cash from these clients, I can use the portfolio I create and hopefully the good words and satisfaction of these clients will result in recommendations to paying clients.

I will not buy any Yellow Page ads or newspaper ads, as the other Web designers in my area have not had any success with them. However, I will post my company's information with three local ISPs to see if I generate any clients through them.

I will use my current portfolio to show my work, but I want to obtain a couple of new, high-profile organizations to boost my portfolio.

My marketing focus will be on midsize manufacturing firms. Since I worked with a manufacturing firm for seven years, I feel that I know enough about this industry to help improve a company's sales through strong Web sites. I also plan to attend the Manufacturers and Metal Designers (MMD) convention and meeting, and will try to present my portfolio to as many business owners as I can.

Once I get my first manufacturing client, I will offer a rebate for other clients that my first satisfied customer refers. As my manufacturing clients get new business, I will request written testimonials to use when approaching others.

In addition to Web site design, XYZ plans to offer high-speed hosting. Since many of the targeted clients are manufacturing firms needing an online catalog, XYZ will offer high-volume database services as well.

Timelines

At the end of the first year of business, XYZ Web Design Shop should have twenty to thirty steady clients. The business should be self-supporting in addition to offering me an income of $30,000.

By the end of the second year, XYZ Web Design Shop should have one hundred clients and I should have an income of $60,000.

By the end of the fifth year, XYZ Web Design Shop should be maintaining 100 to 150 clients. My income level should be between $75,000 and $100,000 per year.

After ten years, I want to be able to find a dependable person who is interested in taking over the business. I don't want to have a larger Web company acquire my business, but rather I would like to see an individual gradually work his or her way into it over a few years. I want someone who will share the same level of concern and responsibility for my clients that I have.

At fifteen years, I want to be retired and have someone else running XYZ Web Design Shop.

Finances

I will start out by charging clients $45 per hour. I base this rate on what I was getting paid at my previous help desk job, plus I factor in taxes, insurance, and benefits that I will lose by leaving my employer. My calculations indicate that I should actually get $55 per hour, but I found out that another local Web designer (from whom I may try to get jobs) is getting $50 per hour, so I want to start out at a lower rate. Once I establish a good reputation, I will increase my rates for new clients at $5 per hour increments until I reach the rate that I want.

In the beginning, I will ask for approximately $400 for designing a small Web site. After I've developed my portfolio and have gained more skills, I will charge an average of $600 for a Web site. If there is extensive database work, the charge will be about $1,500. I will charge $40 per month to host a Web site unless it is a high-volume database server; in this case the charge will be $120 per month. My gross profit will be approximately 25 percent of the hosting fees.

I have about $15,000 in my savings account and this is more money than I will need for start-up expenses. I am willing to use up to two-thirds of this account to help get my business going. Also, if I don't reach my income goal by the third month of business, my savings will supplement my lagging income. If my savings account dips down to $5,000, however, I will close XYZ and get a job either as a help desk associate for the company I am leaving or, if that isn't feasible, I will take other jobs as needed to restore my savings account.

As an alternative to shutting down my Web design business, I will contact head-hunters to inquire about contract assignments. If there is a match, it will help me bridge my income until I can get a steady supply of Web site clients through my own business.

My two primary expenses will be for Web hosting (I will offset this by reselling it) and for various communication services, including a cell phone, two phone lines, and my ISP fees. My Web hosting bill will come each quarter. After the first quarter, I expect to have at least seven hosting clients whom I can bill to cover the cost of the first server. The server costs will grow in proportion to the number of clients I am hosting. This makes my hosting costs, beyond the first server, a variable cost. All of my communication bills are fixed expenses—in other words, they will occur whether I have no clients or numerous clients.

Start-Up Costs

Equipment is absolutely necessary. Here is a list of the items I need and the price I will need to pay for them.

Item	Price
Laptop computer	$2,240
Ink jet printer	$100
Scanner (I have one)	$0
Read/write CD-DVD	$80
Digital camera (with a rechargeable battery and 20 megs of memory)	$240
Cell phone	$125
Professional fees (attorney/accountant)	$1,200
Insurance (liability, property, etc.)	$400
Software (graphics, design)	$2,000
Printing (business cards, letterhead)	$45
Set up Web server space	$290
Phone line installation (two lines)	$150
Office furniture	$370
Office supplies (diskettes, pens, staplers, etc.)	$100
Starting advertising	$0
Licenses/permits	$35
Total	**$7,375**

Operating Profit and Loss

As shown in my Profit and Loss Statement, the business will sustain a loss for the first six months. After that time, it will begin to make a profit. There will be enough funds in my business bank account to cover the period during which XYZ Web Design Shop is operating at a loss.

Insurance

I will obtain liability insurance with a home office rider. I won't take out errors and omissions insurance unless my Web business begins to have substantially more activity in e-commerce sales than is currently indicated. (Errors and omissions insurance protects me from such things as a lawsuit that could be filed against XYZ for a scripting mistake that costs a client thousands of dollars in lost revenue.) Unless I expand into the e-commerce area, the Web sites that I create won't have that much risk. I will also get a rider on my homeowner's policy that will cover my automobile in the event of an accident while doing business for XYZ.

Accounting

My neighbor, a bookkeeper, will maintain my books and review them on a weekly basis. I will also work with the advice of my CPA firm [accounting firm name]. The CPA firm will do the quarterly and year-end tax reports. The firm will also monitor the business to offer advice during the first year's start-up and growth period.

Banking

XYZ Web Design Shop will bank with [bank name]. I have had my personal accounts with this bank and feel I have developed a good relationship with them.

Profit and Loss Statement

Income	Month 1	Month 2	Month 3	Month 4	Month 5
Web sites designed (quantity)	3	3	4	4	5
Web sites designed ($)	1200	1,200	1,600	2,000	2,500
Web sites hosted (quantity)	0	3	7	10	15
Web sites hosted ($)	—	120	280	400	600
Total Income:	**1,200**	**1,320**	**1,880**	**2,400**	**3,100**

Expenses	Month 1	Month 2	Month 3	Month 4	Month 5
Office	0	0	0	0	0
Advertising	0	0	0	0	0
Web server space	195	0	0	0	195
Online connection	20	20	20	20	20
Phone service	45	45	45	45	45
Long distance	15	25	25	10	15
Cell phone	40	40	40	40	40
Electronic and other utilities	15	15	15	15	15
Automobile expenses and parking	25	15	15	25	25
Insurance	115	0	0	0	65
Magazines and periodicals	35	0	0	0	0
Bookkeeping/accounting	215	15	15	35	15
Printing and postage	15	15	15	15	15
Salary	2,500	2,500	2,500	2,500	2,500
Health insurance	0	0	0	0	0
Personal income tax, FICA, etc.	875	875	875	875	875
Total monthly expenses:	**4,110**	**3,565**	**3,565**	**3,580**	**3,825**

	Month 1	Month 2	Month 3	Month 4	Month 5
Profit/Loss	**(2,910)**	**(2,245)**	**(1,685)**	**(1,180)**	**(725)**

Month 6	Month 7	Month 8	Month 9	Month 10	Month 11	Month 12	Total
5	6	6	7	7	8	8	66
2,500	3,600	3,600	4,200	4,200	4,800	4,800	36,200
20	25	30	37	42	50	58	58
800	1,000	1,200	1,480	1,680	2,000	2,320	11,880
3,300	4,600	4,800	5,680	5,880	6,800	7,120	48,080

Month 6	Month 7	Month 8	Month 9	Month 10	Month 11	Month 12	Total
0	0	0	0	0	0	0	0
0	0	0	0	0	0	0	0
0	0	0	195	0	0	0	585
20	20	20	20	20	20	20	240
45	45	45	45	45	45	45	540
15	25	25	25	10	15	15	220
40	40	40	40	40	40	40	480
15	15	15	15	15	15	15	180
25	15	15	15	25	25	25	250
0	0	0	0	0	65	0	245
0	0	0	0	0	0	0	35
15	15	15	15	35	15	15	420
15	15	15	15	15	15	15	180
2,500	2,500	2,500	2,500	2,500	2,500	2,500	30,000
0	0	0	0	0	0	0	0
875	875	875	875	875	875	875	10,500
3,565	3,565	3,656	3,760	3,580	3,630	3,565	43,875
(265)	1,035	1,235	1,920	2,300	3,170	3,555	4,205

Appendix B:
Contract for a
Web Design Business

Contact Information:

Contact name: _____

Phone: _____

Fax: _____

Company/client: _____

Address: _____

E-mail address: _____

Web Site Information:

Present WWW URL (if any): _____

New domain name(s) requested (if applicable): _____

Other choices if first choice not available: _____

1. Definition of Terms.

XYZ WEB DESIGN SHOP: XYZ Web Design Shop, LLC, a Limited Liability Corporation, located at 246 XYZ Drive, Hartford, CT 06555

CLIENT: _____

ISP: XYZ Web Design Shop, LLC

CONTRACT: This agreement and its attachment(s) as listed below.

ATTACHMENT(s): "Web Site Design Worksheet" and "Payment Schedule"

2. Authorization.

The above named CLIENT is engaging XYZ WEB DESIGN SHOP as an independent contractor for the specific project of developing and/or improving a World Wide Web site to be installed on the CLIENT's Web space located on an ISP's computer. The CLIENT hereby authorizes XYZ WEB DESIGN SHOP to access this ISP account, and authorizes the ISP to provide XYZ WEB DESIGN SHOP with any necessary "write permission" for the CLIENT's Web page directory, cgi-bin directory, and any other directories or programs that need to be accessed for this project. The CLIENT also authorizes XYZ WEB DESIGN SHOP to publicize its completed Web site to Web search engines, as well as other Web directories and indexes.

3. Warranties.

XYZ WEB DESIGN SHOP represents and warrants to the CLIENT that it has the experience and ability to perform the services required by this CONTRACT; that it will perform said services in a professional, competent, and timely manner; that it has the power to enter into and perform this CONTRACT; and that its performance of this CONTRACT shall not infringe upon or violate the rights of any third party or violate any federal, state, and municipal laws. However, CLIENT will not determine or exercise control as to general procedures or formats necessary to have these services meet CLIENT's satisfaction.

The CLIENT represents and warrants to XYZ WEB DESIGN SHOP that it will provide CLIENT materials as required in a professional, competent, and timely manner; that it has the power to enter into this Agreement on behalf of CLIENT; and that its performance of this CONTRACT shall not infringe upon or violate the rights of any third party or violate any federal, state, and municipal laws.

4. Standard Web Site Products and Web Site Hosting Services.

The standard **Web site development** as defined through XYZ WEB DESIGN SHOP is as follows:

- E-mail/phone consultation. (Initial planning/development consultation is free.)
- Up to two hours total general Internet orientation, education, marketing strategy, and Web design consultation. Telephone long-distance charges are in addition to rates quoted. Additional education and consultation is at our hourly rate of $xxx.
- Up to six Web pages—for example, a home page, map and directions page, about us page, contact page, products page, and products detail page.
- Text. Final text shall be supplied by the CLIENT. (250 words per Web page approximate maximum and supplied in electronic format. Web pages with more than 1,500 words of text may be subject to additional fees for increased formatting time.)
- Links. Up to an average of five external links per page, and an e-mail response link on each Web page to any e-mail address the CLIENT designates.
- Custom graphics. Company logo or other top-of-page graphic, bullets, lines, colored or textured background, as well as five photos or graphics per page are included. Beyond the five photos or graphics per page, an extra charge will apply for scanning services, photography, and graphic design and modification.
- Installation of Web pages on the CLIENT's ISP host computer.
- A maximum of two revisions to the draft Web site will be included at no extra cost to create the look and feel that is desired. Further revisions will be billed at the normal hourly rate of $xxx.
- Minor updates and changes to existing Web pages for two weeks from completion of Web site (includes up to a half-hour per page total, subject to the limits outlined below).
- Initial registration to the top search engines offering free listings, such as Google, and Yahoo!. The top search engines will be determined by XYZ WEB DESIGN SHOP. At no time does XYZ WEB DESIGN SHOP promise or imply that we guarantee CLIENT's Web site a certain rating in the search engines.

The standard **Web site hosting** as defined through XYZ WEB DESIGN SHOP is as follows:

- As an Internet World Wide Web service provider, XYZ WEB DESIGN SHOP provides a dedicated server computer that is integrated into the Internet.

This server computer will send and receive information as related to the World Wide Web. The CLIENT will be connected to and utilize the hardware and software facilities of XYZ WEB DESIGN SHOP to establish an Internet Web site.

- Domain name search and advice. If a domain name is needed for the Web site, XYZ WEB DESIGN SHOP will suggest appropriate names and do a search to ascertain the availability of those names. The determination of a domain name's availability through the domain name registry does not guarantee it will still be available at the time of registration.

- Domain name registration or transfer. If needed, XYZ WEB DESIGN SHOP will help complete the necessary forms to register or transfer a domain name as selected by the CLIENT. Although XYZ WEB DESIGN SHOP will submit forms to register a requested domain name in a timely fashion, XYZ WEB DESIGN SHOP does not guarantee the availability of any domain name.

- The sending of spam, or Unsolicited Bulk E-mail (UBE), is not permitted on accounts hosted by XYZ WEB DESIGN SHOP.

- Web site hosting includes features and restrictions as found on electronic media at http://www.xyzdesignshopz.com/prices.htm. This information may be updated from time to time.

- Web site hosting runs from the beginning of this contract for a period of three months (known as quarterly) at which time it will be automatically renewed for each subsequent quarter under the same agreement and cost set forth in this contract.

5. Fees.

XYZ WEB DESIGN SHOP will execute this Web site design as specified by the CLIENT requirements as terms of this CONTRACT and incorporated in this CONTRACT. Unless specified otherwise in the ATTACHMENT, this Web site includes up to six Web pages. In case the CLIENT desires additional standard Web pages beyond the original number of pages specified above, the CLIENT agrees to pay XYZ WEB DESIGN SHOP an additional $xxx for each additional Web page. Graphics or photos beyond the allowed average of five per Web page shall be billed at an additional $xxx each. Where custom graphic work (beyond the scope of the "Custom Graphics" detailed above) is requested, it will be billed at the hourly rate of $xxx.

6. Maintenance.

This CONTRACT does not include our maintenance contract. Web page maintenance will be the responsibility of the CLIENT. If a maintenance service agreement is entered into between XYZ WEB DESIGN SHOP and the CLIENT, it will be contained within its own document and not connected to this CONTRACT. However, this CONTRACT does include minor modifications and corrections requested within a two-week period up to an average of one hour per page, including updating links and making minor changes to a sentence or paragraph. It does not include removing nearly all the text from a page and replacing it with new text. If the CLIENT or an agent other than XYZ WEB DESIGN SHOP attempts to update the CLIENT's pages during this time, time to repair the Web pages will be assessed at the hourly rate of $xxx, and is not included as part of the modification time.

7. Payment.

All services agreed to in this CONTRACT shall be sold for the price specified at the end of this document. Payment shall be by cash, check, or money order, in U.S. dollars, and made payable to *"XYZ Web Design Shop, LLC."*

8. Payment Terms.

Unless otherwise stated in the "Payment" document attached to this agreement, the following standard terms apply. A minimum deposit of fifty percent (50%) of the design cost and the total amount of hosting is required to commence work. The site will then be put online on a draft directory of the CLIENT's ISP or of XYZ WEB DESIGN SHOP for the CLIENT's viewing. During this proofing stage, typographical errors, design changes, and other corrections will be made according to the instructions of the CLIENT. The quarterly Web hosting time frame begins when the initial deposit is made and the draft site is put online. Payment for the site must be made in full before the site will be moved to the main directory of the CLIENT's ISP. Marketing of the site in the top ten search engines and directories will occur only after the final payment is made.

9. Completion Date.

XYZ WEB DESIGN SHOP and the CLIENT must work together to complete the Web site in a timely manner. Much of this depends on receiving the appropriate images and text from the CLIENT. We agree to work expeditiously to complete the Web site in a professional and timely fashion.

10. Assignment of Project.

XYZ WEB DESIGN SHOP reserves the right to assign subcontractors to this project to ensure the right fit for the job as well as on-time completion. XYZ WEB DESIGN SHOP will be responsible for the final results of the project.

11. Additional Expenses.

CLIENT agrees to reimburse XYZ WEB DESIGN SHOP for any additional expenses necessary for the completion of the work. Examples would be purchase of special fonts, stock photography, etc.

12. Additional Services.

Any revisions, additions, or redesign CLIENT wishes XYZ WEB DESIGN SHOP to perform not specified in this document shall be considered "additional" and will require a separate Agreement and payment.

13. Copyrights and Trademarks.

The CLIENT represents to XYZ WEB DESIGN SHOP and unconditionally guarantees that any elements of text, graphics, photos, designs, trademarks, or other artwork furnished to XYZ WEB DESIGN SHOP for inclusion in Web pages are owned by the CLIENT, or that the CLIENT has permission from the rightful owner to use each of these elements, and will hold harmless, protect, and defend XYZ WEB DESIGN SHOP and its subcontractors from any claim or suit arising from the use of such elements furnished by the CLIENT.

14. Age.

CLIENT certifies that he or she is at least eighteen years of age.

15. Limited Liability.

CLIENT hereby agrees that any material submitted for publication will not contain anything leading to an abusive or unethical use of the Web Hosting Service or Host Server. Abusive and unethical materials and uses include, but are not limited to, pornography, obscenity, nudity, violations of privacy, computer viruses, any harassing and harmful material or uses, any illegal activity or material advocating illegal activity, and any infringement of privacy or libel.

CLIENT hereby agrees to indemnify and hold harmless XYZ WEB DESIGN SHOP from any claim resulting from CLIENT's publication of material or use of those materials. CLIENT hereby agrees to indemnify and hold harmless XYZ WEB DESIGN SHOP in any claim resulting from the submission of illegal materials.

If XYZ WEB DESIGN SHOP shall acquire an Internet domain name on behalf of the CLIENT, then in such case CLIENT hereby waives any and all claims which it may have against XYZ WEB DESIGN SHOP for any loss, damage, claim, or expense arising out of or in relation to the registration of such domain name in any online or off-line network directories, membership lists, or registration lists, or the release of the domain name from such directories or lists following the termination of the providing of this service by XYZ WEB DESIGN SHOP for any reason.

Under no circumstances, including negligence, shall XYZ WEB DESIGN SHOP, its offices, agents, or anyone else involved in creating, producing, or distributing its services, be liable for any direct, indirect, incidental, special, or consequential damages that result from the use of or inability to use XYZ WEB DESIGN SHOP's services; or that result from mistakes, omissions, interruptions, deletion, or loss of files or data, errors, defects, delays in operation, or of performance, whether or not limited to acts of God, communication failure, theft, destruction, or unauthorized access to XYZ WEB DESIGN SHOP's records, programs, or services. CLIENT maintains sole responsibility for data backups and restoration. CLIENT hereby acknowledges that this paragraph shall apply to all content on XYZ WEB DESIGN SHOP's services.

Notwithstanding the above, CLIENT's exclusive remedies for all damages, losses, and causes of actions whether in CONTRACT, tort including negligence, or otherwise, shall not exceed the aggregate dollar amount that CLIENT paid during the term of this CONTRACT and any reasonable attorney's fee and court costs.

16. Indemnification.

CLIENT agrees that it shall defend, indemnify, save, and hold XYZ WEB DESIGN SHOP harmless from any and all demands, liabilities, losses, costs, and claims, including reasonable attorney's fees ("Liabilities") asserted against XYZ WEB DESIGN SHOP, its agents, clients, servants, officers, and employees, that may arise or result from any service provided or performed or agreed to be performed or any product sold by CLIENT, its agents, employees, or assigns. CLIENT agrees to defend, indemnify, and hold harmless XYZ WEB DESIGN SHOP against Liabilities arising out of any injury to person or property caused by any products or services sold or otherwise distributed in connection with XYZ WEB DESIGN SHOP's service, any material supplied by CLIENT infringing on the proprietary rights of a third party, copyright infringement, and any defective product which CLIENT has sold from the Web site XYZ WEB DESIGN SHOP has designed.

17. Laws Affecting Electronic Commerce.

The CLIENT agrees that the CLIENT is solely responsible for complying with such laws, taxes, and tariffs, and will hold harmless, protect, and defend XYZ WEB DESIGN SHOP and its subcontractors from any claim, suit, penalty, tax, or tariff arising from the CLIENT's use of Internet electronic commerce.

18. Copyright to Web Pages.

Copyright to the finished, assembled work of Web pages produced by XYZ WEB DESIGN SHOP is owned by XYZ WEB DESIGN SHOP. Upon final payment of this CONTRACT, the CLIENT is assigned rights to use as a Web site the design, graphics, and text contained in the finished, assembled Web site. Rights to photos, graphics, source code, work-up files, and computer programs are specifically not transferred to the CLIENT, and remain the property of their respective owners. XYZ WEB DESIGN SHOP and its subcontractors retain the right to display graphics and other Web design elements as examples of their work in their respective portfolios.

19. Authorship Credit.

CLIENT may select that XYZ WEB DESIGN SHOP includes a byline and link on the bottom of their Web page establishing authorship credit. This byline is upon agreement by both CLIENT and XYZ WEB DESIGN SHOP and must be removed at any time upon written request by XYZ WEB DESIGN SHOP.

20. Nondisclosure.

XYZ WEB DESIGN SHOP, its employees, and subcontractors agree that, except as directed by CLIENT, it will not at any time during or after the term of this CONTRACT disclose any Confidential Information to any person whatsoever.

21. Cancellation.

In the event that work is postponed or canceled at the request of the CLIENT by registered letter, XYZ WEB DESIGN SHOP shall have the right to bill pro rata for work completed through the date of that request, while reserving all rights under this CONTRACT. If additional payment is due, this shall be payable within thirty days of the CLIENT's notification to stop work. In the event of cancellation, the CLIENT shall also pay any expenses incurred by XYZ WEB DESIGN SHOP and XYZ WEB DESIGN SHOP shall own all rights to the work. The CLIENT shall assume responsibility for all collection of legal fees necessitated by default in payment.

22. Refund Policy.

If the CLIENT applies by a registered letter for a refund within fifteen (15) days of signing this CONTRACT, work already completed shall be billed at the hourly rate of $xxx and deducted from the initial payment. If the work that has been completed is beyond the amount covered in the initial payment, the CLIENT shall be liable to pay for all work completed at the hourly rate of $xxx.

23. Arbitration.

Any disputes in excess of $1,000 (or the maximum limit for small claims court) arising out of this CONTRACT shall be submitted to binding arbitration before the Joint Ethics Committee or a mutually agreed-upon Arbitrator pursuant to the rules of the American Arbitration Association. The Arbitrator's award shall be final, and judgment may be entered in any court having jurisdiction thereof. The CLIENT shall pay all arbitration and court costs, reasonable attorney's fees, and legal interest on any award or judgment in favor of XYZ WEB DESIGN SHOP.

24. Payment of Fees.

In order for XYZ WEB DESIGN SHOP to remain in business, payments must be made promptly. Invoices are due upon receipt. Delinquent bills will be assessed a $15 charge if payment is not received within ten days of the due date. If an amount remains delinquent thirty days after its due date, an additional five percent (5%) penalty will be added for each month of delinquency. XYZ WEB DESIGN SHOP reserves the right to remove Web pages from viewing on the Internet until final payment is made. In case collection proves necessary, the CLIENT agrees to pay all fees incurred by that process. This CONTRACT becomes effective only when signed by XYZ WEB DESIGN SHOP. Regardless of the place of signing of this CONTRACT, the CLIENT agrees that for purposes of venue, this CONTRACT was entered into in Hartford County, Connecticut, and any dispute will be litigated or arbitrated in Hartford County, Connecticut. Please pay on time.

25. Entire Understanding.

This CONTRACT constitutes the sole agreement between XYZ WEB DESIGN SHOP and the CLIENT regarding its Web Design Service. It becomes effective only when signed by both parties. This CONTRACT shall be governed and construed in accordance with the laws of the State of Connecticut. The parties agree that if any part, term, or provision of this Agreement shall be found illegal or in conflict with any valid controlling law, the validity of the remaining provisions shall not be affected thereby.

The undersigned agrees to the terms of this CONTRACT on behalf of his or her organization or business.

On behalf of the CLIENT:

_____   Date _____

On behalf of XYZ WEB DESIGN SHOP:

_____   Date _____

WEB SITE DESIGN WORKSHEET

In conjunction with the contract, the following outlines the details for the Web site design work.

Pages:

- Home page
- About Us page
  Client to provide six to ten paragraphs of material
- Testimonials page
  From existing page
- Product Safety Statement page
  Two pages—convert current pages into PDF for downloading
- Contractor's proposal page
  Based upon existing proposal—client to provide extra details
- Links page
  Link addresses (maximum links: 16) and brief descriptions to be supplied by client
- CLIENT will develop a logo and submit it to XYZ WEB DESIGN SHOP in a JPG file for inclusion in Web site.
- XYZ WEB DESIGN SHOP will create a domain name and link it to a commercial-grade XYZ WEB DESIGN SHOP server. Note: CLIENT will be responsible for registering an additional domain name (xyz.com).
- XYZ WEB DESIGN SHOP will provide a link from the Product Safety Statement page to that domain as part of this agreement.
- Insert a temporary "coming soon" home page.
- XYZ WEB DESIGN SHOP will create a draft directory on the server to develop new Web site that is available for previewing.
- Upon completion of the Web site and payment in full, XYZ WEB DESIGN SHOP will transfer the site to the main directory of the Web site.
- XYZ WEB DESIGN SHOP will confirm proper functionality of all links and actions of the Web site.
- XYZ WEB DESIGN SHOP will contact three major search engines with related information.

PAYMENT SCHEDULE

$ xxxx   Total cost* for entire Web design project including the first quarter of Web hosting.

_____

*The total cost above does not include the estimated charge of $xxx that CLIENT will pay to create a logo nor of an extra domain name registration that will be taken care of by the CLIENT. Those are not a part of this contract, but are mentioned here and are understood as being an additional charge.

$ xxxx   Total at beginning, upon signing of contract

Includes:

       $xxx   Hosting setup

       $xxx   Domain name registration (good for two years)

       $xxx $xxx per month x three months of Web hosting

       $xxx   50 percent of design work in advance

* * *

$ xxxx   Balance due upon completion of Web site design
          (plus applicable taxes)

Includes:

$xxx   50 percent of design work upon completion

Appendix C:
Start-Up Checklist

This checklist is a tool that you can use to help in starting your Web design business. It should be modified to add anything that might be specific to your particular business, but it should be helpful as a starting point.

Equipment:

☐ Computer (PC or Mac)
☐ Printer
☐ CD/DVD burner
☐ Digital camera
☐ Scanner
☐ Answering machine or voice mail service
☐ Cell phone
☐
☐

Software:

☐ HTML editor
☐ File Transfer Protocol (FTP) program
☐ Bookkeeping software or manual bookkeeping system
☐ Antivirus program and firewall to protect your computer
☐ Graphic design program
☐
☐

Support Team:

☐ Attorney
☐ Bookkeeper and/or accountant
☐

Other Needs:

☐ Your business plan
☐ Your portfolio of work you've done
☐ Customers
☐ Web host for customers
☐ Work area
☐ Customer meeting area
☐ Your own Web site
☐ Customer billing and payment arrangements
☐ Your rates
☐ Your own domain name
☐
☐

Appendix D: Frequently Asked Questions

How Much Handholding Is Too Much to Offer?

I know of some Web designers who charge for every phone call and everything that they do. I know others who charge for an initial Web site and then offer lots of free advice, help, and updates after that. You will eventually need to create your own comfort zone of how much free advice you will offer. If a client wants to know about an e-mail he got from an Internet company promising thousands of search engine listings, I want him to feel free to call me. I can tell him my opinion of that offer and perhaps steer him to some of my more effective services. Likewise, if he's having difficulty with his e-mail, I don't want him to assume it is a problem with my service and go elsewhere. I want him to call and ask me about it. There are some times when it becomes evident that the problem is with the client's computer, but I feel that is an unspoken part of my service to offer some basic troubleshooting for e-mail problems.

If you find that you have a client who is taking up too much of your time, there may be some nonabrasive ways to deal with the problem. Suggest that you are busy and perhaps she can send you an e-mail so you can look at it when you get a chance. You can be just heading out the door, but if it is a brief question maybe you can help. If you answer a phone call for help and feel it is time to gently steer the request for help into a paid consultation, here's what works for me. At the beginning of the call, I interrupt and tell my client that I have a couple of projects that I'm working on and wonder if this is a quick question or something that needs some of my billable time. Usually the call becomes a very brief request for advice, and this also reminds the client that if he wants to consult with me, my time is billable.

What's a Request for Proposal (RFP), and How Do I Prepare One?

A Request for Proposal is just what it sounds like, a request by a potential client for you to put together a proposal for her. I typically don't use them, and I have only received a few RFPs since I've been doing design work. Most of my clients are smaller businesses and wouldn't take time out of their schedule to read through a formal proposal if I sent it to them. Two of the people who sent me RFPs read somewhere that designers expect to be asked for a proposal, and so they formally asked for one. Another RFP was from a small company accustomed to dealing with government contracts and wanted to know what I'd charge to build a Web site. For others, I felt that they already knew who they were going to hire and just wanted to get their quota of three quotes. I sent each prospect a breakdown of what it would cost for his or her project and what I would need (money and materials). I did this in my usual contract format in the worksheet page. In a formal cover sheet titled "Proposal for Web Design for XYZ Company," I referred to the various sections of my contract.

One client called for a follow-up phone meeting and confessed that of the six RFPs he sent, no one else had responded. It made my selling job easier. He admitted that he was totally confused and wanted someone he could depend on. Since I had already convinced him of my dependability, I helped demystify the process for him and the rest fell into place. Another RFP was for a group that decided to do the work themselves (or they planned to do it themselves anyway and were fishing for ideas). And one group got my "official RFP" and hired me.

I give you these stories because you may get an RFP from a huge organization wanting an elaborate proposal. Consider whether the project might be larger than you want to handle. You might be spending a lot of time putting together a proposal and end up with nothing to show for it in the end if they go elsewhere. For larger design houses, that risk is built into their larger prices. For a small business, it is enough to put a large dent in your time and income.

If I spent the time putting together a detailed RFP with a resume, justification as to why I am most qualified to get the job, and how I'm going to complete the job, I could spend as much time on the RFP as I would on the job. At that point, I need to either charge twice as much to make up for the time I spent putting the RFP together or end up with half as much money as usual due to the time I spent on the RFP.

If you want some good ideas for proposals, go to www.secretsites.com/ and read what Dave Siegel has to say in his archives. Although he doesn't like RFPs, his book and his archived Web site have some good tips on alternatives such as setting up a "questionnaire" for clients. I tried formalizing my setup using ideas from his book, *Secrets of Successful Web Sites* (it is somewhat outdated now but is still a good book). However, most of my clients are much smaller than his and are less likely to spend much time deciding what they want. They assume I should already know what they want; this means I must do my homework without handing them a questionnaire.

How Often Should I Bill My Clients?

I bill my hosting clients quarterly. That is spread out enough that I don't feel I'm being a nuisance by making them pay each month. I usually do not encourage annual hosting payments, though. I've found that if I invoice annually, that is how often my clients are reminded that I exist. When I send out invoices quarterly, that is frequently how a client remembers to get something on his Web site updated (more money for me!). So quarterly works best for my clients and me.

Am I Too Young to Be Taken Seriously as a Web Designer?

At a young age you might have some image obstacles to overcome in selling your services; some business owners may feel that you don't know enough about their business to put a site together for them. However, if you keep doing some free sites and push those satisfied free customers to recommend you, you will soon find doors start opening. The key is to make sure you offer something that others don't so as to entice potential clients. Can you offer lower prices than a full-fledged Web designer? Or, because of your age, can you offer some youthful insight that others may miss? Or can you give a business owner extra time to make sure everything is done correctly as opposed to some designer coming in and doing a quick throw-together job?

Make sure your own Web site is representative of what you will be doing for a business owner. Then use that as proof of what you can do. It doesn't have to be fancy, it only has to do its job. Remember that to a business owner, glitter and fancy stuff don't matter as much as being able to get customers in the door. Your Web site is a good starting point. Keep polishing it and making it a magnet for the customers you are after and then start sending potential customers there for a look. Point them in that direction and then let it sell for you!

Am I Too Old to Start Designing Web Sites?

Whether you are forty, fifty, or seventy and retired doesn't matter; the issue is what your goals are. You have a learning curve ahead of you. If you enjoy this business and are interested in it, there is no reason you can't jump in. As you get older (and I speak from experience!), you will find that some "kids" can run circles around you with their computers. It is important that you don't try to compete with the work that they do for after-school pocket change. Use your age as an asset! Position yourself as much more mature and able to bring assets that the kids don't have to the negotiation table.

Most business owners are not kids, but more mature men and women. They are more likely to take someone our age seriously rather than a fourteen-year-old (who might be better at some techie stuff, but perhaps is not percevied to be as wise or is thought to have less business sense).

Would a business person rather have some impetuous young kid without worldly experience design his Web site, or someone who has been around for a while and has a lifetime of experiences to offer? Here's a related experience I had that deserves sharing.

A self-taught eighteen-year-old had designed and been maintaining a Web site for a company for more than four years and was doing a great job of it. Meanwhile the company had grown from a small start-up into a major public distributor with international sales teams. The CEO decided that she was nervous about a "kid" being in charge of the Web site and wanted someone more mature.

When I was approached, I figured out that the solution was easy. Instead of the kid getting a low rate without a contract to do a great job of managing a major site, the company now has a more mature person (myself) overseeing the Web site. I bill out at a rate that allows me to pay the same "kid" as a subcontractor more than double what he was getting on his own, and I, in turn, get paid to make sure the workflow is sustained. Everyone is happy.

What has changed? The kid is still in charge of the Web site. But the corporate director feels that she has an older and more stable person in charge of her Web site. She is happy because she gets a feeling of stability, the kid is happy because he gets a big raise, and I am happy because I get paid for my work. The CEO put much value on having an older person involved in maintaining her Web site. Yes, I've got some experience that the kid may be lacking, but the kid can run circles around me in PHP and any programming and scripting stuff. Together we are a strong team, able to take care of the client's needs.

I Don't Have a Fancy Degree or Even a Webmaster Certificate. Is That a Problem?

A certificate or degree can be a handy marketing tool to show you "know your stuff," but it is not absolutely essential. Even with a certificate or degree, your main means for establishing credibility is not those but a strong portfolio of work you've done. The certificate can be bought and might not impress most business owners. However, the portfolio is most revealing—it shows the work you've done and for whom. By the way, I don't have any "fancy degrees" or certificates. I built my portfolio one client at a time, so you can tell what my bias is.

If a Client Doesn't Want to Sign a Contract, What Should I Do?

If someone suggests that I work without a written agreement, I'll run the other way! If you are asked to work "on a handshake" or without a contract, or someone is hounding you to drop your guard, that is the time to use a thorough contract!

If your client wants you to shorten the contract, ask him what part he objects to. Would he rather fight a lawsuit due to miscommunication over copyright infringements? Or maybe over late payments? Or due to a not-so-clear definition of the responsibilities? It is a mutual benefit to have a thorough contract.

This reminds me of the kid mowing my lawn who wanted a key to my house so he could get a glass of water while I was away. I told him I'd leave him some refreshments on the step. He then wanted the key to use the bathroom while I was away. I said no. The more he insisted that I violate my sense of security, the more concerned and cautious I became. I found out later that some neighbors had experienced problems with missing items when he had access to their homes. Don't be afraid to stick with your policies unless there is very good reason not to.

The only time I vary my contract is if there is a good reason to cross out and initial a section. That way, there is no doubt that everything else applies and this is a one-time exception.

How Do I Give a Client a Nudge to Get Materials to Me?

Part of customer service is allowing my clients to create or gather the content for their Web site at their pace rather than based on a deadline that is convenient for me. Although most clients are eager to get their Web sites up and running, occasionally getting the necessary materials or approvals drags on for a long time. During times of tight cash flow I view it as annoying and other times I view it as future cash in the bank. But I don't have a perfect solution to it.

Here are some tips that I've used to nudge clients, though. First, I remind myself that their focus is on running their business, not completing their Web site. Eventually someone or something is going to remind them that they have already invested a lot of money in developing a Web site and have nothing to show for it other than a half-completed site in draft mode. An important customer of theirs may ask them what their Web address is; that might do it. Or they are getting ready to send out a mass mailing (which has happened to me a couple of times) and suddenly they're scrambling to complete the site. Whatever triggers it, when I have a couple of unfinished Web sites I send periodic notes saying, "I know you are very busy, but I just wanted to let you know I'm not ignoring you, and if you have a chance I'm available next week if you want to complete your Web site. Keep in touch." That is a friendly way of nudging them without being nasty or a pest.

Once in a while I'll have a client suddenly contact me in a panic to complete her site while I'm in the midst of other stuff, but usually I've got her site to a point that I can complete it in between other jobs. Of course, I still subtly let her know it's a monumental favor I'm doing to put a rush on it. Once she asks me to put her back into my "extremely busy" schedule, she usually is happy to give me everything I need to complete the site and is very grateful that I'm fitting her in, just to meet her urgent need. Such clients usually become my best customers because they see that I'm willing to go the extra mile for them in time of need.

Periodically I'll find a client who creates a "self-imposed" deadline. For example, I had a client who, after several months of feet dragging, set up an advertising campaign to begin "this Friday." The week before his advertising campaign began, I got an urgent phone call to see if I could complete the Web site in time. I had to shuffle a couple of smaller non-time-sensitive jobs, but I was delighted to finally complete the site. And the client was extremely grateful. After completing the Web site and letting the dust settle, I asked him why he put this mailing campaign up with such short notice. He gave me what was probably the most honest answer I've heard: "We have trouble finding time to complete stuff like this without a pending deadline and once we knew that the mailing was ready to go out, we panicked and realized we had to complete the Web site so new customers wouldn't see our half-completed Web site."

Here's another tip to give a client a nudge, which I would only use carefully or it may backfire. I had a client who was selling gifts through her shop and she wanted to display them online. She was a gung-ho starter and yet a nonfinisher. I mentioned this to a couple of friends who loved the shop and used to buy stuff there all the time. After I told the tale of the incomplete and stalled Web site, each time they'd go in, my friends would ask if some new line of jewelry was online yet. When the owner made the time to complete the site, she told me that she needed to complete it because several of her customers were using the Web site. She was correct; I just unintentionally gave it a little boost.

Another time I had a client dragging his feet and, unprompted by me, a friend kept calling the receptionist to ask if they had a map and directions on their Web site or if the hours of the business were posted there. Word got back to the boss that they should finish the Web site so people wouldn't keep calling to ask for directions. I got a phone call shortly after that to complete the Web site.

Of course, those were not nudges that I instigated, but I suppose they could be done intentionally to prod a slow mover. Like I said, I'd be very careful if you do try something like that because it could very easily backfire and create some ill-will if the client ever tied it back to you.

Sometimes I don't find out until much later that a high-level customer or a government contract or something provided the extra push. But sooner or later, it will happen. If you've been paid enough money up front, the ending payment should be insignificant to the total and make the client feel he's already paid for almost the entire site in advance. Sometimes you can help the process along, but most of the time the best thing is to keep yourself in front of the client so he finds you to be ready to help when he has a few minutes to catch his breath while trying to keep his own business running smoothly.

Some designers put penalties in their contracts, but I have found it creates ill feelings, excuses, and improperly placed blame (on me!), and doesn't accomplish my goal of having and keeping a good relationship with the client. For that reason there are no penalties in my contracts for not meeting deadlines.

A Client Wants to Take Credit Cards without Using a Secure Server. What Can I Do to Convince Her to Pay for Security?

Most Internet users are now aware that if they go to a Web site and are asked for a credit card, that little padlock at the bottom of the browser better be locked or they should not enter the transaction. I knew of one site that lost its secure server and tried to get away without it. The company had so many customers complain that they figured out that they were losing a lot of sales by taking a shortcut.

If a client wants to take that risk, it is up to you whether to aid her in that endeavor. I do everything that I can to discourage clients from such a risky practice. If they still want to take credit cards without appropriate security measures, I step down from helping them. I don't know whether I might be caught up in a problem their actions may cause, but I don't think it is worth the risk.

Here is some sage advice my attorney, F. W. O'Connor, offered when we were discussing a similar matter:

> If my wife, who is not as Internet savvy as you or I, went online and made a purchase, and as a result had her credit card number stolen because someone intercepted the unsecure transmission, she'd be very upset. When she got that upset, I'd be upset also. My next course of action would be to check and see if the company she bought from was using reasonable safety precautions such as using a secure server and encrypted e-mail. If they were using commercially reasonable measures to protect credit cards, I'd chalk it up to an unfortunate situation.
>
> However, if I discovered that the company hadn't taken commercially reasonable and prudent measures to protect credit cards, I would consider litigation against the company itself and all those associated with the company, including whoever designed the Web site.

Then my attorney got to the point that I needed (but didn't want) to hear:

> If you designed the site and there was any documentation indicating that you told them about the danger of unsecure transmission, you may be in trouble. If you think you can wash your hands of it as an outside consultant, regardless of what your contractual agreement says, you are wrong. If it can be demonstrated that you are aware of a problem and yet agree to be a party to the transaction you may be in trouble. If, after I take you through the courts, you can spend enough money to prove to a jury otherwise, so be it, but I wouldn't count on it. Either way, you should make sure you never agree to take on a client without being sure you are not aiding that client in an irresponsible action.

My attorney then concluded the sobering conversation by telling me that if it were a paying client who came to him instead of its being his wife that he was representing, he could make some money *plus* make sure someone learned that she should use "reasonable care" in taking credit cards. He then said:

> If you assist a client in setting up an unsecure credit card site anyway, you better make sure you either put lots of big scary warnings on the site telling visitors that it isn't secure and that it uses unencrypted e-mail that could be intercepted, or charge enough to make it well worth your while.

After that, I decided those jobs are not worth it!

Even Though My Prices Are Low, I'm Afraid Some Customers Will Think I'm Too Expensive. What Can I Do?

Here's a "game" to play. Find a make-believe customer—someone who is willing to do some role playing. Don't tell him what to say or do other than to do some serious role playing as a reluctant customer thinking about a Web site. When prices comes up (it should with any reluctant customer), triple your normal rate! Do so with a straight face. Explain the reasons. Embrace that price. Get used to it. Justify it.

Now when you talk prices with a "real" potential client, you'll find your "real" price is becoming more comfortable to you. If the other person isn't comfortable with the price, offer to let her shop around. Give her some ideas of what others in the area are charging. Be sensitive to her concerns but don't let her shrewd negotiation ability short-sell you. Learn how to negotiate a fair deal for yourself the same way you had to learn how to create tables in HTML. It's a necessary part of conducting your business.

What Is E&O Insurance? Do I Need It?

Errors & Omissions (E&O) is professional liability insurance. I can't advise you on whether you should have it or not as that should be something you need to decide after a discussion with your insurance agent and your attorney. It is very costly for a Web designer just starting out, but it is important to make a decision one way or the other rather than just ignoring the risk. Dan Goldfarb of Anderson-Meyer Insurance in Glastonbury, Connecticut, explains it this way:

E&O coverage for a Web site designer will depend on the exact type of work being done. The thing to keep in mind is that E&O coverage normally only comes into play for economic losses suffered by the claimant. A typical claim in this area might be something like "the Web site does not collect orders properly and has caused us to pay overtime to our Customer Service Representatives to process the orders correctly." Costs for this E&O coverage can vary for a small "one-person shop" with limited revenues, at $1,000 to $1,500 or so per year, to a larger company with premiums in the tens of thousands of dollars.

Should I Offer a Do-It-Yourself Web Site Builder or Editor Along with My Other Services?

If a client wants to build his own Web site, there's not a lot of service you can offer other than telling him the advantages to having you take care of it. Many times I'll suggest that I'll build it for him and then turn it over to him to make updates and changes. That way he gets a great Web site that is completed in a timely fashion that can be a good foundation on which to make his edits. That way he feels he is ultimately in control of it. If he likes the idea of having me build it and then turn it over to him, I've found some editors that work well for my clients.

First, there is a solution that keeps them on my server with an open source Web-based editor called Joomla. This is also known as a Content Management System (CMS) because the content is separated from the layout. It is not a simple solution for someone wanting a few pages, but for clients with a lot of content to take care of, this is a powerful editor package.

I also use an online editor called ContentSeed (www.contentseed.com) that can be installed on the server and costs $150. To pop up the password-protected editor, the client simply clicks Control-y, puts in the password, and starts editing that page. It comes in PHP or ASP, and a bit of programming will come in handy if you use it on multiple Web sites.

The other program I use for clients wanting to do it themselves is Contribute by Adobe (www.adobe.com/products/contribute/). You will need Dreamweaver and your own copy of Contribute to make the best use of this editor. Your clients will pay $199 for the software. You can buy groups of licenses at a slight discount, but I've found it works better to have my clients go there and purchase it themselves.

That way, they can look to Adobe for support rather than going through me. With Contribute, you use your administrator access to Contribute through Dreamweaver to create an access key, which you e-mail to your clients. With that key, they can go in to their Web site and make changes to the content without breaking the layout or navigation. Keep a copy of their key for that day when they call to say they got a new computer and can't find their key.

You may find some clients who want to use Microsoft Word to update their Web site. I suggest you strongly discourage that. Word and some other word processing programs can save files in HTML, but they create very bloated and poorly coded pages. You can show your clients the difference in source code if they are skeptical.

If desired, your clients can build an entire Web site from scratch using any of these products; however there isn't much money to be made by you. In my experience there is another reason I no longer encourage clients to build an entire Web site using these editors. They start building it and contact me with a "quick question": how to make that image go to the left side of the screen, or what are the Meta tags it talks about, or why the font won't get any larger.

I've found it to be cumbersome to do nickel-and-dime consulting charges (billing $3 for a three-minute phone call), and much of what they are asking me is how to do something that I normally would charge them to do right. Fixing their mistakes would cost them more than for me to build it and therefore sets us both up to be unsatisfied in the end.

However, if I've designed and set up the Web site, I have already made my money and don't mind helping them set up an editor to make their own changes. Chances are when they have big changes to make, they will come back to me anyway. Additionally, at a client's request I will frequently set up an editor on a site I've built only to have the client e-mail me the next set of changes. I make those changes and bill her for that. The client then realizes how much more convenient it is to send stuff to me rather than making the changes herself. After that positive experience, she never uses the editor that she wanted so badly in the beginning.

Can I Get an Electronic Version of Your Sample Contract?

Because I've had many requests for this, I've posted it on my Blarneystone Web site at www.blarneystone.com/designbusiness/. From this page you will find a link to an electronic version of the contract. I do not want you to copy it to use it as it is. It is there so you can download it, make your own notes and changes to it, double-space it, print it, and then sit down with your attorney and go over it together to make any appropriate changes to meet your needs. My sample contract should be a starting point for you to have a discussion with your attorney—it is not a finished product for you to copy and use.

How Do I Tell a Potential Client That His Web Site Stinks?

As you probably know, if you want to criticize someone's Web site you need to be very cautious; if you bash a business owner's Web site and then find that his daughter is the proud designer, you won't score any points.

The most important thing to do is to try to find a tie-in with that company. If you see a large candy-manufacturing firm in your area is still advertising special Christmas candy boxes in April, you know they need help. See if you can find any leads into the company. Do your homework. Ask friends and business associates if they know someone who knows someone there. If you find a foothold that way, you are much more likely to get some time with the decision maker.

If you can find no contact at all within the company, is it a place where you can pose as a customer (or even become a customer!)? Have a friend call and ask if the company has a Web site. My wife loves to do that for me. If someone says, "Yeah, we do have a Web site at www.rottenoldsite.com, but it really isn't very good," my wife says, "Hey, I know someone who can help with that." Then she asks who could her friend talk to? Bingo, I have a contact name.

Since you don't want to offend someone at the company, use some sensitivity while maneuvering the company owner to say something bad about the site. I am frequently surprised at how well owners beat up their own Web sites if given the opportunity without being put on the defensive. They usually know the site stinks. They've been trying to get their Web designer off the beach and in for a meeting to get the updates completed. They don't want to go from one headache to another, so it is up to you to have some testimonials from current clients that say, "Heidi has been responsible for my Web site for over a year now (month now?). Any time I need changes, I simply e-mail her and it is done!"

There are lots of Web designers out there jumping into the field. A few are good and stay with it. Many are looking for an easy way to make money without too much energy and will abandon their clients after a while. If you can come across as one of the ones who is in it for the long haul, you will start to find more and more of these abandoned and outdated Web sites. The owners are usually both overly cautious and desperate for help. If they feel that you can take care of their concerns and hire you, they will see how much better you are than that "other guy," and they eventually become part of your cheering section and a great springboard for more business.

How Do I Fire a Customer?

When you've been in business for a while, firing a client will unfortunately become a part of your business. As tempting as it is to tell an unruly or unreasonable client just what you think of him, you should handle it very carefully. Before gleefully ditching unwanted clients, here are a few things to consider:

1. If you leave on less than stellar terms, your ex-client might become a word-of-mouth nightmare. Don't give him any extra ammo to use against you!

2. If you part company with a client, make sure you leave no contracted obligation unfinished. A disgruntled ex-client with a greedy lawyer can make your life miserable and your bank account empty.

3. Are you being paid well? Do you need the money? Sometimes it is worth it to do some artistically challenged (ugly) work just to get enough money to do some fun stuff for less money later. Don't fire a client just because he wants it done his way.

4. Are you charging enough? Are you billing by the hour for everything? One of my clients got his Web site completed and then thought I'd give him lots of free advice and updates thereafter. I do a lot of handholding with novice clients, so I don't mind. However, when he was calling several times every week and taking up way too much of my time, I finally asked him at the beginning of one of the calls if this was a quick question or a billable consultation. His conversation was brief and somewhat less chatty than before. Reminding a client that he is paying consulting fees can extremely shorten a requested task.

5. Is this a Web site that you started for the client and it is going on forever without apparent end (and no extra money)? Check your contract (if you don't have one, get one ASAP!). Is there a clearly defined completion point? If so, do that and end it. If you haven't clearly defined the terms of your agreement, do so as soon as possible and as tactfully as possible. You may take a hit by having to do some extra work you hadn't anticipated, but (1) you are learning a very valuable lesson for future contracts, and (2) by

doing so, you now can set a clear end point to work toward. Make sure you get the client involved in the process so you both agree on a completion point. For example:

Mrs. Pita, I know you would like to see this Web site completed, so I want to make sure we both recognize how that will happen. I have a couple of big projects coming up and I don't want to leave you hanging while I work on other things. So let's see where we are and what we need to do to finish this. To consider this Web site completed, you want the "About Us" page revamped to match the info you sent me. You want a couple of photos put in on the home page. And you want the three extra projects you've been working on to be included. Is there anything else we need in order to complete this project?

That should take care of any lingering issues with a client wanting to keep the momentum going. If there are other things beyond the scope of the contract (outside of the initial agreement as you've both just agreed on), those extras should be billed as extras.

Some time ago I had a client who was heading down the road to late payments and quibbling over every cost. At one time when she was complaining about the cost of hosting, I offered to help find a cheaper alternative for her. I acted very professionally in helping transition her to a $10/month Web host and even offered to erase the last month's hosting bill she owed me. She was very happy and (hopefully) never knew how glad I was to get rid of her. I know from experience that it sometimes is necessary to gather some of those marginal clients in the beginning when things are lean and there's enough extra time to deal with a few headaches. Just remember that it won't always be that way. Some day you can cheerfully offer to help clients pursue their low-cost alternatives.

When I'm having difficulty with a client, I find it helps if I remind myself that I am not an employee of this client. I am a professional there to do a specific task as agreed upon in writing in advance for a preset amount of money. Once that obligation is completed, that client and I have no further obligation to each other. If he wants to enter into another contract with me, I can either become very busy, or I can price the work according to its value to me. I can also say no if necessary.

Glossary

browser A software program that allows you to search for and display a Web page. The two most popular browsers are Internet Explorer and Firefox.
If you design a business Web site that looks best when viewed with one particular browser, you are doing a disservice to your client. Always try to make the sites cross-browser friendly (able to be viewed on a variety of types and versions of browsers).

burner A CD and/or DVD drive that can be used to copy or "burn" information to a disk. CD burners are either recordable (CD-R) or rewritable (CD-RW). The CD-R can only record once onto a blank disk, while a CD-RW can be reused many times, similar to a floppy disk.

business suit A symbol of the personality trait needed to be a good decision maker for a Web design business. This trait also personifies the neat, well-organized, hard-nosed negotiator.

cascading style sheet (CSS) A file or series of files that contain information about the style or the layout of the various elements within one or more Web pages, such as links and font sizes. "Cascading" means that these files can be combined in a sequence based upon rules of hierarchy.

CD-ROM Defined as *compact disk, read-only memory*, this disk can store 650 to 700 megabytes of information—over 700 floppy disks' worth of data. Some CDs are read-only, while others are recordable and also rewritable, which means they can be reused many times.

domain name A Web name that is referenced to an IP address. Rather than typing in four long numbers to designate an address (for example,

161.58.215.166), domain names were created to make the task easier. Many names end in "dot-com," although there are several others such as "dot-org" and "dot-net." There are also an abundance of two letter country codes such as ".ca" for Canada and ".ie" for Ireland.

DVD A digital video disk is a disc storage media similar in appearance to a CD. However, DVDs are encoded in a different format and at a much higher density. While a CD holds 650 to 700 megabytes of data, a DVD can store 4.7 gigabytes, and a dual layer DVD allows up to 8.5 gigabytes of data storage.

e-commerce Electronic commerce or e-commerce is the buying and selling of goods and services over the Internet. For the purposes of most definitions, an e-commerce site can take an order and accept payment for it, as opposed to an online catalog that is for viewing merchandise but not for placing a direct order.

FAQ Frequently Asked Question or FAQs (pronounced either "FAX" or F-A-Qs). Lists of common questions that every newcomer asks when first coming to a mail list or online forum. Anyone first learning about a list should find out where the FAQs are. This prevents asking the same questions that have been answered thousands of times before. *For a business Web site, you can suggest a FAQ section for your client to answer all of those questions that everyone first asks about the business, such as where they are located, what their hours are, what their return policy is, etc. Each business has its own unique set of FAQs, and if you are having trouble finding out what they are, ask the person(s) that answer the incoming phone calls; that should give you plenty of FAQs to work with.*

flash drive A USB data storage device that is taking over where floppy disks left off. With storage capability thousands of times greater than a standard floppy disk, these units are small and sturdy enough to be carried on a key ring or in a pocket. They plug into a USB port and have no moving parts so they are robust and very convenient.

forum See *newsgroups*.

FTP File Transfer Protocol. This is the primary method of transferring files from your computer to the Web server on the Internet. Technically, FTP is a protocol rather than a method of transferring files, but unless you are in a deep discussion with someone in an overactive geek mode, you can use the terms interchangeably.

gif Graphics Interchange Format (pronounced either "jiff" or "gif"). One of three popular file types used for graphics in Web sites *(see also jpg and png)* whose extension ends in .gif. Typically, a gif file is used for logos and graphics with only a few colors.

green visor cap A symbol used to signify a sharp accountant.
In the first chapter of this book, I describe the personality traits of a green visor cap that are vital to a Web design shop.

home page The page through which a Web site's visitors enter. The home page is usually named index.htm, index.html, or sometimes default.htm. Although a Web server can be configured to bring up other beginning Web pages, the three listed are the most common ones.

host The computer(s) that is directly connected to the Internet. Usually files for Web sites on the Internet are stored on host computers. A "Web host" is a company that provides host computers for its customers. Many Web designers provide Web hosting services for their customers.

HTML HyperText Markup Language (pronounced using each letter "H-T-M-L"). The language that is used to design Web sites. It is based largely upon using codes inside of brackets to turn features on such as using <b> **to turn bold type on, and using brackets with a slash like this** </b> to turn bold type off. Using your browser, go to VIEW and SOURCE to see the HTML code for any Web site.

HTTP HyperText Transfer Protocol. This tells the receiving computer that the file is a Web page. In designing a Web site, you will usually start links with http:// or https:// for secure pages.

IP address A numeric address written as four numbers separated by periods. Each number can be zero to 255. For example, 161.58.215.166 could be an IP address.

Java The high-level programming language developed by Sun Microsystems.
In using Java on Web pages, there are many small applications known as Java applets that can be found on the Internet. If you are like me and would rather drink your Java than code it in, you can frequently find ready-to-use Java applets on programmers' Web sites. Most of these are either very inexpensive or free. To avoid being recognized as a rookie, don't interchangeably use the terms Java and JavaScript (see JavaScript).

JavaScript A relatively basic scripting language used frequently in Web site design. *JavaScript and Java are frequently thought to be the same or similar but are completely different. JavaScript is a script or group of commands that is created within the HTML page, whereas Java is a complete programming language. (When you roll your mouse over a button on a Web page and it changes color or shape, this is usually a JavaScript known as a mouseover.)*

jpg Also known as JPEG files (pronounced jay-peg). This is one of three types of graphic files normally used in designing Web sites *(see also gif and png)*. JPG uses a special compression technique that is well suited for photographs and other color-intensive graphics on Web sites.

mail list An automated application so subscribers can send e-mail to one e-mail address, and then their message is copied and sent to all of the other subscribers of the mail list. A popular one to install on your client's Web server is Majordomo at www.greatcircle.com/majordomo/.

newsgroups Discussion groups on the Internet in which individuals exchange electronic messages about a common interest. There are thousands of these groups on the Internet that share information on topics about anything imaginable. They are also known as *forums*.

Optical Character Resolution (OCR) A software program that converts printed text into material your computer can recognize.
OCR can save some time for Web designers. If a client gives you hard copies of text that are to go into a Web site, rather than retyping all of the text, you can scan the pages, run the OCR program, and get an output that should be in a usable format. Note that you probably will still need to check for spelling errors and you might need to make some formatting changes.

png One of three popular file types *(see gif and jpg)* for images and typically pronounced P-N-G. It was developed as a step up from gif files. It can have a transparent background like gif files and generally has better compression (which means it is a smaller file size).

ponytail A term used to describe the artistic side of Web designers. Ponytails are usually creative and enjoy the design aspect of Web sites.

portfolio In the Web design business, as in many other businesses, a portfolio is a sampling of Web sites that a Web designer has done. A portfolio can be either a notebook with shots of the Web sites or an online portfolio with links to Web sites a designer has created.

In starting your home-based Web design business, a portfolio may consist only of Web sites done for friends and associates that were not for payment. However, as you complete more jobs, your portfolio may be expanded to demonstrate the work you've done for paying clients.

propeller-head A term used to describe programmers and technicians. Propeller-heads are the diligent and brilliant individuals who frequently work behind the scenes to create programs, keep the electronic machinery going, and protect and maintain a Web site's security system.

rainmaker A term used to describe a salesperson.

search engine A generic term used to describe applications that find words and phrases on the Internet.

Most people use the term "search engine" for all Internet search tools. After you have become more familiar with the Internet, you will draw distinctions between different search engines such as AltaVista and Google, and directories such as Yahoo!.

server Also referred to as a Web server, this is a computer that serves or delivers Web pages to the Internet.

There are also mail servers and others, but for Web designs, when we talk about a server, it is a Web server connected to the Internet.

social network A generic term for many of the networks such as LinkedIn, Twitter, MySpace, and Facebook that allow people to build their own Web presence and interact with each other.

surfing A term used for moving from one page or site to another on the Internet.

URL Uniform Resource Locator. A term, pronounced U-R-L, which means a Web address, such as "http://www.bpmug.org/events/index.htm." The URL usually includes the domain name (for example, bpmug.org/), possibly some directories (event/), and a filename (index.htm). If you want a Web address from a customer, don't ask for the URL—unless you are trying to intimidate them with jargon — just ask for the Web address.

value added reseller (VAR) In Web design, a person who adds value or add-ons to products and services.

As a Web designer, you may wish to become a VAR for add-ons like domain names and hosting. A client, of course, can select a less expensive provider for hosting. However, with your hosting you can add much value with features such as a guarantee of up time, the expertise and knowledge to pick the best of many hosts, and much more. If you take a service or product and turn around and resell it for a higher price without adding something of value, you may find your clients are going directly to the same source you use. Add value and they will frequently (not always) choose value over price.

Web page A single document on the Internet. Each Web page has its own URL or Web address.

Web site A compilation of Web pages, scripts, and other things on the Internet. A Web site can be as small as a single page or as large as many thousands of pages. The site typically begins with a home page.

Webmaster The individual who designs a Web site. A Webmaster is also in charge of adding and modifying Web pages, making sure the servers are up and running, checking and analyzing the statistics for the site, repairing or removing links that are no longer active, and much more.

Most small businesses can't afford a full-time Webmaster, so they depend upon the use of the Web designer for other tasks as well. Although I include many of the services of a Webmaster in my Web design business, I also work with some Webmasters to create or modify portions of clients' sites.

zip drive A large-capacity floppy disk drive that accepts large disks that can hold almost seventy times more than a standard floppy.

Although you may still find a client using a zip drive, for the most part CD and DVD burners and USB flash drives have made zip drivers obsolete.

Index

About the Author

Jim Smith is an accomplished Web designer and trainer whose home-based business, Blarneystone, LLC, designs and hosts Web sites for small to midsize companies. For three years he served as training specialist and Webmaster for United HealthCare Learning Institute, during which time he launched and maintained the institute's Web site and created and delivered Web-related training seminars and classes. He is also Webmaster and on the board of directors for the Business and Professional Microcomputer User Group (BPMUG), where he conducts monthly special interest groups on the Internet. He has written a number of Internet-related pieces for the BPMUG's *Help Key* newsletter.

Jim speaks frequently to groups on Internet-related subjects. His presentations range from introductory training sessions at local libraries to Internet seminars and workshops for Fortune 500 companies.

Jim lives and works in Connecticut, and his Web site is www.blarneystone .com.